TWO STORY HOMES
Colonial • Tudor • French • Spanish • Georgian Styles

HOME PLANNERS, INC.

Contents

Edited by: Net Gingras

Published by Home Planners, Inc., 23761 Research Drive, Farmington Hills, Michigan 48024.
All designs and illustrative material Copyright © MCMLXXXVI by Home Planners, Inc. All
rights reserved. Reproduction in any manner or form not permitted. Printed in the United
States of America. International Standard Book Number (ISBN): 0-918894-50-6.

Index to Designs

On the Cover: Cover design can be found on page 108.

How To Read Floor Plans and Blueprints

Selecting the most suitable house plan for your family is a matter of matching your needs, tastes, and life-style against the many designs we offer. When you study the floor plans in this issue, and the blueprints that you may subsequently order, remember that they are simply a two-dimensional representation of what will eventually be a three-dimensional reality.

Floor plans are easy to read. Rooms are clearly labeled, with dimensions given in feet and inches. Most symbols are logical and self-explanatory: The location of bathroom fixtures, planters, fireplaces, tile floors, cabinets and counters, sinks, appliances, closets, sloped or beamed ceilings will be obvious.

A blueprint, although much more detailed, is also easy to read; all it demands is concentration. The blueprints that we offer come in many large sheets, each one of which contains a different kind of information. One sheet contains foundation and excavation drawings, another has a precise plot plan. An elevations sheet deals with the exterior walls of the house; section drawings show precise dimensions, fittings, doors, windows, and roof structures. Our detailed floor plans give the construction information needed by your contractor. And each set of blueprints contains a lengthy materials list with size and quantities of all necessary components. Using this list, a contractor and suppliers can make a start at calculating costs for you.

When you first study a floor plan or blueprint, imagine that you are walking through the house. By mentally visualizing each room in three dimensions, you can transform the technical data and symbols into something more real.

Start at the front door. It's preferable to have a foyer or entrance hall in which to receive guests. A closet here is desirable; a powder room is a plus.

Look for good traffic circulation as you study the floor plan. You should not have to pass all the way through one main room to reach another. From the entrance area you should have direct access to the three principal areas of a house—the living, work, and sleeping zones. For example, a foyer might provide separate entrances to the living room, kitchen, patio, and a hallway or staircase leading to the bedrooms.

Study the layout of each zone. Most people expect the living room to be protected from cross traffic. The kitchen, on the other hand, should connect with the dining room—and perhaps also the utility room, basement, garage, patio or deck, or a secondary entrance. A homemaker whose workday centers in the kitchen may have special requirements: a window that faces the backyard; a clear view of the family room where children play; a garage or driveway entrance that allows for a short trip with groceries; laundry facilities close at hand. Check for efficient placement of kitchen cabinets, counters, and appliances. Is there enough room in the kitchen for additional appliances, for eating in? Is there a dining nook?

Perhaps this part of the house contains a family room or a den/bedroom/office. It's advantageous to have a bathroom or powder room in this section.

As you study the plan, you may encounter a staircase, indicated by a group of parallel lines, the number of lines equaling the number of steps. Arrows labeled "up" mean that the staircase leads to a higher level, and those pointing down mean it leads to a lower one. Staircases in a split-level will have both up and down arrows on one staircase because two levels are depicted in one drawing and an extra level in another.

Notice the location of the stairways. Is too much floor space lost to them? Will you find yourself making too many trips?

Study the sleeping quarters. Are the bedrooms situated as you like? You may want the master bedroom near the kids, or you may want it as far away as possible. Is there at least one closet per person in each bedroom or a double one for a couple? Bathrooms should be convenient to each bedroom—if not adjoining, then with hallway access and on the same floor.

Once you are familiar with the relative positions of the rooms, look for such structural details as:

- Sufficient uninterrupted wall space for furniture arrangement.
- Adequate room dimensions.
- Potential heating or cooling problems—i.e., a room over a garage or next to the laundry.
- Window and door placement for good ventilation and natural light.
- Location of doorways—avoid having a basement staircase or a bathroom in view of the dining room.
- Adequate auxiliary space—closets, storage, bathrooms, countertops.
- Separation of activity areas. (Will noise from the recreation room disturb sleeping children or a parent at work?)

As you complete your mental walk through the house, bear in mind your family's long-range needs. A good house plan will allow for some adjustments now and additions in the future.

Each member of your family may find the listing of his, or her, favorite features a most helpful exercise. Why not try it?

How To Choose a Contractor

A contractor is part craftsman, part businessman, and part magician. As the person who will transform your dreams and drawings into a finished house, he will be responsible for the final cost of the structure, for the quality of the workmanship, and for the solving of all problems that occur quite naturally in the course of construction. Choose him as carefully as you would a business partner, because for the next several months that will be his role in your life.

As soon as you have a building site and house plans, start looking for a contractor, even if you do not plan to break ground for several months. Finding one suitable to build your house can take time, and once you have found him, you will have to be worked into his schedule. Those who are good are in demand and, where the season is short, they are often scheduling work up to a year in advance.

There are two types of residential contractors: the construction company and the carpenter-builder, often called a general contractor. Each of these has its advantages and disadvantages.

The carpenter-builder works directly on the job as the field foreman. Because his background is that of a craftsman, his workmanship is probably good—but his paperwork may be slow or sloppy. His overhead—which you pay for—is less than that of a large construction company. However, if the job drags on for any reason, his interest may flag because your project is overlapping his next job and eroding his profits.

Construction companies handle several projects concurrently. They have an office staff to keep the paperwork moving and an army of subcontractors they know they can count on. Though you can be confident that they will meet deadlines, they may sacrifice workmanship in order to do so. Because they emphasize efficiency, they are less personal to work with than a general contractor. Many will not work with an individual unless he is represented by an architect. The company and the architect speak the same language; it requires far more time to deal directly with a homeowner.

To find a reliable contractor, start by asking friends who have built homes for recommendations. Check with local lumber yards and building supply outlets for names of possible candidates.

Once you have several names in hand, ask the Chamber of Commerce, Better Business Bureau, or local department of consumer affairs for any information they might have on each of them. Keep in mind that these watchdog organizations can give only the number of complaints filed; they cannot tell you what percent of those claims were valid. Remember, too, that a large-volume operation is logically going to have more complaints against it than will an independent contractor.

Set up an interview with each of the potential candidates. Find out what his specialty is—custom houses, development houses, remodeling, or office buildings. Ask each to take you into—not just to the site of—houses he has built. Ask to see projects that are complete as well as work in progress, emphasizing that you are interested in projects comparable to yours. A $300,000 dentist's office will give you little insight into a contractor's craftsmanship.

Ask each contractor for bank references from both his commercial bank and any other lender he has worked with. If he is in good financial standing, he should have no qualms about giving you this information. Also ask if he offers a warranty on his work. Most will give you a one-year warranty on the structure; some offer as much as a ten-year warranty.

Ask for references, even though no contractor will give you the name of a dissatisfied customer. While previous clients may be pleased with a contractor's work overall, they may, for example, have had to wait three months after they moved in before they had any closet doors. Ask about his follow-through. Did he clean up the building site, or did the owner have to dispose of the refuse? Ask about his business organization. Did the paperwork go smoothly, or was there a delay in hooking up the sewer because he forgot to apply for a permit?

Talk to each of the candidates about fees. Most work on a "cost plus" basis; that is, the basic cost of the project—materials, subcontractors' services, wages of those working directly on the project, but not office help—plus his fee. Some have a fixed fee; others work on a percentage of the basic cost. A fixed fee is usually better for you if you can get one. If a contractor works on a percentage, ask for a cost breakdown of his best estimate and keep very careful track as the work progresses. A crafty contractor can always use a cost overrun to his advantage when working on a percentage.

Do not be overly suspicious of a contractor who won't work on a fixed fee. One who is very good and in great demand may not be willing to do so. He may also refuse to submit a competitive bid.

If the top two or three candidates are willing to submit competitive bids, give each a copy of the plans and your specifications for materials. If they are not each working from the same guidelines, the competitive bids will be of little value. Give each the same deadline for turning in a bid; two or three weeks is a reasonable period of time. If you are willing to go with the lowest bid, make an appointment with all of them and open the envelopes in front of them.

If one bid is remarkably low, the contractor may have made an honest error in his estimate. Do not try to hold him to it if he wants to withdraw his bid. Forcing him to build at too low a price could be disastrous for both you and him.

Though the above method sounds very fair and orderly, it is not always the best approach, especially if you are inexperienced. You may want to review the bids with your architect, if you have one, or with your lender to discuss which to accept. They may not recommend the lowest. A low bid does not necessarily mean that you will get quality with economy.

If the bids are relatively close, the most important consideration may not be money at all. How easily you can talk with a contractor and whether or not he inspires confidence are very important considerations. Any sign of a personality conflict between you and a contractor should be weighed when making a decision.

Once you have financing, you can sign a contract with the builder. Most have their own contract forms, but it is advisable to have a lawyer draw one up or, at the very least, review the standard contract. This usually costs a small flat fee.

A good contract should include the following:
• Plans and sketches of the work to be done, subject to your approval.
• A list of materials, including quantity, brand names, style or serial numbers. (Do not permit any "or equal" clause that will allow the contractor to make substitutions.)
• The terms—who (you or the lender) pays whom and when.
• A production schedule.
• The contractor's certification of insurance for workmen's compensation, damage, and liability.
• A rider stating that all changes, whether or not they increase the cost, must be submitted and approved in writing.

Of course, this list represents the least a contract should include. Once you have signed it, your plans are on the way to becoming a home.

A frequently asked question is: "Should I become my own general contractor?" Unless you have knowledge of construction, material purchasing, and experience supervising subcontractors, we do not recommend this route.

How To Shop For Mortgage Money

Most people who are in the market for a new home spend months searching for the right house plan and building site. Ironically, these same people often invest very little time shopping for the money to finance their new home, though the majority will have to live with the terms of their mortgage for as long as they live in the house.

The fact is that all banks are not alike, nor are the loans that they offer—and banks are not the only financial institutions that lend money for housing. The amount of down payment, interest rate, and period of the mortgage are all, to some extent, negotiable.

• Lending practices vary from one city and state to another. If you are a first-time builder or are new to an area, it is wise to hire a real estate (not divorce or general practice) attorney to help you unravel the maze of your specific area's laws, ordinances, and customs.

• Before talking with lenders, write down all your questions. Take notes during the conversation so you can make accurate comparisons.

• Do not be intimidated by financial officers. Keep in mind that you are not begging for money, you are buying it. Do not hesitate to reveal what other institutions are offering; they may be challenged to meet or better the terms.

• Use whatever clout you have. If you or your family have been banking with the same firm for years, let them know that they could lose your business if you can get a better deal elsewhere.

• Know your credit rights. The law prohibits lenders from considering only the husband's income when determining eligibility, a practice that previously kept many people out of the housing market. If you are turned down for a loan, you have a right to see a summary of the credit report and change any errors in it.

A GUIDE TO LENDERS

Where can you turn for home financing? Here is a list of sources for you to approach:

Savings and loan associations are the best place to start because they write well over half the mortgages in the United States on dwellings that house from one to four families. They generally offer favorable interest rates, require lower down payments, and allow more time to pay off loans than do other banks.

Savings banks, sometimes called mutual savings banks, are your next best bet. Like savings and loan associations, much of their business is concentrated in home mortgages.

Commercial banks write mortgages as a sideline, and when money is tight many will not write mortgages at all. They do hold about 15 percent of the mortgages in the country, however, and when the market is right, they can be very competitive.

Mortgage banking companies use the money of private investors to write home loans. They do a brisk business in government-backed loans, which other banks are reluctant to handle because of the time and paperwork required.

Some credit unions are now allowed to grant mortgages. A few insurance companies, pension funds, unions, and fraternal organizations also offer mortgage money to their membership, often at terms more favorable than those available in the commercial marketplace.

A GUIDE TO MORTGAGES

The types of mortgages available are far more various than most potential home buyers realize.

Traditional Loans

Conventional home loans have a fixed interest rate and fixed monthly payments. About 80 percent of the mortgage money in the United States is lent in this manner. Made by private lending institutions, these fixed rate loans are available to anyone whom the bank officials consider a good credit risk. The interest rate depends on the prevailing market for money and is slightly negotiable if you are willing to put down a large down payment. Most down payments range from 15 to 33 percent.

You can borrow as much money as the lender believes you can afford to pay off over the negotiated period of time—usually 20 to 30 years. However, a 15 year mortgage can save you considerably and enable you to own your home in half the time. For example, a 30 year, $60,800 mortgage at 12% interest will have a monthly payment of $625.40 per month vs $729.72 per month for a 15 year loan at the same interest rate. At the end of 30 years you have paid $164,344 in interest vs $70,550 for the 15 year. Remember - this is only $104.32 more per month. Along with saving with a 15 year mortgage, additional savings

can be realized with a biweekly payment plan. So be sure to consult your borrowing institution for all of your options.

The FHA does not write loans; it insures them against default in order to encourage lenders to write loans for first-time buyers and people with limited incomes. The terms of these loans make them very attractive, and you may be allowed to take as long as 25 to 30 years to pay it off.

The down payment also is substantially lower with an FHA-backed loan. At present it is set at 3 percent of the first $25,000 and 5 percent of the remainder, up to the $75,300 limit. This means that a loan on a $75,300 house would require a $750 down payment on the first $25,000 plus $2,515 on the remainder, for a total down payment of $3,265. In contrast, the down payment for the same house financed with a conventional loan could run as high as $20,000.

Anyone may apply for an FHA-insured loan, but both the borrower and the house must qualify.

The VA guarantees loans for eligible veterans, and the husbands and wives of those who died while in the service or from a service-related disability. The VA guarantees up to 60 percent of the loan or $27,500, whichever is less. Like the FHA, the VA determines the appraised value of the house, though with a VA loan, you can borrow any amount up to the appraised value.

The Farmers Home Administration offers the only loans made directly by the government. Families with limited incomes in rural areas can qualify if the house is in a community of less than 10,000 people and is outside of a large metropolitan area; if their income is less than $18,000; and if they can prove that they do not qualify for a conventional loan.

For more information, write Farmers Home Administration, Department of Agriculture, Washington, D.C. 20250, or your local office.

New loan instruments

If you think that the escalating cost of housing has squeezed you out of the market, take a look at the following new types of mortgages.

The graduated payment mortgage features a monthly obligation that gradually increases over a negotiated period of time—usually five to ten years. Though the payments begin lower, they stabilize at a higher monthly rate than a standard fixed rate mortgage. Little or no equity is built in the first years, a disadvantage if you decide to sell early in the mortgage period.

These loans are aimed at young people who can anticipate income increases that will enable them to meet the escalating payments. The size of the down payment is about the same or slightly higher than for a conventional loan, but you can qualify with a lower income. As of last year, savings and loan associations can write these loans, and the FHA now insures five different types.

The flexible loan insurance program (FLIP) requires that part of the down payment, which is about the same as a conventional loan, be placed in a pledged savings account. During the first five years of the mortgage, funds are drawn from this account to supplement the lower monthly payments.

The deferred interest mortgage, another graduated program, allows you to pay a lower rate of interest during the first few years and a higher rate in the later years of the mortgage. If the house is sold, the borrower must pay back all the interest, often with a prepayment penalty. Both the FLIP and deferred interest loans are very new and not yet widely available.

The variable rate mortgage is most widely available in California, but its popularity is growing. This instrument features a fluctuating interest rate that is linked to an economic indicator—usually the lender's cost of obtaining funds for lending. To protect the consumer against a sudden and disastrous increase, regulations limit the amount that the interest rate can increase over a given period of time.

To make these loans attractive, lenders offer them without prepayment penalties and with "assumption" clauses that allow another buyer to assume your mortgage should you sell.

Flexible payment mortgages allow young people who can anticipate rising incomes to enter the housing market sooner. They pay only the interest during the first few years; then the mortgage is amortized and the payments go up. This is a valuable option only for those people who intend to keep their home for several years because no equity is built in the lower payment period.

The reverse annuity mortgage is targeted for older people who have fixed incomes. This new loan allows those who qualify to tap into the equity on their houses. The lender pays them each month and collects the loan when the house is sold or the owner dies.

HERITAGE HOUSES . . .

as delightfully featured on the following pages reflect the charm of our country's rich architectural history. These early American styles ranged from the stark Medieval and Tudor influences of the 17th-Century through the later periods of Georgian and Federal styles. Saltbox, Gambrel, Garrison, Cape Cod, Williamsburg and Southern Colonial adaptations added to the diversity in exterior appearances. The appealing proportions of these historical houses have lent themselves to the up-dating of the old floor plans to satisfy today's current standards of family livability. This marriage of the old and the new results in a picturesque and practical selection of home designs.

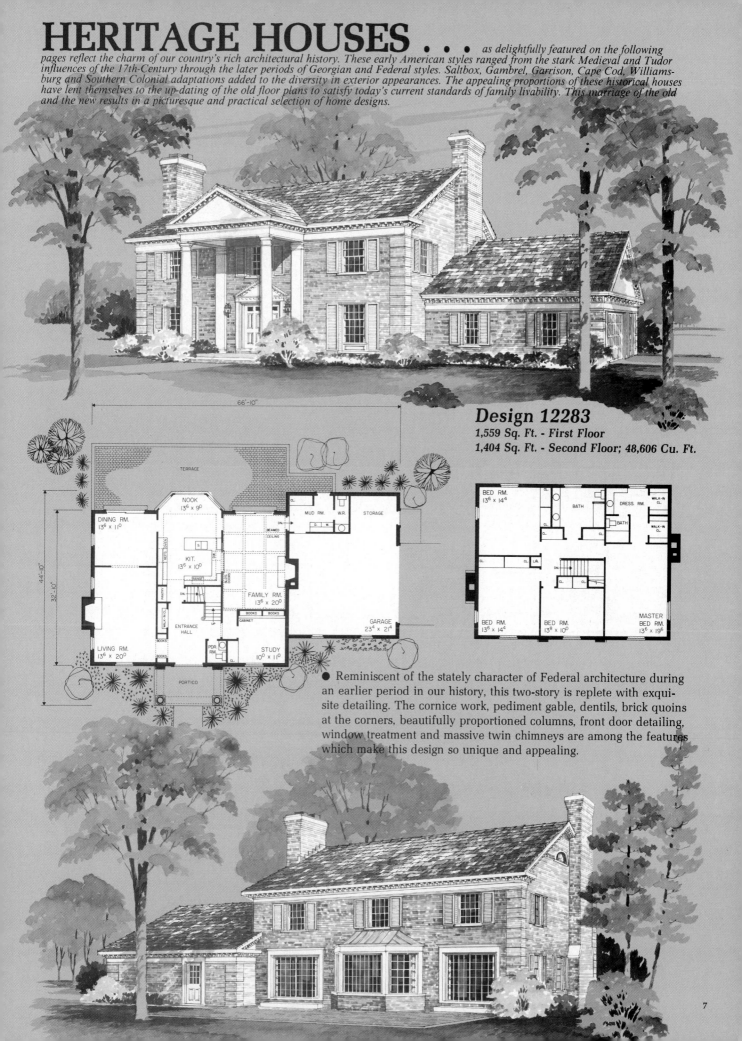

Design 12283
1,559 Sq. Ft. - First Floor
1,404 Sq. Ft. - Second Floor; 48,606 Cu. Ft.

● Reminiscent of the stately character of Federal architecture during an earlier period in our history, this two-story is replete with exquisite detailing. The cornice work, pediment gable, dentils, brick quoins at the corners, beautifully proportioned columns, front door detailing, window treatment and massive twin chimneys are among the features which make this design so unique and appealing.

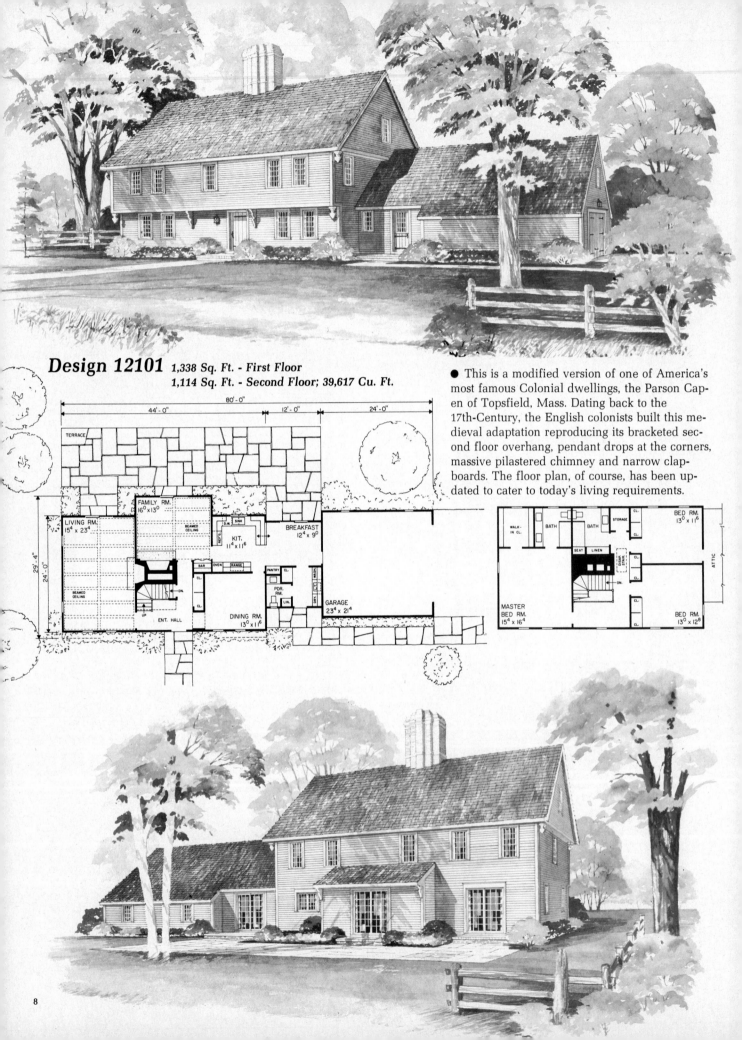

Design 12101
1,338 Sq. Ft. - First Floor
1,114 Sq. Ft. - Second Floor; 39,617 Cu. Ft.

● This is a modified version of one of America's most famous Colonial dwellings, the Parson Capen of Topsfield, Mass. Dating back to the 17th-Century, the English colonists built this medieval adaptation reproducing its bracketed second floor overhang, pendant drops at the corners, massive pilastered chimney and narrow clapboards. The floor plan, of course, has been updated to cater to today's living requirements.

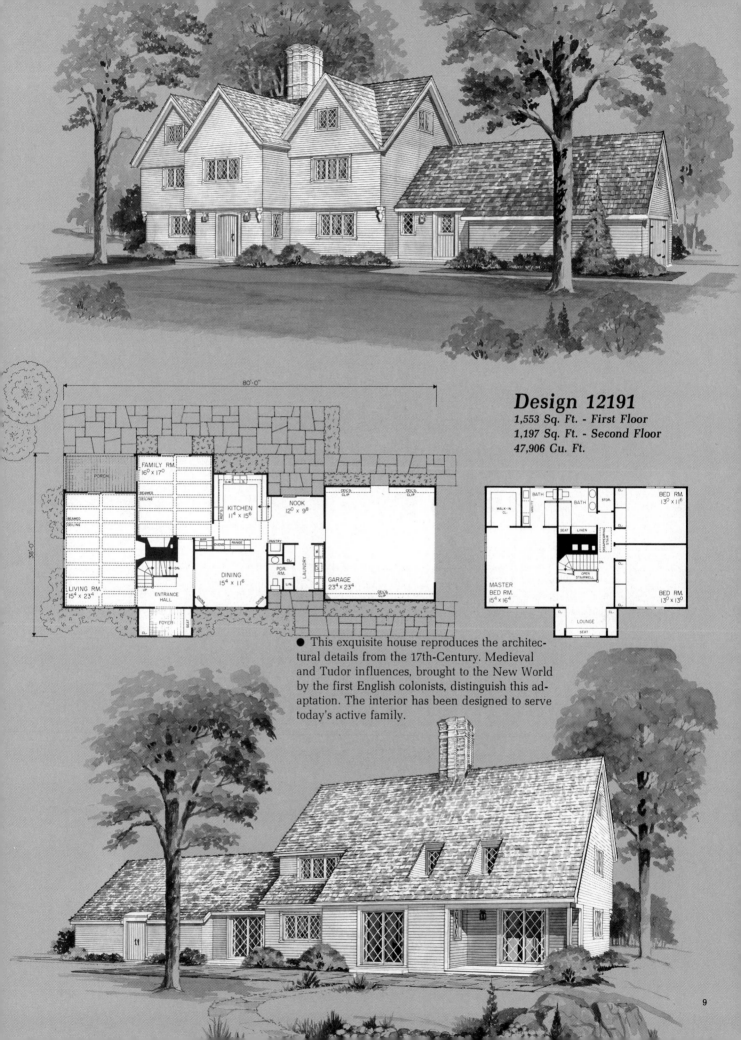

Design 12191

1,553 Sq. Ft. - First Floor
1,197 Sq. Ft. - Second Floor
47,906 Cu. Ft.

● This exquisite house reproduces the architectural details from the 17th-Century. Medieval and Tudor influences, brought to the New World by the first English colonists, distinguish this adaptation. The interior has been designed to serve today's active family.

9

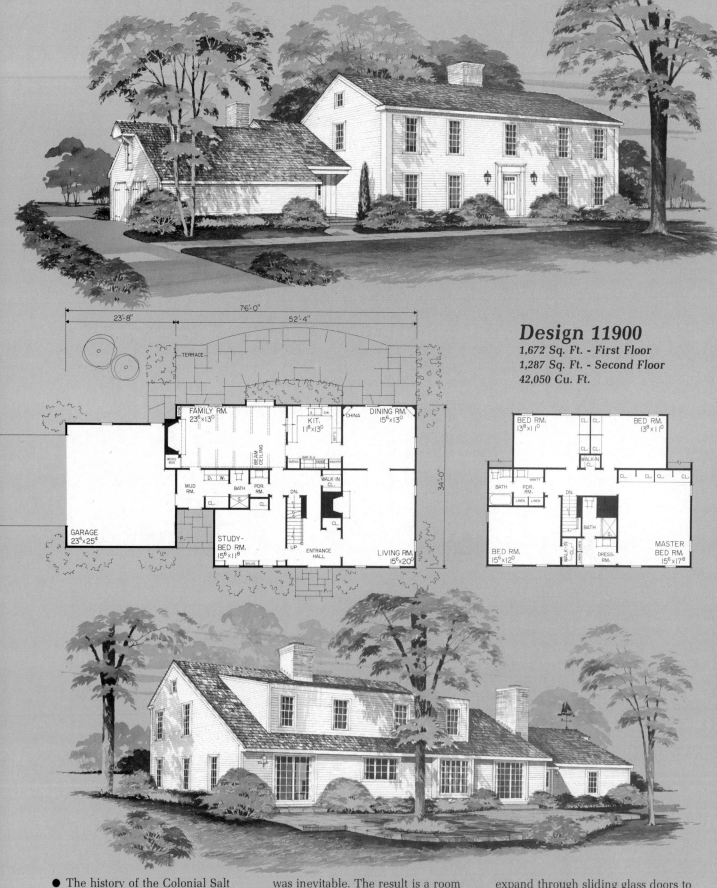

Design 11900

1,672 Sq. Ft. - First Floor
1,287 Sq. Ft. - Second Floor
42,050 Cu. Ft.

● The history of the Colonial Salt Box goes back some 200 years. This unusually authentic adaptation captures all the warmth and charm of the early days both inside as well as outside. To reflect today's living patterns, an up-dating of the floor plan was inevitable. The result is a room arrangement which will serve the active family wonderfully. Formal living and dining take place at one end of the house which is free of cross-room traffic. Informal living activities will center around the family room and expand through sliding glass doors to the terrace. The mud room area is strategically located and includes the laundry and a full bath. An extra study/bedroom supplements four bedrooms upstairs. Count the closets and the other storage areas.

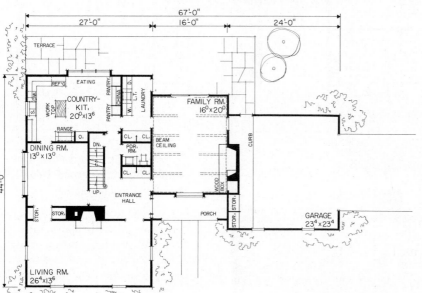

Design 11887

1,518 Sq. Ft. - First Floor
1,144 Sq. Ft. - Second Floor
40,108 Cu. Ft.

● This Gambrel roof Colonial is steeped in history. And well it should be, for its pleasing proportions are a delight to the eye. The various roof planes, the window treatment, and the rambling nature of the entire house revive a picture of rural New England. The covered porch protects the front door which opens into a spacious entrance hall. Traffic then flows in an orderly fashion to the end living room, the separate dining room, the cozy family room, and to the spacious country-kitchen. There is a first floor laundry, plenty of coat closets, and a handy powder room. Two fireplaces enliven the decor of the living areas. Upstairs there is an exceptional master bedroom layout, and abundant storage. Note the walk-in closets.

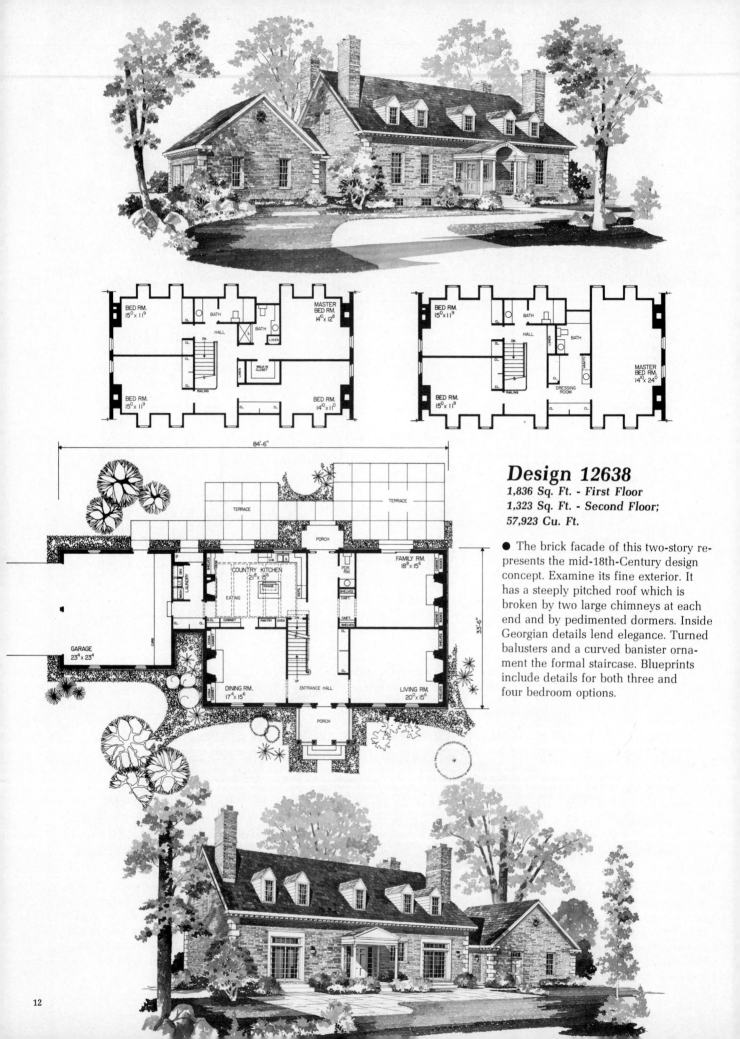

BED RM. 15⁰ x 11⁹

BATH

CL

HALL

MASTER BED RM. 14⁰ x 12⁸

BATH

LINEN

DN.

CL

CL

CL

LINEN

WALK IN CLOSET

RAILING

BED RM. 15⁰ x 11⁹

CL

CL

BED RM. 14¹⁰ x 11⁰

BED RM. 15⁰ x 11⁹

BATH

CL

HALL

LINEN

BATH

DN.

CL

CL

VANITY

DRESSING ROOM

MASTER BED RM. 14⁰ x 24⁰

RAILING

CL

CL

84'-6"

TERRACE

TERRACE

PORCH

P

WASH

DRY

LAUNDRY

COUNTRY KITCHEN 21⁸ x 15⁶

SHELVES

D.W.

RANGE

REFG.

FAMILY RM. 18⁸ x 15⁶

PDR. RM.

CABINET

CABINET

EATING

SHELVES

CAB'T

CABINET

BOOKS

33'-6"

CL

B.CL.

CABINET

PANTRY

OVEN

DN.

CAB'T

SHELVES

CL

GARAGE 23⁴ x 23⁴

CHINA CABINET

CL

DINING RM. 17⁴ x 15⁶

UP

ENTRANCE HALL

SHELVES

CL

LIVING RM. 20⁰ x 15⁶

PORCH

Design 12638
1,836 Sq. Ft. - First Floor
1,323 Sq. Ft. - Second Floor;
57,923 Cu. Ft.

● The brick facade of this two-story represents the mid-18th-Century design concept. Examine its fine exterior. It has a steeply pitched roof which is broken by two large chimneys at each end and by pedimented dormers. Inside Georgian details lend elegance. Turned balusters and a curved banister ornament the formal staircase. Blueprints include details for both three and four bedroom options.

Design 12132

1,958 Sq. Ft. - First Floor
1,305 Sq. Ft. - Second Floor
51,428 Cu. Ft.

● Another Georgian adaptation with a great heritage dating back to 18th-Century America. Exquisite and symmetrical detailing set the character of this impressive home. Don't overlook such features as the two fireplaces, the laundry, the beamed ceiling, the built-in china cabinets and the oversized garage.

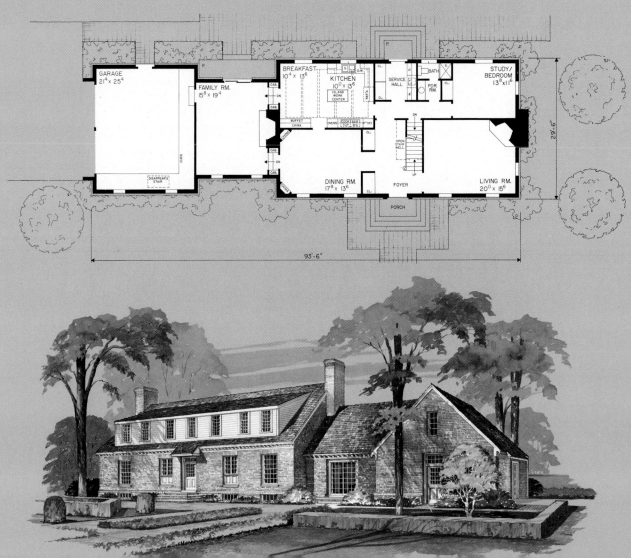

Design 12655
893 Sq. Ft. - First Floor
652 Sq. Ft. - Second Floor; 22,555 Cu. Ft.

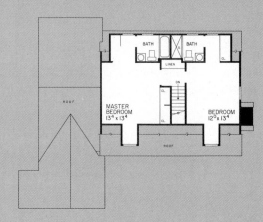

● Wonderful things can be enclosed in small packages. This is the case for this two-story design. The total square footage is a mere 1,545 square feet yet its features are many, indeed. Its exterior appeal is very eye-pleasing with horizontal lines and two second story dormers. Livability will be enjoyed in this plan. The front study is ideal for a quiet escape. Nearby is a powder room also convenient to the kitchen and breakfast room. Two bedrooms and two full baths are located on the second floor.

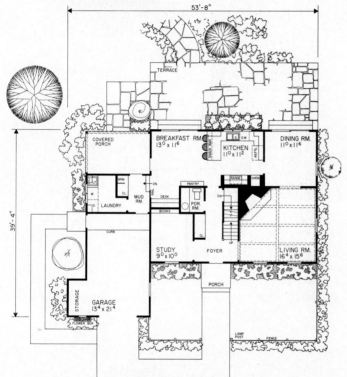

53'-8"

TERRACE

COVERED PORCH

BREAKFAST RM. 13⁰ x 11⁶

KITCHEN 11⁰ x 11²

DINING RM. 11⁰ x 11⁶

39'-4"

BRM

MUD RM.

LAUNDRY

PANTRY

DESK

PDR. RM.

BOOKS

RANGE OVEN

STUDY 9⁰ x 10⁰

FOYER

LIVING RM. 16⁴ x 15⁶

CURB

STORAGE

GARAGE 13⁴ x 21⁴

PORCH

FLOWER BOX

LAMP POST

FENCE

Design 12656 1,122 Sq. Ft. - First Floor
884 Sq. Ft. - Second Floor; 31,845 Cu. Ft.

ROOF

BEDROOM 12⁰ x 13⁰

BATH

LIN

LINEN

MASTER BEDROOM 12⁸ x 16⁰

DN

RAIL

BEDROOM 12⁰ x 11⁰

DRESSING RM.

BATH

ROOF

● This charming Cape cottage possesses a great sense of shelter through its gambrel roof. Dormers at front and rear pierce the gambrel roof to provide generous, well-lit living space on the second floor which houses three bedrooms. This design's first floor layout is not far different from that of the Cape cottages of the 18th century. The large kitchen and adjoining dining room recall cottage keeping rooms both in function and in location at the rear of the house.

Design 12641
1,672 Sq. Ft. - First Floor
1,248 Sq. Ft. - Second Floor; 45,306 Cu. Ft.

● This Georgian adaptation is from the early 18th-Century and has plenty of historical background. The classical details are sedately stated. The plan promises up-to-date livability. The size of your site need not be large, either.

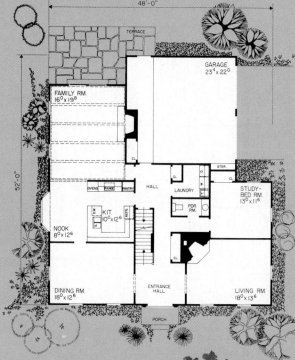

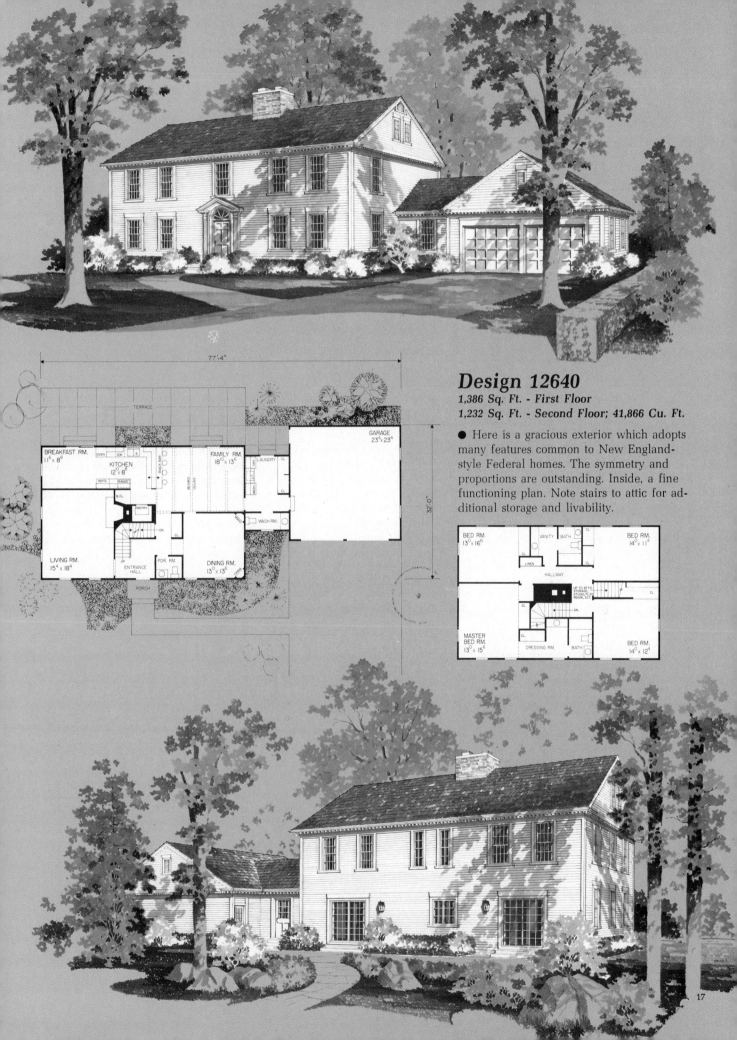

Design 12640

1,386 Sq. Ft. - First Floor
1,232 Sq. Ft. - Second Floor; 41,866 Cu. Ft.

● Here is a gracious exterior which adopts many features common to New England-style Federal homes. The symmetry and proportions are outstanding. Inside, a fine functioning plan. Note stairs to attic for additional storage and livability.

First Floor Plan

77'-4"
32'-0"

TERRACE

BREAKFAST RM. 11'⁶ x 8'⁸
OVEN DW S
KITCHEN 12'⁰ x 8'⁸
REFR. RANGE
B. CL.
PANTRY
SNACK BAR
FAMILY RM. 18'¹⁰ x 13'⁶
BEAMED CEILING
LAUNDRY CL.
CL.
WASH RM.
GARAGE 23'⁴ x 23'⁴

LIVING RM. 15'⁴ x 18'⁴
UP DN
ENTRANCE HALL
PDR. RM.
CL.
DINING RM. 13'⁰ x 13'⁶
PORCH

Second Floor Plan

BED RM. 13'⁰ x 16'⁶
VANITY BATH
LINEN
BED RM. 14'⁰ x 11'⁴
HALLWAY
MASTER BED RM. 13'⁰ x 15'⁶
UP TO ATTIC STORAGE, STUDIO, PLAY ROOM, ECT.
CL.
DN.
CL.
DRESSING RM. BATH
BED RM. 14'⁰ x 12'⁴

17

A Mount Vernon Reminiscence

● This magnificent manor's streetview illustrates a centralized mansion connected by curving galleries to matching wings. What a grand presentation this home will make! The origin of this house dates back to 1787 and George Washington's stately Mount Vernon. The underlying aesthetics for this design come from the rational balancing of porticoes, fenestration and chimneys. The rear elevation of this home also deserves mention. Six two-story columns, along with four sets of French doors, highlight this view. Study all of the intricate detailing that is featured all around these exteriors.

The flanking wings create a large formal courtyard where guests of today can park their cars. This home, designed from architecture of the past, is efficient and compact enough to fit many suburban lots. Its interior has been well planned and is ready to serve a family of any size.

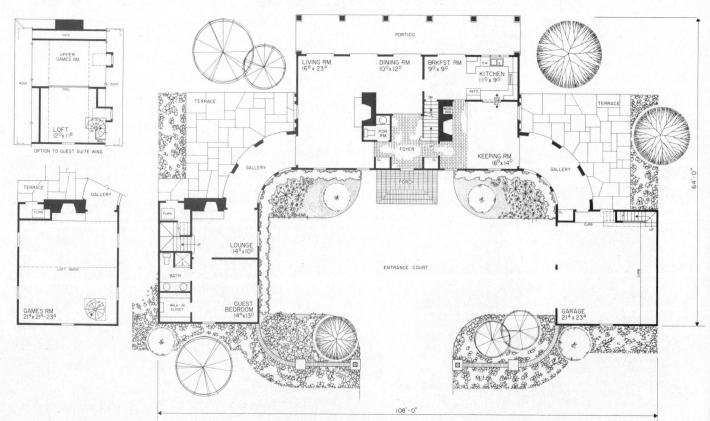

Design 12665 1,152 Sq. Ft. - First Floor

1,152 Sq. Ft. - Second Floor; 38,754 Cu. Ft. (Excludes Guest Suite and Galleries)

● The main, two-story section of this home houses the living areas. First - there is the large, tiled foyer with two closets and powder room. Then there is the living room which is the entire width of the house. This room has a fireplace and leads into the formal dining room. Three sets of double French doors lead to the rear portico from this formal area. The kitchen and breakfast room will function together. There is a pass-thru from the kitchen to the keeping room. All of the sleeping facilities, four bedrooms, are on the second floor. The gallery on the right leads to the garage; the one on the left, to a lounge and guest suite with studio above. The square and cubic footages quoted above do not include the guest suite or gallery areas. The first floor of the guest suite contains 688 sq. ft.; the second floor studio, 306 sq. ft. The optional plan shows a game room with a loft above having 162 sq. ft.

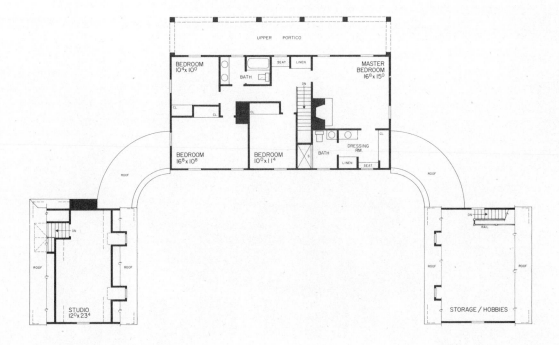

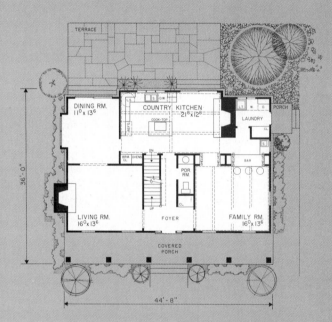

● The exterior of this full two-story is highlighted by the covered porch and balcony. Many enjoyable hours will be spent at these outdoor areas. The interior is highlighted by a spacious country kitchen. Be sure to notice its island cook-top, fireplace and the beamed ceiling. A built-in bar is in the family room.

Design 12664
1,308 Sq. Ft. - First Floor
1,262 Sq. Ft. - Second Floor; 49,215 Cu. Ft.

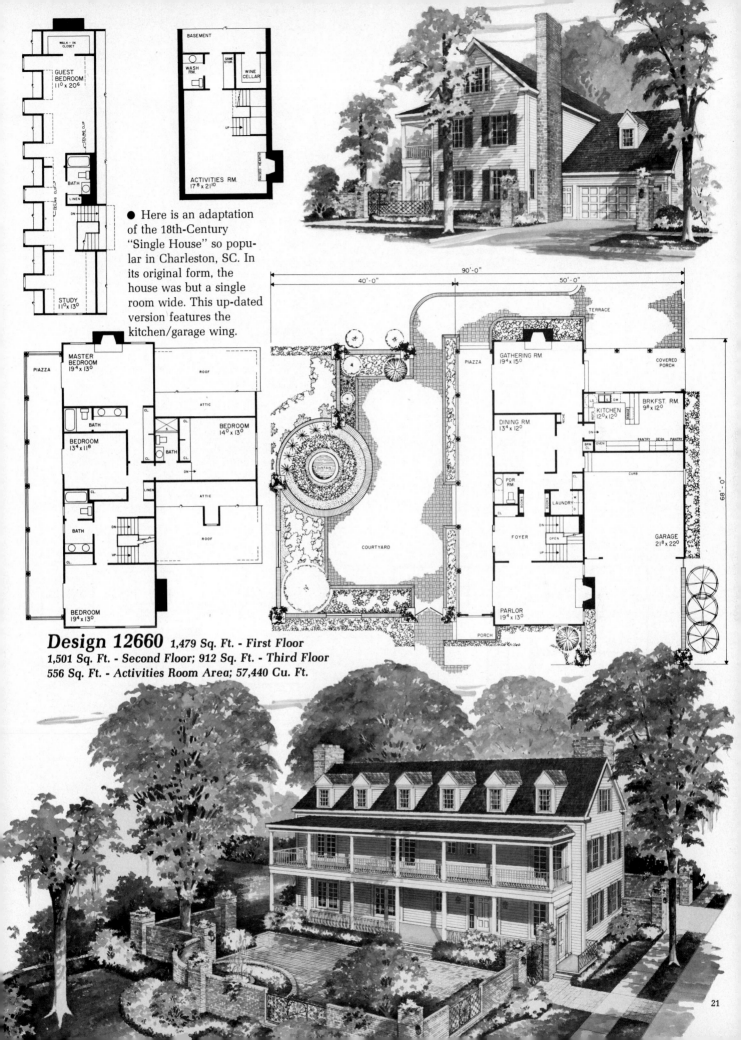

WALK - IN CLOSET

GUEST BEDROOM 11⁰ x 20⁶

BATH

LINEN

DN

STUDY 11⁰ x 13⁰

BASEMENT

WASH RM.

GAME STOR.

WINE CELLAR

UP

RAISED HEARTH

ACTIVITIES RM. 17⁸ x 21¹⁰

● Here is an adaptation of the 18th-Century "Single House" so popular in Charleston, SC. In its original form, the house was but a single room wide. This up-dated version features the kitchen/garage wing.

PIAZZA

MASTER BEDROOM 19⁴ x 13⁰

ROOF

ATTIC

BATH

BEDROOM 13⁴ x 11⁸

BATH

CL.

BEDROOM 14⁰ x 13⁰

CL.

LINEN

ATTIC

BATH

DN

ROOF

UP

CL.

BEDROOM 19⁴ x 13⁰

90'-0"

40'-0"   50'-0"

TERRACE

PIAZZA

GATHERING RM. 19⁴ x 15⁰

COVERED PORCH

DINING RM. 13⁴ x 12⁰

KITCHEN 12⁰ x 12⁰

BRKFST. RM. 9⁸ x 12⁰

PANTRY DESK PANTRY

FOUNTAIN

NICHE

OVEN

PDR. RM.

BOOKS

CURB

BOOKS

LAUNDRY

FOYER

DN

OPEN

COURTYARD

UP

GARAGE 21⁸ x 22⁰

PARLOR 19⁴ x 13⁰

PORCH

68'-0"

Design 12660 1,479 Sq. Ft. - First Floor
1,501 Sq. Ft. - Second Floor; 912 Sq. Ft. - Third Floor
556 Sq. Ft. - Activities Room Area; 57,440 Cu. Ft.

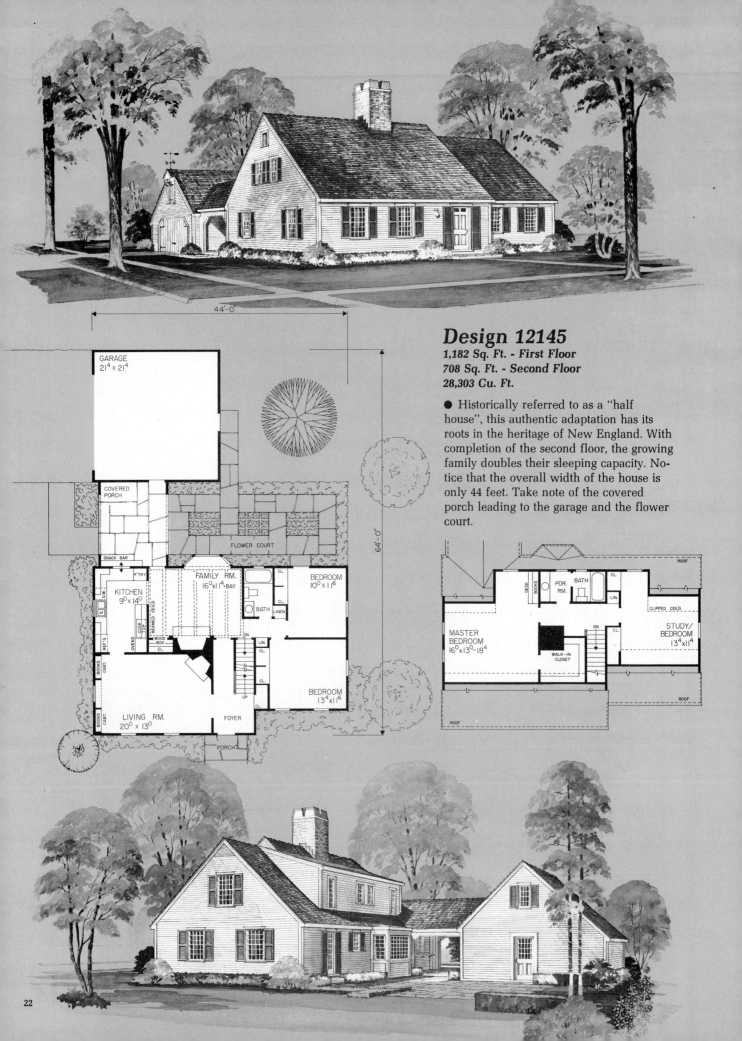

Design 12145

1,182 Sq. Ft. - First Floor
708 Sq. Ft. - Second Floor
28,303 Cu. Ft.

● Historically referred to as a "half house", this authentic adaptation has its roots in the heritage of New England. With completion of the second floor, the growing family doubles their sleeping capacity. Notice that the overall width of the house is only 44 feet. Take note of the covered porch leading to the garage and the flower court.

GARAGE
21⁴ x 21⁴

COVERED PORCH

FLOWER COURT

SNACK BAR

KITCHEN
9⁰ x 14⁰

P'TRY

COOK TOP

OVENS

WOOD BOX

FAMILY RM.
16⁰ x 11⁴ BAY

BATH

LINEN

BEDROOM
10⁰ x 11⁶

BEDROOM
13⁴ x 11⁶

BOOKS

CABT.

REF'G.

D.W.

LIVING RM.
20⁰ x 13⁰

FOYER

UP

DN

PORCH

44'-0"

64'-0"

DESK

BOOKS

PDR. RM.

BATH

LIN.

ROOF

CLIPPED CEIL'G

MASTER BEDROOM
16⁰ x 13⁰-18⁴

WALK-IN CLOSET

DN

STUDY/ BEDROOM
13⁴ x 11⁴

ROOF

ROOF

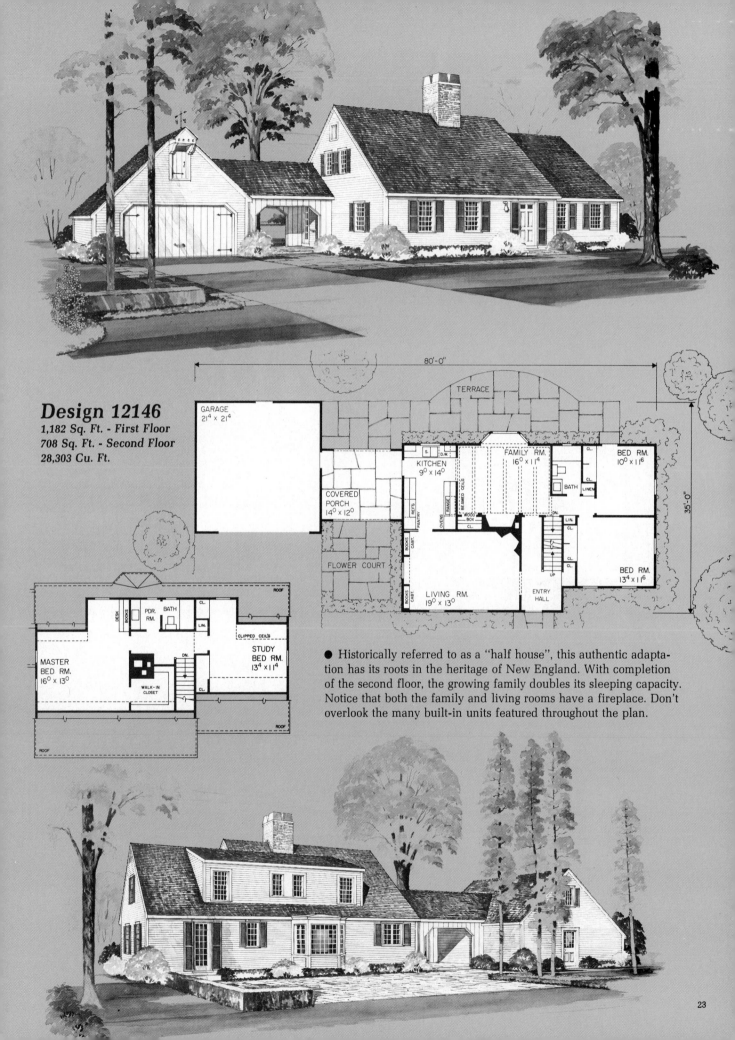

Design 12146

1,182 Sq. Ft. - First Floor
708 Sq. Ft. - Second Floor
28,303 Cu. Ft.

GARAGE 21⁴ x 21⁴

TERRACE

KITCHEN 9⁰ x 14⁰

FAMILY RM. 16⁰ x 11⁴

BED RM. 10⁰ x 11⁶

BATH

LINEN

COVERED PORCH 14⁰ x 12⁰

OVENS
RANGE
REF'S
PANTRY
WOOD BOX
CL.
LIN.
CL.
CL.
DN.
UP

BED RM. 13⁴ x 11⁶

FLOWER COURT

BOOKS
CABT.
BOOKS
CABT.

LIVING RM. 19⁰ x 13⁰

ENTRY HALL

80'-0"

35'-0"

ROOF
DESK
BOOKS
PDR. RM.
BATH
CL.
LIN.
CLIPPED CEIL'G
ROOF

MASTER BED RM. 16⁰ x 13⁰

DN.

WALK-IN CLOSET

STUDY BED RM. 13⁴ x 11⁴

ROOF

● Historically referred to as a "half house", this authentic adaptation has its roots in the heritage of New England. With completion of the second floor, the growing family doubles its sleeping capacity. Notice that both the family and living rooms have a fireplace. Don't overlook the many built-in units featured throughout the plan.

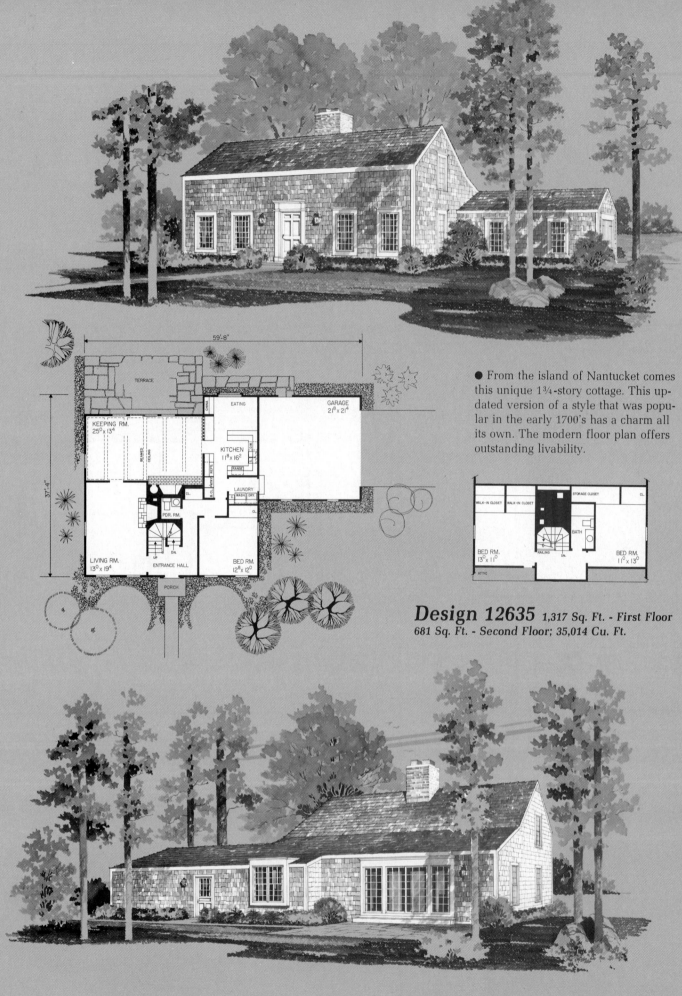

TERRACE

59'-8"

37'-4"

KEEPING RM.
25⁰ x 13⁴

BEAMED CEILING

EATING

GARAGE
21⁸ x 21⁴

CHINA

KITCHEN
11⁸ x 16²

RANGE

B.CL. PANTRY REF'G.

LAUNDRY
WASH. DRY.

CL.

CL.

PDR. RM.

UP   DN.

LIVING RM.
13⁰ x 19⁴

ENTRANCE HALL

BED RM.
12⁸ x 12⁰

PORCH

● From the island of Nantucket comes this unique 1¾-story cottage. This updated version of a style that was popular in the early 1700's has a charm all its own. The modern floor plan offers outstanding livability.

WALK-IN CLOSET WALK-IN CLOSET STORAGE CLOSET CL.

BED RM.
13⁰ x 11⁰

RAILING DN.

BATH

BED RM.
11⁰ x 13⁰

ATTIC

Design 12635 1,317 Sq. Ft. - First Floor
681 Sq. Ft. - Second Floor; 35,014 Cu. Ft.

● Another 1¾-story home - a type of house favored by many of Cape Cod's early whalers. The compact floor plan will be economical to build and surely an energy saver. An excellent house to finish-off in stages.

STORAGE

MASTER BED RM. 16⁴ x 14⁸

BATH

LINEN

SHELVES DESK

DN.

WALK-IN CLOSET

BED RM. 12⁸ x 13⁴

HALL

STORAGE

Design 12636 1,211 Sq. Ft. - First Floor
747 Sq. Ft. - Second Floor; 28,681 Cu. Ft.

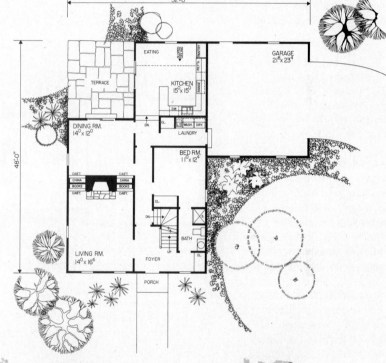

52'-0"

48'-0"

EATING

TERRACE

KITCHEN 15⁰ x 15⁰

GARAGE 21⁸ x 23⁴

DINING RM. 14⁰ x 12⁰

DN.

LAUNDRY

WASH. DRY.

BED RM. 11⁴ x 12⁰

CL.

CHINA BOOKS

CHINA BOOKS

CAB'T.

CAB'T.

CL.

DN.

BATH

LIVING RM. 14⁰ x 16⁶

FOYER

UP

PORCH

Design 12192

1,884 Sq. Ft. - First Floor
1,521 Sq. Ft. - Second Floor
58,380 Cu. Ft.

● This is surely a fine adaptation from the 18th-Century when formality and elegance were by-words. The authentic detailing of this design centers around the fine proportions, the dentils, the window symmetry, the front door and entranceway, the massive chimneys and the masonry work. The rear elevation retains all the grandeur exemplary of exquisite architecture. The appeal of this outstanding home does not end with its exterior elevations. Consider the formal living room with its corner fireplace. Also, the library with its wall of bookshelves and cabinets. Further, the dining room highlights corner china cabinets. Continue to study this elegant plan.

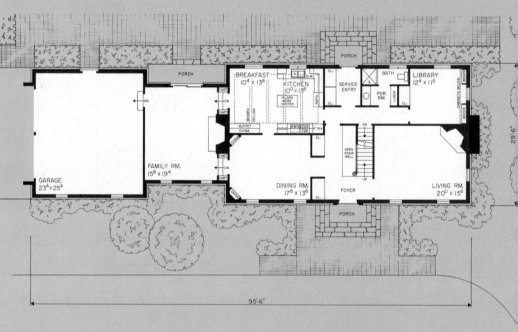

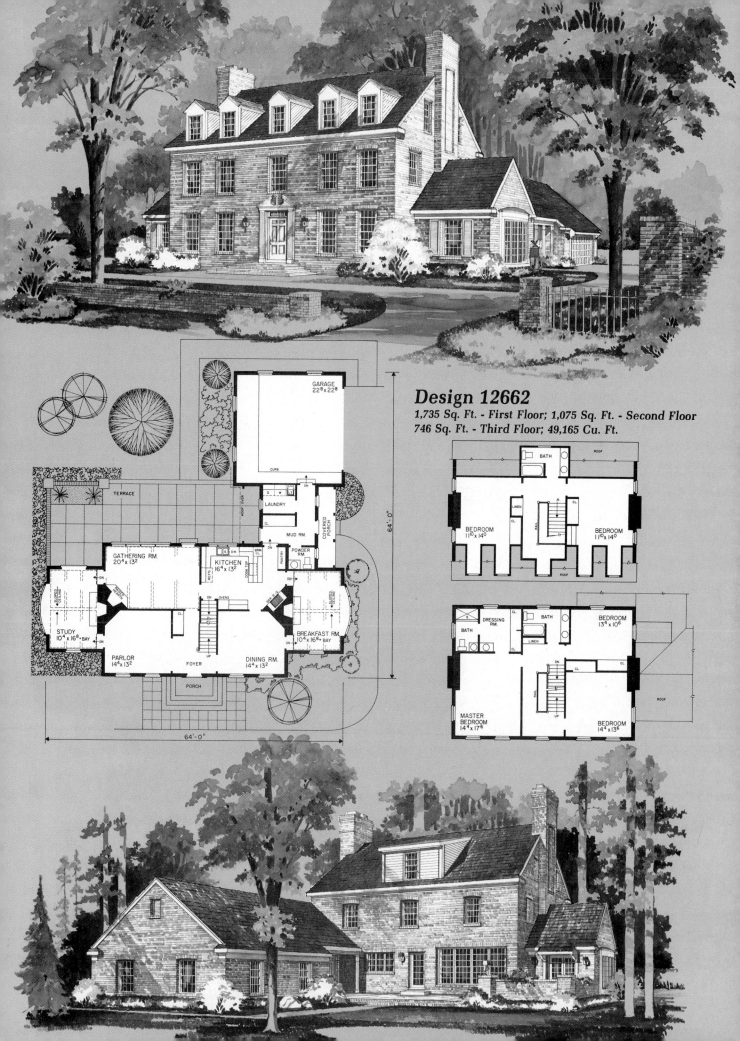

Design 12662

1,735 Sq. Ft. - First Floor; 1,075 Sq. Ft. - Second Floor
746 Sq. Ft. - Third Floor; 49,165 Cu. Ft.

GARAGE
22⁸ x 22⁸

LAUNDRY

MUD RM.

COVERED PORCH

POWDER RM.

PANTRY

TERRACE

GATHERING RM.
20⁴ x 13²

KITCHEN
16⁴ x 13²

STUDY
10⁴ x 16⁸ BAY

PARLOR
14⁴ x 13²

FOYER

DINING RM.
14⁴ x 13²

BREAKFAST RM.
10⁴ x 16⁸ BAY

PORCH

64'-0"

BATH

BEDROOM
11¹⁰ x 14⁰

BEDROOM
11¹⁰ x 14⁰

LINEN

ROOF

DRESSING RM.

BATH

BATH

LINEN

BEDROOM
13⁴ x 10⁶

MASTER BEDROOM
14⁴ x 17⁶

BEDROOM
14⁴ x 13⁶

ROOF

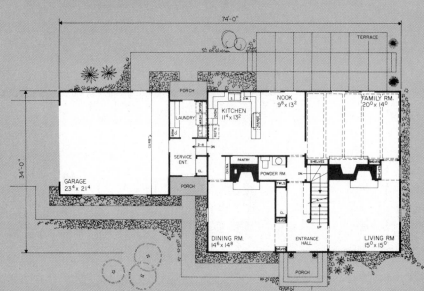

● Here is a New England Georgian adaptation with an elevated doorway highlighted by pilasters and a pediment. It gives way to a second-story Palladian window, capped in turn by a pediment projecting from the hipped roof. The interior is decidely up-to-date with even an upstairs lounge.

Design 12639 1,556 Sq. Ft. - First Floor; 1,428 Sq. Ft. - Second Floor; 46,115 Cu. Ft.

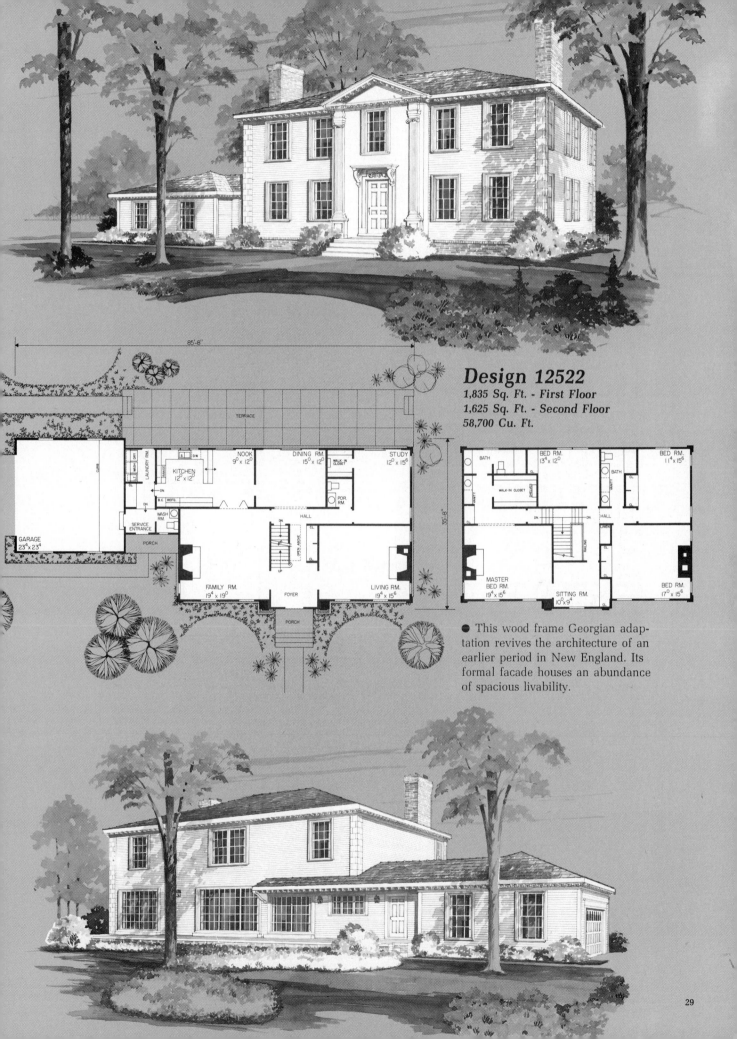

Design 12522

1,835 Sq. Ft. - First Floor
1,625 Sq. Ft. - Second Floor
58,700 Cu. Ft.

85'-8"

35'-8"

TERRACE

GARAGE
23⁴ x 23⁴

LAUNDRY RM.

KITCHEN
12⁰ x 12⁰

NOOK
9⁰ x 12⁰

DINING RM.
15⁰ x 12⁰

WALK-IN CLOSET

STUDY
12⁰ x 15⁶

PDR. RM.

SERVICE ENTRANCE

WASH RM.

PORCH

HALL

OPEN ABOVE

UP
DN

B.C.

REFG.

FAMILY RM.
19⁴ x 19⁰

FOYER

LIVING RM.
19⁴ x 15⁶

PORCH

BATH

BED RM.
13⁴ x 12⁰

BED RM.
11⁴ x 15⁶

WALK-IN CLOSET

BATH

VANITY

HALL

LINEN

DN
DN

RAILING

MASTER BED RM.
19⁴ x 15⁶

SITTING RM.
10⁰ x 9⁴

BED RM.
17⁰ x 15⁶

● This wood frame Georgian adaptation revives the architecture of an earlier period in New England. Its formal facade houses an abundance of spacious livability.

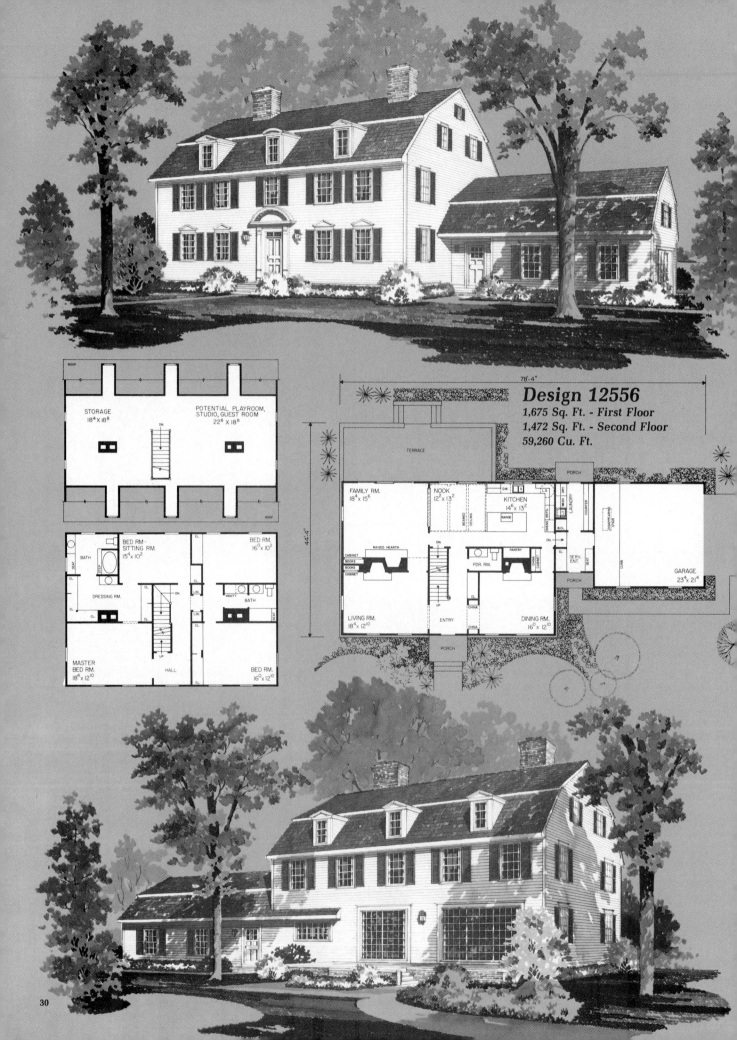

Design 12556

1,675 Sq. Ft. - First Floor
1,472 Sq. Ft. - Second Floor
59,260 Cu. Ft.

78'-4"

44'-4"

STORAGE
18⁴ x 18⁸

POTENTIAL PLAYROOM,
STUDIO, GUEST ROOM
22⁸ x 18⁸

ROOF

ROOF

DN.

BED RM. -
SITTING RM.
15⁴ x 10²

BED RM.
16⁰ x 10²

BATH

DRESSING RM.

DN.

LIN.

LIN.

VANITY

BATH

CL.

CL.

CL.

CL.

SEAT

MASTER
BED RM.
18⁴ x 12¹⁰

HALL

UP

BED RM.
16 x 12¹⁰

TERRACE

FAMILY RM.
18⁴ x 15⁶

NOOK
12² x 13²

KITCHEN
14⁶ x 13²

RANGE

D.W.

BEAMED
CEILING

OVEN REFR.

W.B.CL.

WASH DRY.

LAUNDRY

COUNTER

PORCH

DISAPPEARING
STAIR

CURB

GARAGE
23⁴ x 21⁴

CABINET
BOOKS
BOOKS
CABINET

RAISED HEARTH

DN.

PDR. RM.

PANTRY

CHINA
CABINET

SERV.
ENT.

SEAT

CL.

DN.

LIVING RM.
18⁴ x 12¹⁰

UP

ENTRY

CHINA

CL.

CHINA

DINING RM.
16⁰ x 12¹⁰

PORCH

PORCH

30

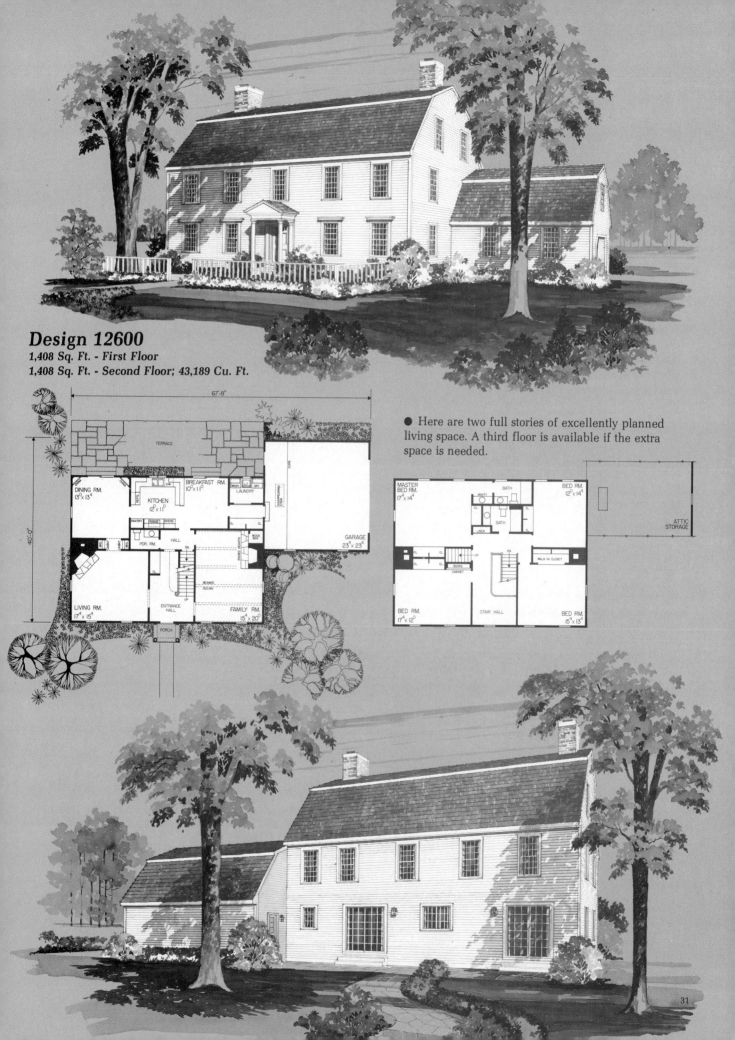

Design 12600
1,408 Sq. Ft. - First Floor
1,408 Sq. Ft. - Second Floor; 43,189 Cu. Ft.

67'-8"

TERRACE

DINING RM.
13⁰ x 13⁴

KITCHEN
12 x 11⁰

BREAKFAST RM.
10⁰ x 11⁰

LAUNDRY

GARAGE
23⁴ x 23⁴

40'-0"

PANTRY   RANGE   OVENS

PDR. RM.   HALL

WOOD BOX

LIVING RM.
17⁴ x 15⁴

ENTRANCE HALL

BEAMED CEILING

RAISED HEARTH

FAMILY RM.
15⁴ x 20⁰

PORCH

● Here are two full stories of excellently planned living space. A third floor is available if the extra space is needed.

MASTER BED RM.
17⁴ x 14⁴

VANITY   BATH

BATH

LINEN

BED RM.
12⁰ x 14⁴

ATTIC STORAGE

CL   BOOKS   CABINET

UP   DN

WALK-IN CLOSET

BED RM.
17⁴ x 12⁰

STAIR HALL

BED RM.
15⁴ x 13⁴

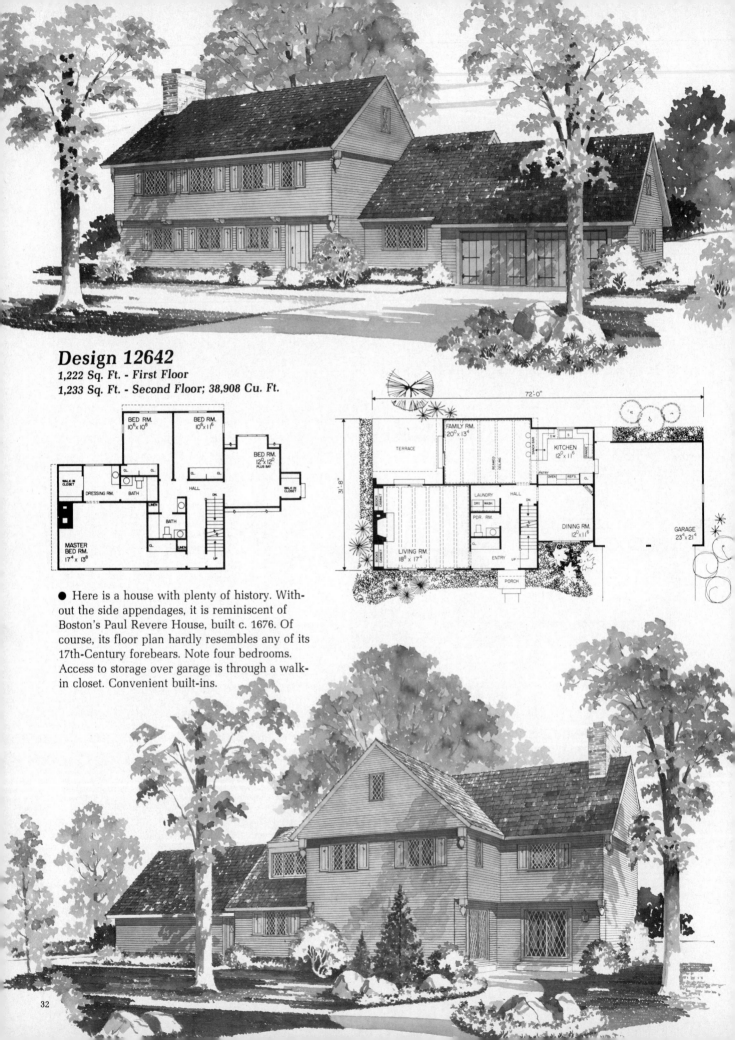

Design 12642

1,222 Sq. Ft. - First Floor
1,233 Sq. Ft. - Second Floor; 38,908 Cu. Ft.

● Here is a house with plenty of history. Without the side appendages, it is reminiscent of Boston's Paul Revere House, built c. 1676. Of course, its floor plan hardly resembles any of its 17th-Century forebears. Note four bedrooms. Access to storage over garage is through a walk-in closet. Convenient built-ins.

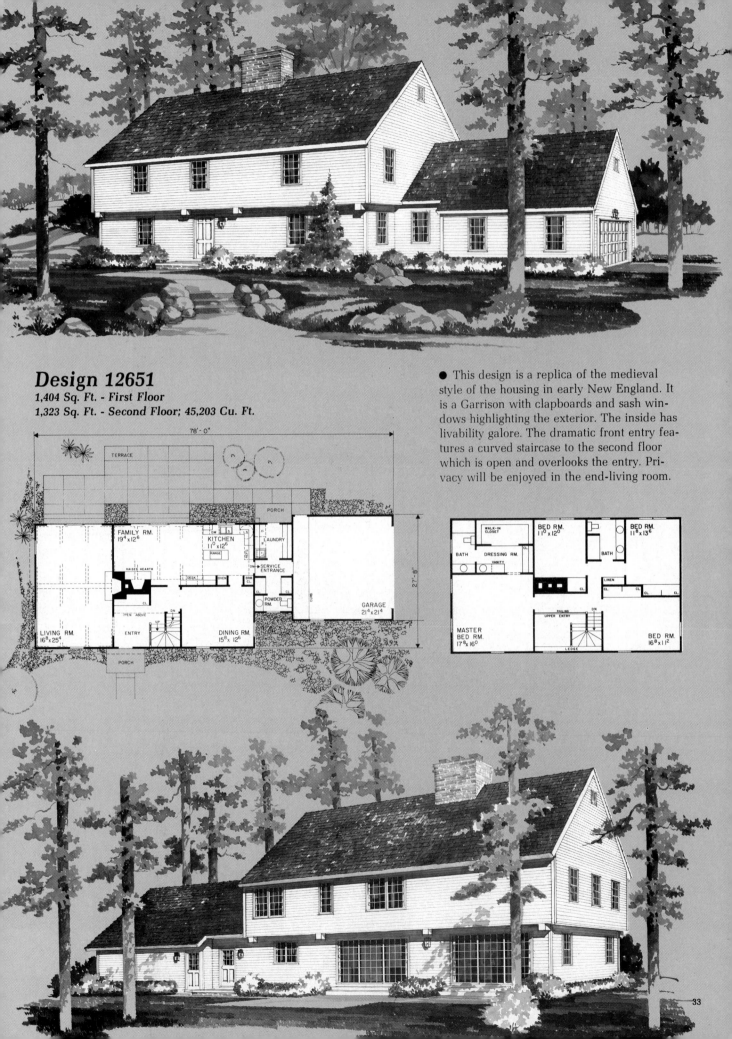

Design 12651

1,404 Sq. Ft. - First Floor
1,323 Sq. Ft. - Second Floor; 45,203 Cu. Ft.

● This design is a replica of the medieval style of the housing in early New England. It is a Garrison with clapboards and sash windows highlighting the exterior. The inside has livability galore. The dramatic front entry features a curved staircase to the second floor which is open and overlooks the entry. Privacy will be enjoyed in the end-living room.

First floor plan labels:
- 78'-0"
- TERRACE
- PORCH
- FAMILY RM. 19⁴ x 12⁶
- KITCHEN 11⁰ x 12⁶
- RANGE
- LAUNDRY
- REF.
- SERVICE ENTRANCE
- RAISED HEARTH
- DESK
- OVEN
- BRM CL.
- POWDER RM.
- CL.
- GARAGE 21⁴ x 21⁴
- LIVING RM. 16⁸ x 25⁴
- OPEN ABOVE
- ENTRY
- UP
- DN
- DINING RM. 15⁸ x 12⁶
- PORCH
- 27'-8"

Second floor plan labels:
- WALK-IN CLOSET
- BATH
- DRESSING RM.
- VANITY
- BED RM. 11⁰ x 12⁰
- BED RM. 11⁸ x 13⁶
- BATH
- LINEN
- CL. CL. CL.
- UPPER ENTRY
- RAILING
- DN
- MASTER BED RM. 17⁸ x 16⁰
- LEDGE
- BED RM. 16⁸ x 11¹²

33

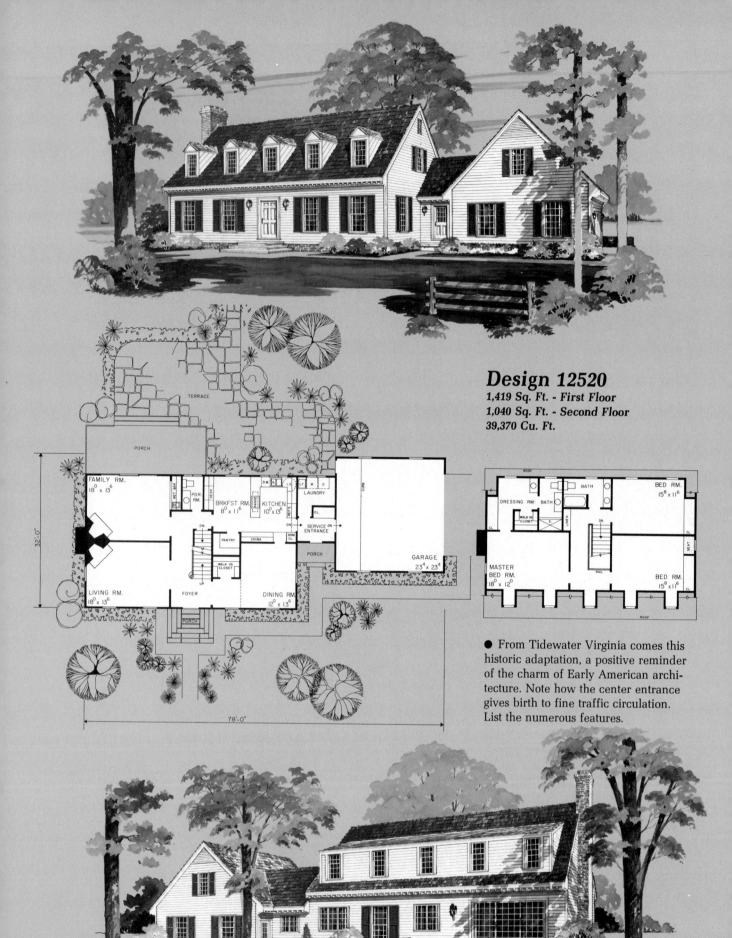

Design 12520

1,419 Sq. Ft. - First Floor
1,040 Sq. Ft. - Second Floor
39,370 Cu. Ft.

● From Tidewater Virginia comes this historic adaptation, a positive reminder of the charm of Early American architecture. Note how the center entrance gives birth to fine traffic circulation. List the numerous features.

Design 11970

1,664 Sq. Ft. - First Floor
1,116 Sq. Ft. - Second Floor
41,912 Cu. Ft.

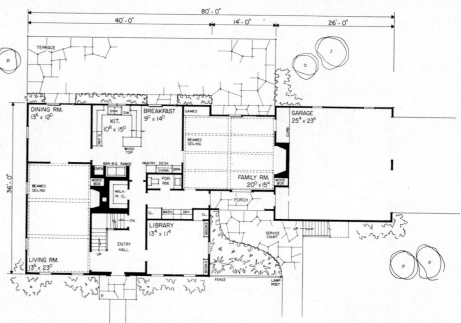

● The prototype of this Colonial house was an integral part of the 18th-Century New England landscape; the updated version is a welcome addition to any suburban scene. The main entry wing, patterned after a classic Cape Cod cottage design, is two stories high but has a pleasing groundhugging look. The steeply pitched roof, triple dormers, and a massive central chimney anchor the house firmly to its site. Entry elevation is symmetrically balanced; doorway, middle dormer, and chimney are in perfect alignment. The one story wing between the main house and the garage is a spacious, beam-ceilinged family room with splay-walled entry porch at the front elevation and sliding glass windows at the rear opening to terrace, which is the full length of the house.

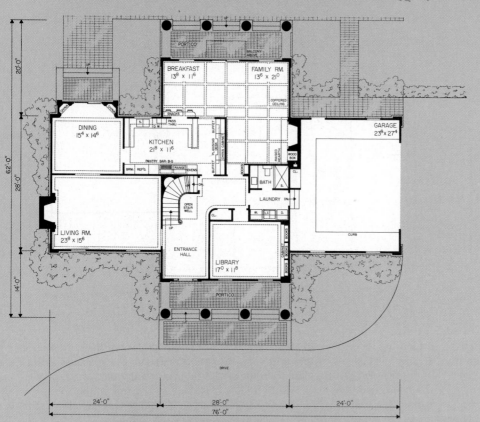

Portico

BREAKFAST
13⁸ x 11⁶

FAMILY RM.
13⁶ x 21⁰

BALCONY
ABOVE

COFFERED
CEILING

DINING
15⁴ x 14⁶

KITCHEN
21⁸ x 11⁶

PASS THRU
SNACKS

PANTRY BAR-B-Q

RANGE   OVENS

GARAGE
23⁸ x 27⁴

RAISED
HEARTH

WOOD
BOX

BATH

LAUNDRY

LIVING RM.
23⁸ x 15⁶

OPEN
STAIR
WELL

CURB

ENTRANCE
HALL

LIBRARY
17⁰ x 11⁸

Portico

DRIVE

24'-0"   28'-0"   24'-0"
76'-0"

20'-0"   62'-0"   28'-0"   14'-0"

UPPER PORTICO

BALCONY

LOUNGE

MASTER
BED RM.
SUITE
27⁴ x 15⁴

CABINET
BOOKS   BOOKS

LINEN

BATH

DRESSING
RM.

BATH

WALK-IN
CL.

STAIR
WELL

BED RM.
13⁰ x 12⁰

BED RM.
11⁶ x 15⁶

UPPER PORTICO

Design 12184

1,999 Sq. Ft. - First Floor
1,288 Sq. Ft. - Second Floor
58,441 Cu. Ft.

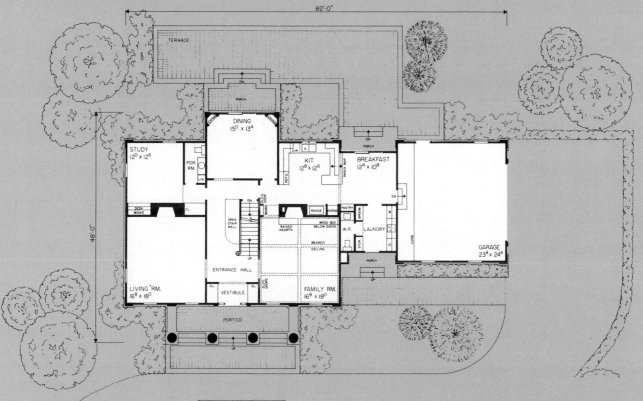

Design 12185 1,916 Sq. Ft. - First Floor
1,564 Sq. Ft. - Second Floor; 59,649 Cu. Ft.

● The elements of Greek Revival architecture when adapted to present day standards can be impressive, indeed. A study of this floor plan will reveal its similarity to that on the opposite page. There is a vestibule which leads to a wonderfully spacious entrance hall. The open stairwell is most dramatic. As it affords a view of the four bedroom, two bath second floor. The study and family room will be favorite spots for family relaxation. Both the dining and living rooms can be made to function as formally as you wish.

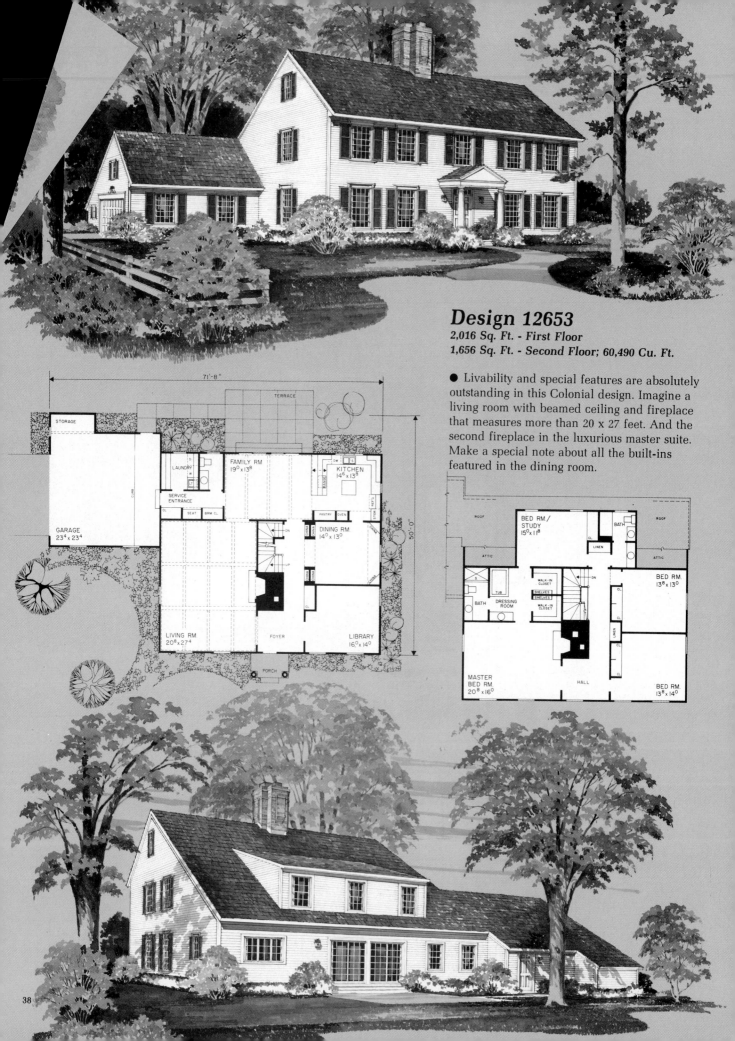

Design 12653
2,016 Sq. Ft. - First Floor
1,656 Sq. Ft. - Second Floor; 60,490 Cu. Ft.

● Livability and special features are absolutely
outstanding in this Colonial design. Imagine a
living room with beamed ceiling and fireplace
that measures more than 20 x 27 feet. And the
second fireplace in the luxurious master suite.
Make a special note about all the built-ins
featured in the dining room.

Design 12643

1,446 Sq. Ft. - First Floor
1,281 Sq. Ft. - Second Floor; 41,299 Cu. Ft.

● Four fireplaces! One to serve each of the main rooms on the first floor. Plus an impressive front and rear entrance hall to lead the way through the rest of the interior. Now note the exterior. The main house is identical from the front and back view. This house could hardly be more symmetrical.

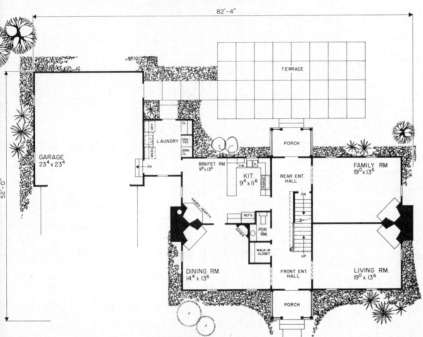

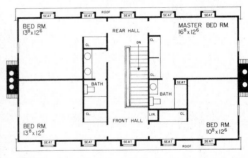

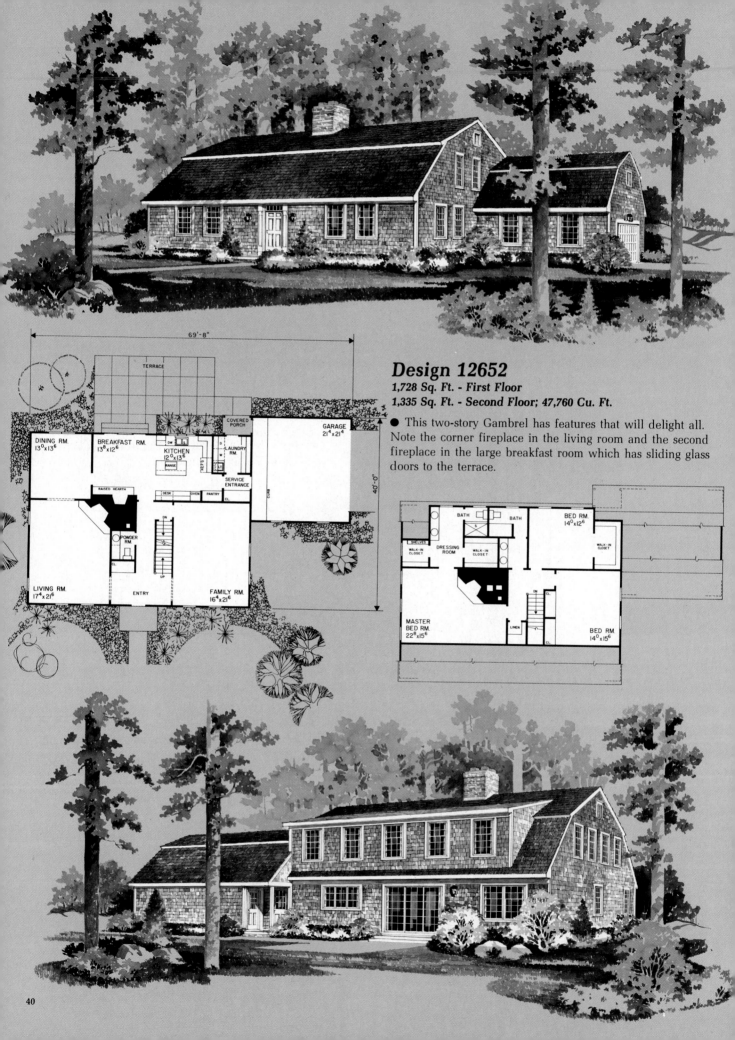

Design 12652

1,728 Sq. Ft. - First Floor
1,335 Sq. Ft. - Second Floor; 47,760 Cu. Ft.

● This two-story Gambrel has features that will delight all. Note the corner fireplace in the living room and the second fireplace in the large breakfast room which has sliding glass doors to the terrace.

First Floor

69'-8"

TERRACE

DINING RM.
13⁰x13⁶

BREAKFAST RM.
13⁸x12⁶

COVERED PORCH

GARAGE
21⁴x21⁴

KITCHEN
12⁰x13⁶

DW

RANGE

REF'G

D
W

LAUNDRY RM.

40'-0"

RAISED HEARTH

DESK   OVEN   PANTRY

SERVICE ENTRANCE

CURB

CL.

POWDER RM.

DN

UP

CL.

LIVING RM.
17⁴x21⁶

ENTRY

FAMILY RM.
16⁴x21⁶

Second Floor

BATH   BATH

BED RM.
14⁰x12⁶

SHELVES

WALK-IN CLOSET

DRESSING ROOM

WALK-IN CLOSET

WALK-IN CLOSET

DN   CL.

MASTER BED RM.
22⁸x15⁶

LINEN

CL.

BED RM.
14⁰x15⁶

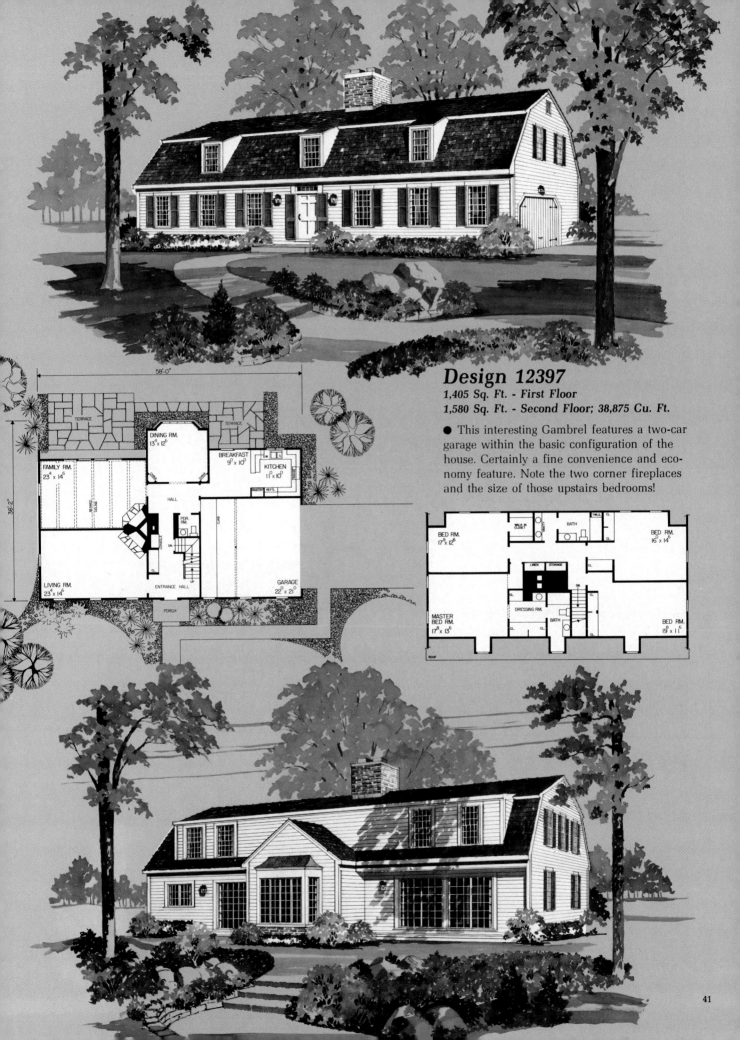

Design 12397

1,405 Sq. Ft. - First Floor
1,580 Sq. Ft. - Second Floor; 38,875 Cu. Ft.

● This interesting Gambrel features a two-car garage within the basic configuration of the house. Certainly a fine convenience and economy feature. Note the two corner fireplaces and the size of those upstairs bedrooms!

First Floor Plan

58'-0"
38'-2"

TERRACE
DINING RM. 13'⁴ x 12'⁶
TERRACE
BREAKFAST 9'⁰ x 10'⁰
KITCHEN 11' x 10'⁰
FAMILY RM. 23'⁴ x 14'⁶
PANTRY   REFG.
HALL
PDR. RM.
LIVING RM. 23'⁴ x 14'⁶
ENTRANCE HALL
GARAGE 22' x 21'⁰
PORCH

Second Floor Plan

BED RM. 17'⁸ x 12'⁸
WALK IN CLOSET
VANITY
BATH
TWLS. CL.
BED RM. 16' x 14'⁶
LINEN   STORAGE
CL.
DRESSING RM.
MASTER BED RM. 17'⁸ x 13'⁶
BATH
BED RM. 19'⁸ x 11'⁶
ROOF

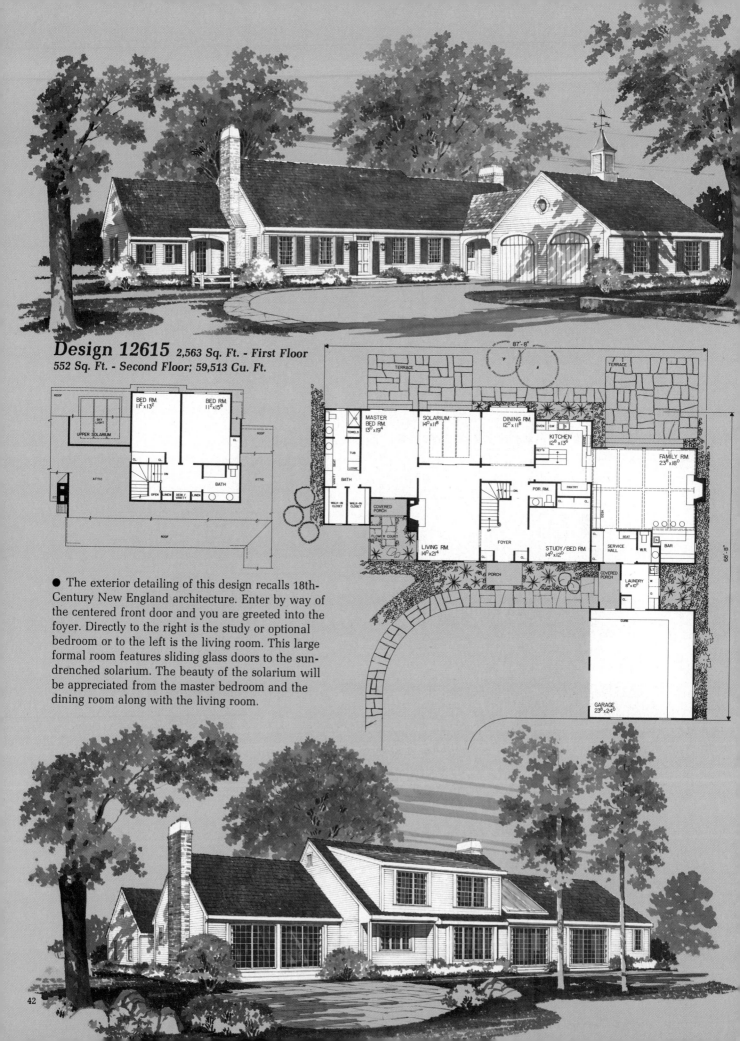

Design 12615 2,563 Sq. Ft. - First Floor
552 Sq. Ft. - Second Floor; 59,513 Cu. Ft.

● The exterior detailing of this design recalls 18th-Century New England architecture. Enter by way of the centered front door and you are greeted into the foyer. Directly to the right is the study or optional bedroom or to the left is the living room. This large formal room features sliding glass doors to the sun-drenched solarium. The beauty of the solarium will be appreciated from the master bedroom and the dining room along with the living room.

Design 12395
1,481 Sq. Ft. - First Floor
861 Sq. Ft. - Second Floor; 34,487 Cu. Ft.

● New England revisited. The appeal of this type of home is ageless. As for its livability, it will serve its occupants admirably for generations to come. With two bedrooms downstairs, you may want to finish off the second floor at a later date.

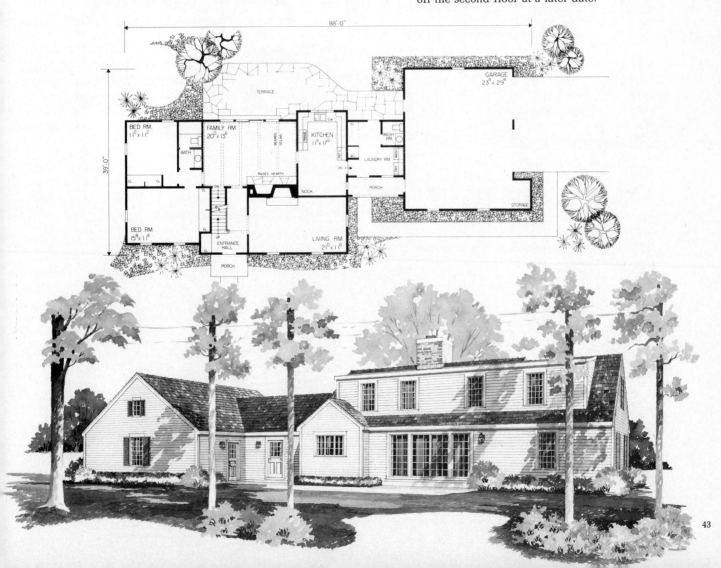

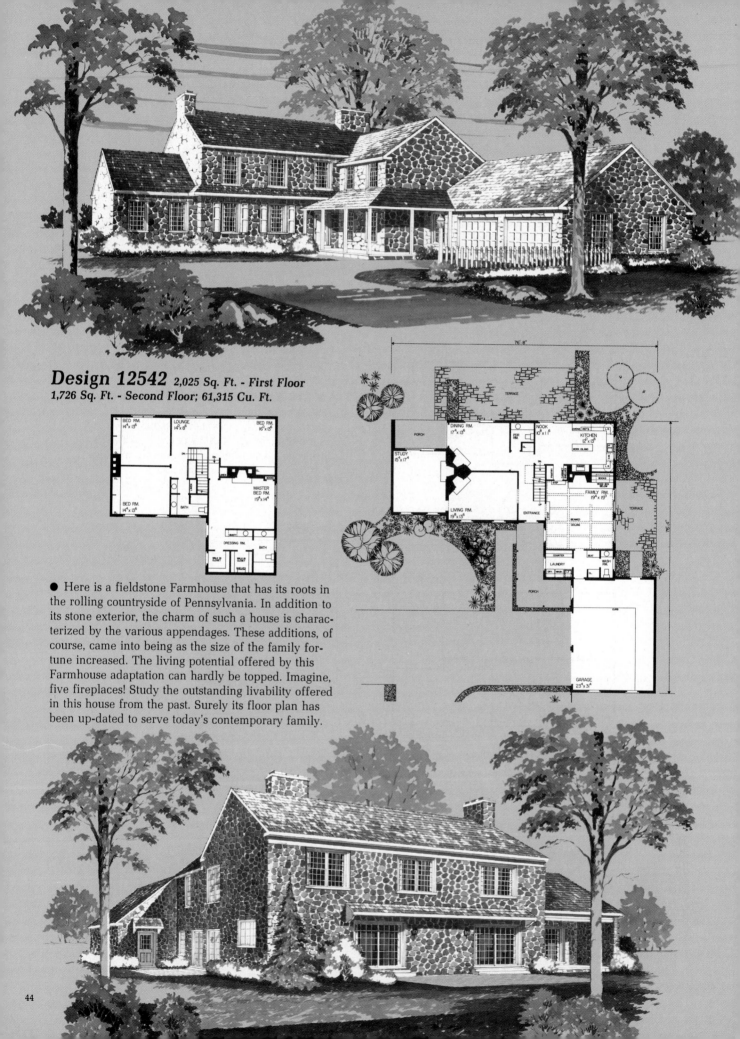

Design 12542 2,025 Sq. Ft. - First Floor
1,726 Sq. Ft. - Second Floor; 61,315 Cu. Ft.

● Here is a fieldstone Farmhouse that has its roots in the rolling countryside of Pennsylvania. In addition to its stone exterior, the charm of such a house is characterized by the various appendages. These additions, of course, came into being as the size of the family fortune increased. The living potential offered by this Farmhouse adaptation can hardly be topped. Imagine, five fireplaces! Study the outstanding livability offered in this house from the past. Surely its floor plan has been up-dated to serve today's contemporary family.

Design 12633

1,338 Sq. Ft. - First Floor
1,200 Sq. Ft. - Second Floor
506 Sq. Ft. - Third Floor
44,525 Cu. Ft.

● This is certainly a pleasing Georgian. Its facade features a front porch with a roof supported by 12'' diameter wooden columns. The garage wing has a sheltered service entry and brick facing which complements the design. Sliding glass doors link the terrace and family room, providing an indoor/outdoor area for entertaining as pictured in the rear elevation. The floor plan has been designed to serve the family efficiently. The stairway in the foyer leads to four second-floor bedrooms. The third floor is windowed and can be used as a studio and study.

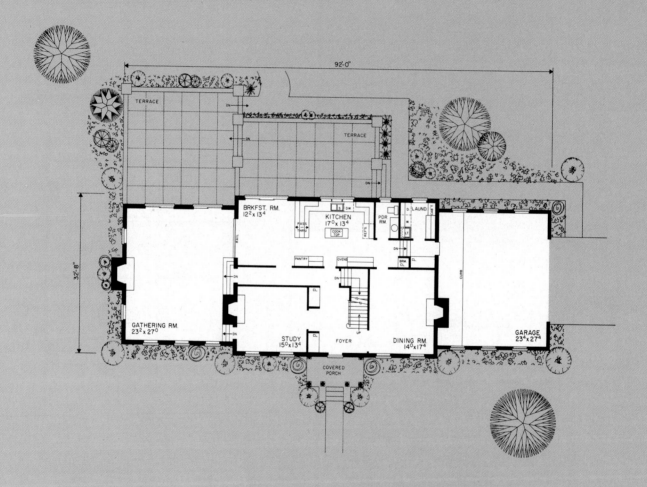

Design 12683 2,126 Sq. Ft. - First Floor; 1,424 Sq. Ft. - Second Floor; 78,828 Cu.Ft.

● This historical Georgian home has its roots in the 18th-Century. Dignified symmetry is a hallmark of both front and rear elevations. The full two-story center section is delightfully complimented by the 1½-story wings. Interior livability has been planned to serve today's active family. The elegant gathering room, three steps down from the rest of the house, has ample space for entertaining on a grand scale. It fills an entire wing and is dead-ended so that traffic does not pass through it. Guests and family alike will enjoy the two rooms flanking the foyer, the study and formal dining room. Each of these rooms will have a fireplace as its highlight. The breakfast room, kitchen, powder room and laundry are arranged for maximum efficiency. This area will always have that desired light and airy atmosphere with the sliding glass door and the triple window over the kitchen sink. The second floor houses the family bedrooms. Take special note of the spacious master bedroom suite. It has a deluxe bath, fireplace and sunken lounge with dressing room and walk-in closet. Surely an area to be appreciated.

Georgian Elegance from the Past

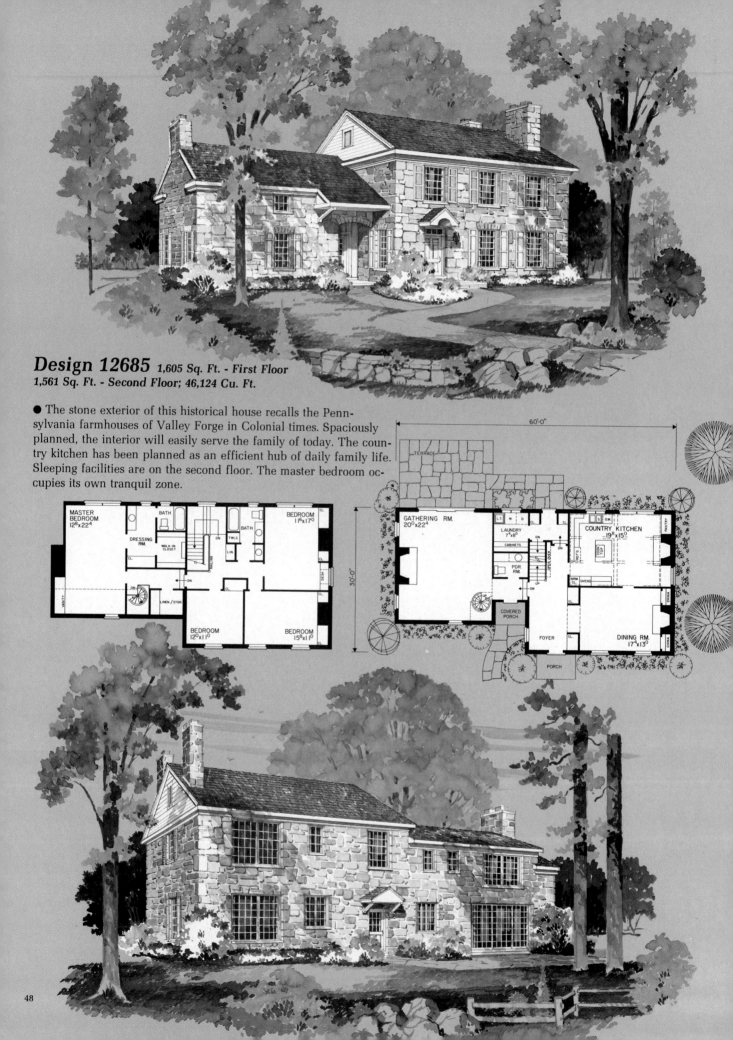

Design 12685 *1,605 Sq. Ft. - First Floor*
1,561 Sq. Ft. - Second Floor; 46,124 Cu. Ft.

● The stone exterior of this historical house recalls the Pennsylvania farmhouses of Valley Forge in Colonial times. Spaciously planned, the interior will easily serve the family of today. The country kitchen has been planned as an efficient hub of daily family life. Sleeping facilities are on the second floor. The master bedroom occupies its own tranquil zone.

MASTER BEDROOM 12⁸x22⁴

DRESSING RM.

WALK-IN CLOSET

BATH

BEDROOM 11⁶x17⁰

BEDROOM 12⁰x11⁰

BEDROOM 15⁸x11⁰

LINEN / STOR.

60'-0"

TERRACE

GATHERING RM. 20⁰x22⁴

LAUNDRY 7⁴x8⁰

CABINETS

PDR. RM.

COUNTRY KITCHEN 19⁸x15⁰

PANTRY

30'-0"

COVERED PORCH

FOYER

PORCH

DINING RM. 17⁴x13⁰

Design 12521
1,272 Sq. Ft. - First Floor
1,139 Sq. Ft. - Second Floor; 37,262 Cu. Ft.

● Here is a house to remind one of the weather-beaten facades of Nantucket. The active family plan is as up-to-date as tomorrow. Along with formal and informal areas on the first floor, there is a music alcove. If a music alcove is not needed, this area would make an ideal intimate sitting area.

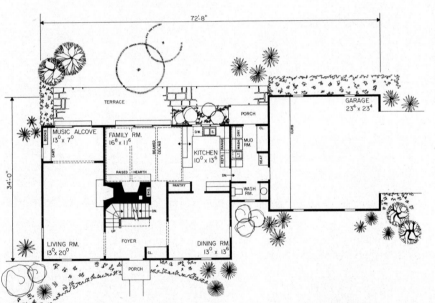

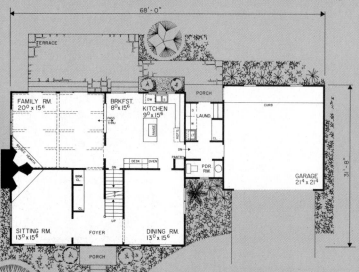

Design 12644

1,349 Sq. Ft. - First Floor
836 Sq. Ft. - Second Floor
36,510 Cu. Ft.

68'-0"

TERRACE

FAMILY RM.
20⁰ x 15⁶

BRKFST.
8⁰ x 15⁶

KITCHEN
9⁰ x 15⁶

PORCH

LAUND.

PASS THRU

CL.

RAISED HEARTH

BRM. CL.

DESK OVEN

PANTRY

PDR. RM.

CL.

DN

GARAGE
21⁴ x 21⁴

CURB

31'-8"

SITTING RM.
13⁰ x 15⁶

FOYER

UP

DINING RM.
13⁰ x 15⁶

PORCH

ROOF

BEDROOM
11⁰ x 10⁶

CL.

BATH

LINEN

BATH

SHLVS

WALK-IN CLOSET

DN

CL.

BEDROOM
17⁸ x 10⁶

WALK-IN CLOSET

MASTER BEDROOM
13⁰ x 14⁸

ROOF

● What a delightful, compact two-story this is! This design has many fine features tucked within its framework. The bowed roofline of this house stems from late 17th-Century architecture.

50

Design 12661

1,020 Sq. Ft. - First Floor
777 Sq. Ft. - Second Floor; 30,745 Cu. Ft.

● Any other starter house or retirement home couldn't have more charm than this design. Its compact frame houses a very livable plan. An outstanding feature of the first floor is the large country kitchen. Its fine attractions include a beamed ceiling, raised hearth fireplace, built-in window seat and a door leading to the outdoors. A living room is in the front of the plan and has another fireplace which shares the single chimney. The rear dormered second floor houses the sleeping and bath facilities.

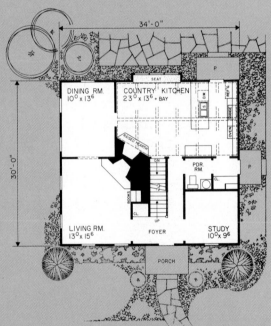

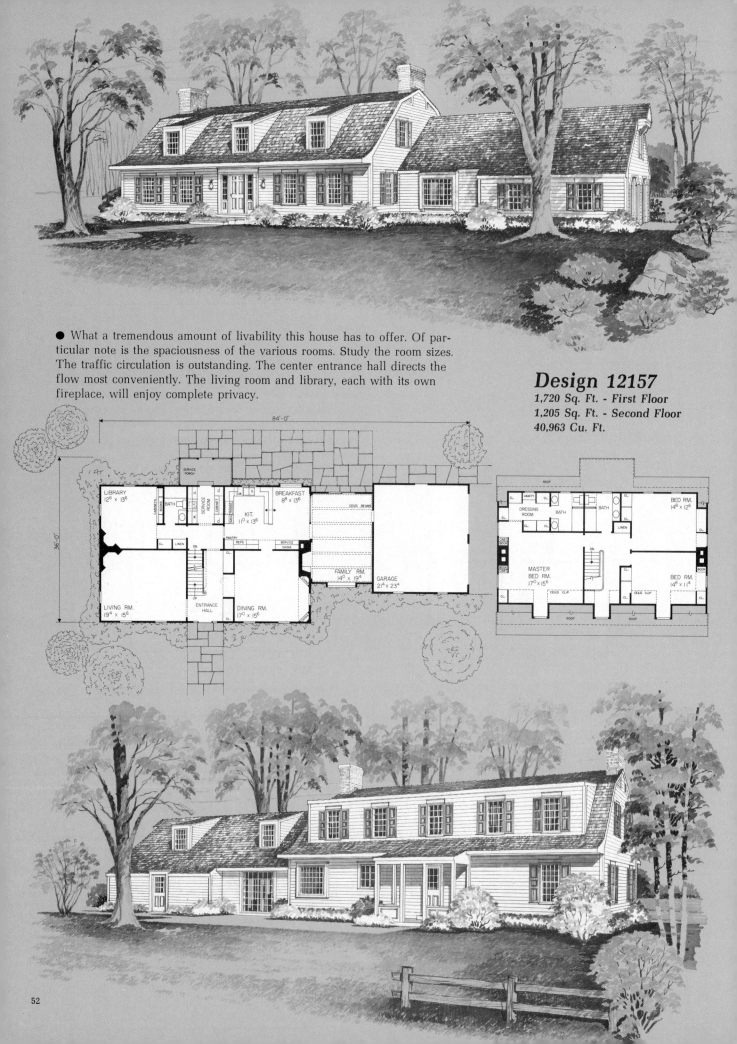

● What a tremendous amount of livability this house has to offer. Of particular note is the spaciousness of the various rooms. Study the room sizes. The traffic circulation is outstanding. The center entrance hall directs the flow most conveniently. The living room and library, each with its own fireplace, will enjoy complete privacy.

Design 12157

1,720 Sq. Ft. - First Floor
1,205 Sq. Ft. - Second Floor
40,963 Cu. Ft.

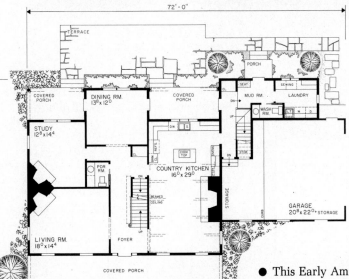

Design 12680

1,707 Sq. Ft. - First Floor
1,439 Sq. Ft. - Second Floor; 53,865 Cu. Ft.

● This Early American, Dutch Colonial not only has charm, but offers many fine features. The foyer allows easy access to all rooms on the first floor - excellent livability. Note the large country kitchen with beamed ceiling, fireplace and island cook top. A large, formal dining room and powder room are only a few steps away. A fireplace also will be found in the study and living room. The service area, mud room, wash room and laundry are tucked near the garage. Two bedrooms, full bath and master bedroom suite will be found on the second floor. A fourth bedroom and bath are accessible through the master bedroom or stairs in the service entrance.

Design 12649

1,501 Sq. Ft. - First Floor
1,280 Sq. Ft. - Second Floor; 43,537 Cu. Ft.

● This design's front exterior is highlighted by four pedimented nine-over-nine windows, five second-story eyebrow windows and a massive central chimney. Note the spacious kitchen of the interior. It is large in size and features an island range, pantry and broom closets, breakfast room with sliding glass doors to the rear porch and an adjacent laundry room which has access to the garage.

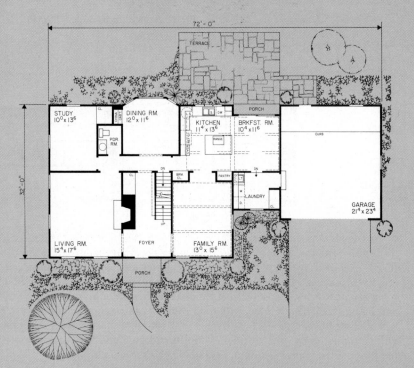

Design 12616 1,415 Sq. Ft. - First Floor
1,106 Sq. Ft. - Second Floor; 36,880 Cu. Ft.

● Unlike the majority of the Salt Boxes of Colonial New England, this design has a distinguishing feature: a saw-tooth-shaped side wing that shares the same rear roofline as the house to which it was appended. History is exquisitely detailed in this exterior yet its floor plan has been planned to serve today's family conveniently.

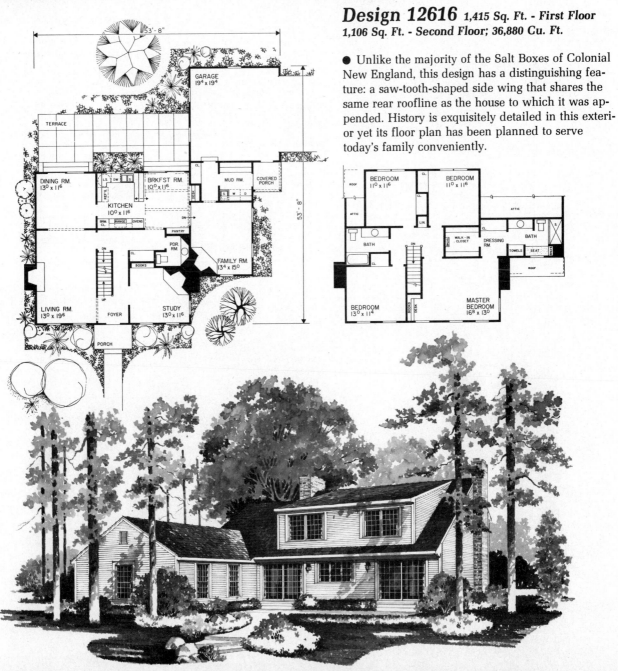

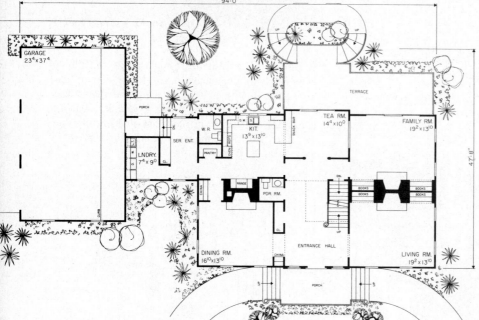

Design 12301

2,044 Sq. Ft. - First Floor
1,815 Sq. Ft. - Second Floor
69,925 Cu. Ft.

● Reminiscent of architecture with roots in the deep South, this finely detailed home is exquisite, indeed. Study the contemporary floor plan and the living patterns it offers.

Design 12667 *1,827 Sq. Ft. - First Floor*
697 Sq. Ft. - Second Floor; 46,290 Cu. Ft.

● Two one-story wings flank the two-story center section of this design which echoes the architectural forms of 18th-Century Tidewater Virginia. The left wing is a huge living room; the right, the master bedroom suite, service area and garage. Kitchen, dining room and family room are centrally located with the three bedrooms above. Study both plans and envision your family occupying them.

Expanding the Half-House

Design 12682 976 Sq. Ft. - First Floor (Basic Plan)
1,230 Sq. Ft. - First Floor (Expanded Plan); 744 Sq. Ft. - Second Floor (Both Plans)
29,355 Cu. Ft. Basic Plan; 35,084 Cu. Ft. Expanded Plan

● Here is an expandable Colonial with a full measure of Cape Cod Charm. For those who wish to build the basic house, there is an abundance of low-budget livability. Twin fireplaces serve the formal living room and the informal country kitchen. Note the spaciousness of both areas. A dining room and powder room are also on the first floor of this basic plan. Upstairs three bedrooms and two full baths.

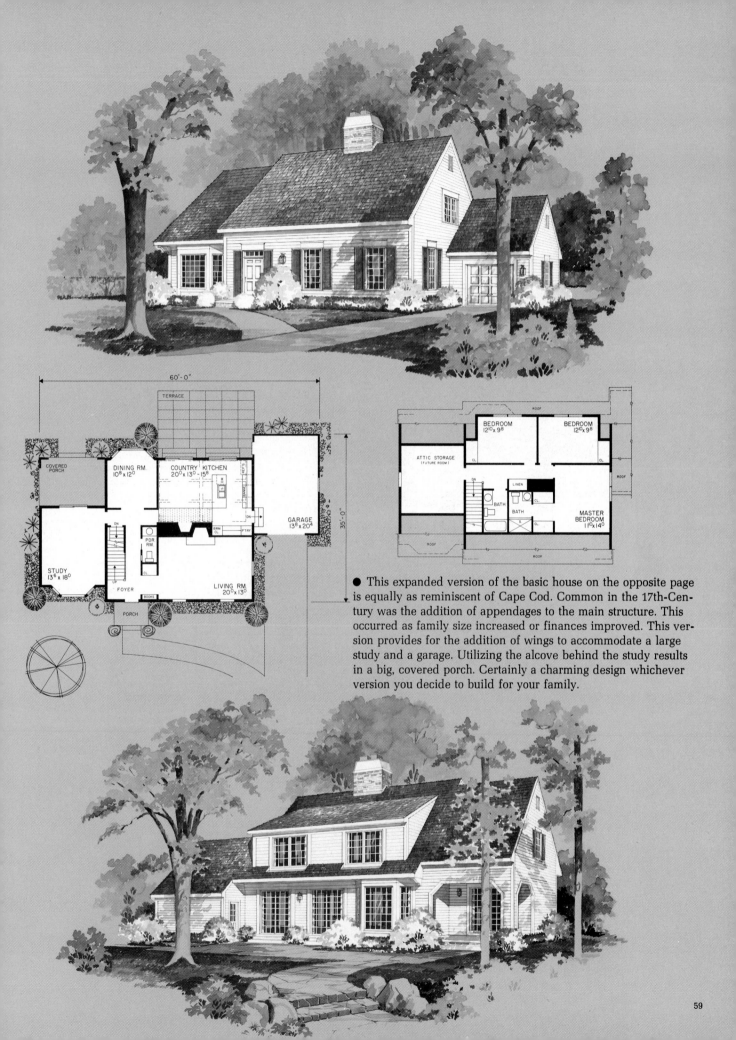

TERRACE

60'-0"

COVERED PORCH

DINING RM.
10⁸ x 12⁰

COUNTRY KITCHEN
20⁰ x 13⁰ - 15⁸

GARAGE
13⁸ x 20⁴

35'-0"

STUDY
13⁶ x 18⁰

PDR. RM.

BRM. CL.

P'TRY

FOYER

BOOKS

LIVING RM.
20⁰ x 13⁰

PORCH

ATTIC STORAGE
(FUTURE ROOM)

ROOF

BEDROOM
12¹⁰ x 9⁸

BEDROOM
12¹⁰ x 9⁸

CL.

CL.

ROOF

LINEN

DN

BATH

BATH

CL.

MASTER BEDROOM
11⁶ x 14⁰

ROOF

ROOF

● This expanded version of the basic house on the opposite page is equally as reminiscent of Cape Cod. Common in the 17th-Century was the addition of appendages to the main structure. This occurred as family size increased or finances improved. This version provides for the addition of wings to accommodate a large study and a garage. Utilizing the alcove behind the study results in a big, covered porch. Certainly a charming design whichever version you decide to build for your family.

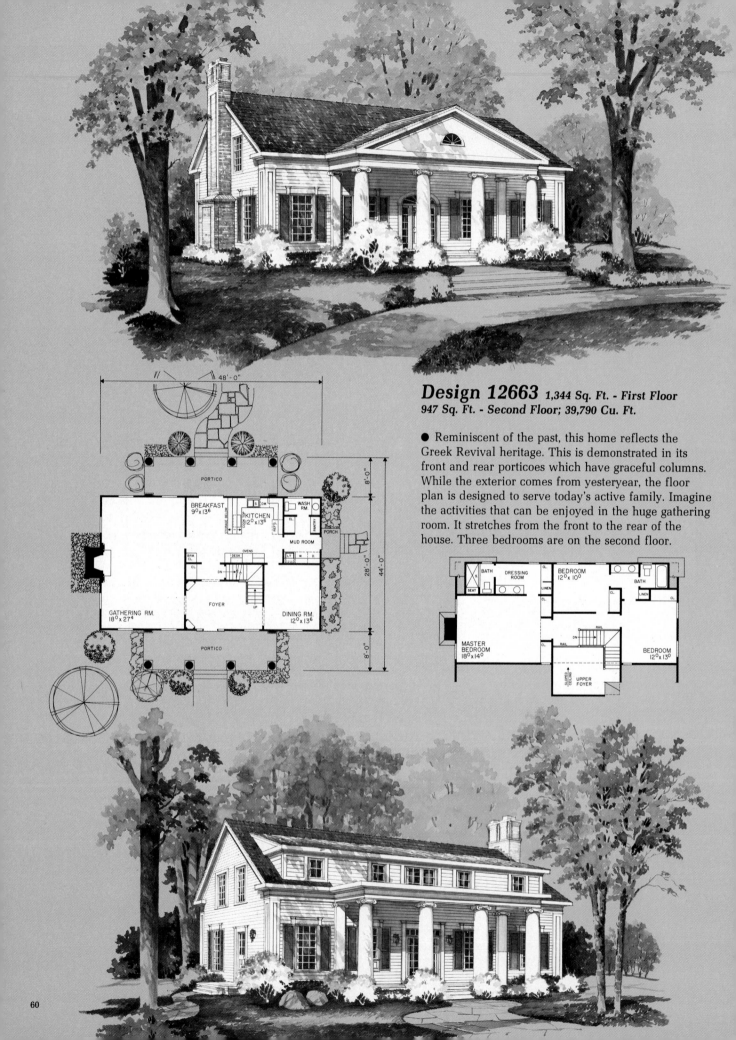

Design 12663 *1,344 Sq. Ft. - First Floor*
947 Sq. Ft. - Second Floor; 39,790 Cu. Ft.

● Reminiscent of the past, this home reflects the Greek Revival heritage. This is demonstrated in its front and rear porticoes which have graceful columns. While the exterior comes from yesteryear, the floor plan is designed to serve today's active family. Imagine the activities that can be enjoyed in the huge gathering room. It stretches from the front to the rear of the house. Three bedrooms are on the second floor.

48'-0"

PORTICO

BREAKFAST 9⁰x13⁶

KITCHEN 12⁰x13⁶

WASH RM.

MUD ROOM

PANTRY

PORCH

OVENS

DESK

BRM CL.

DN

UP

GATHERING RM. 18⁰x27⁴

FOYER

DINING RM. 12⁰x13⁶

PORTICO

8'-0"   28'-0"   44'-0"   8'-0"

BATH

DRESSING ROOM

BEDROOM 12⁰x10⁰

BATH

MASTER BEDROOM 18⁰x14⁰

DN

RAIL

RAIL

BEDROOM 12⁰x13⁰

SLOPED CEILING

UPPER FOYER

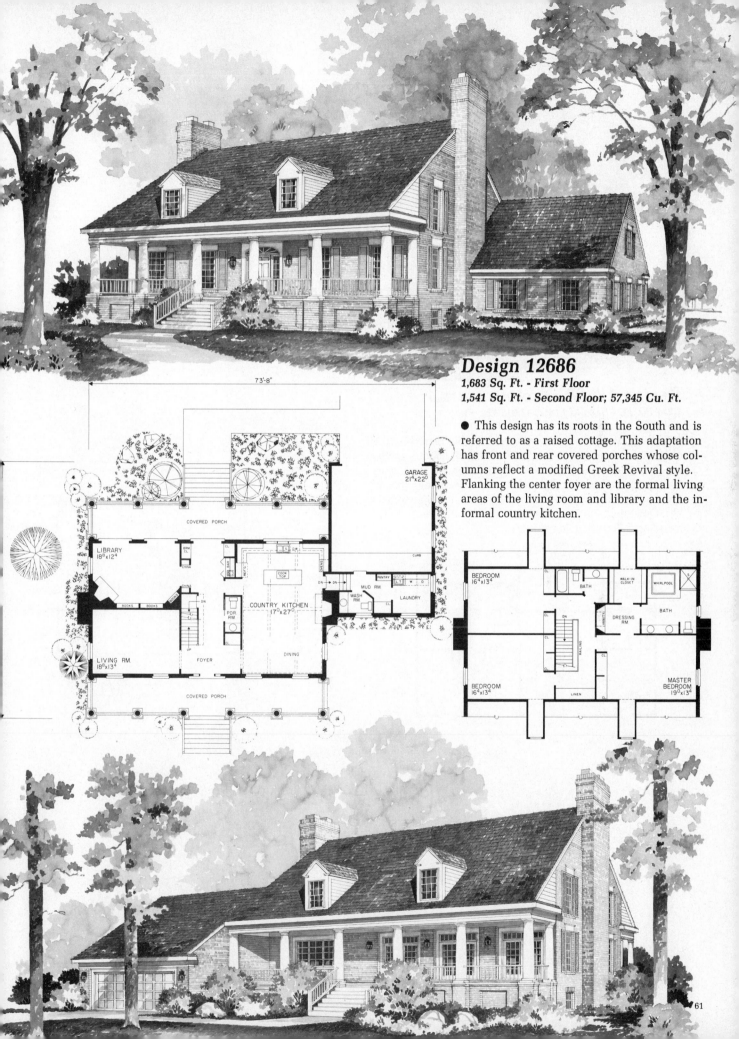

Design 12686

1,683 Sq. Ft. - First Floor
1,541 Sq. Ft. - Second Floor; 57,345 Cu. Ft.

● This design has its roots in the South and is referred to as a raised cottage. This adaptation has front and rear covered porches whose columns reflect a modified Greek Revival style. Flanking the center foyer are the formal living areas of the living room and library and the informal country kitchen.

73'-8"

GARAGE
21⁴x22⁰

COVERED PORCH

LIBRARY
18⁶x12⁴

BRM
CL

CHINA

CL

COOK TOP

OVENS

CURB

PANTRY

LT

W   D

CHINA

BOOKS   BOOKS

DN   DN

MUD RM.

WASH
RM.

LAUNDRY

POR
RM.

COUNTRY KITCHEN
17⁰x27⁰

UP

LIVING RM.
18⁶x13⁴

FOYER

DINING

COVERED PORCH

BEDROOM
16⁴x13⁴

BATH

WALK-IN
CLOSET

WHIRLPOOL

BATH

DRESSING
RM.

DN

CL

RAILING

BEDROOM
16⁴x13⁴

LINEN

MASTER
BEDROOM
19⁰x13⁴

Design 12668
1,206 Sq. Ft. - First Floor
1,254 Sq. Ft. - Second Floor; 47,915 Cu. Ft.

● This elegant exterior houses a very livable plan. Every bit of space has been put to good use. The front country kitchen is a good place to begin. It is efficiently planned with its island cook top, built-ins and pass-thru to the dining room. The large great room will be the center of all family activities. Quiet times can be enjoyed in the front library. Study the second floor sleeping areas.

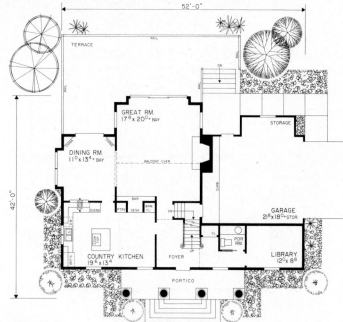

Design 12230

2,288 Sq. Ft. - First Floor
1,863 Sq. Ft. - Second Floor
79,736 Cu. Ft.

● The gracefulness and appeal of this southern adaptation will be everlasting. The imposing two-story portico is truly dramatic. Notice the authentic detailing of the tapered Doric columns, the balustraded roof deck, the denticulated cornice, the front entrance and the shuttered windows. The architecture of the rear is no less appealing with its formal symmetry and smaller Doric portico. The impressive exterior of this two-story houses a total of 4,151 square feet. The spacious, formal front entrance hall provides a fitting introduction to the scale and elegance of the interior.

● Clapboard siding and shuttered, multi-paned windows create the delightful detailing of this two-story gambrel. Beamed ceilings and a thru-fireplace highlight the living and family rooms. The work centers, kitchen and laundry, are clustered together for greater convenience. The formal dining room is nearby to make the serving of meals easy. The second floor houses all of the sleeping facilities.

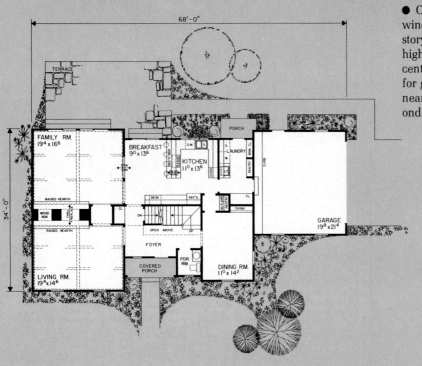

Design 12632
1,460 Sq. Ft. - First Floor
912 Sq. Ft. - Second Floor; 39,205 Cu. Ft.

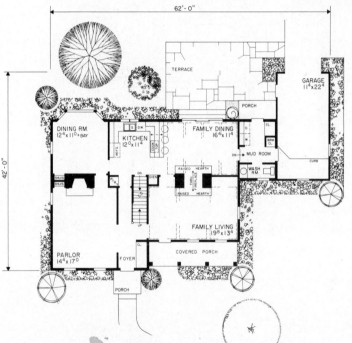

Design 12681 1,350 Sq. Ft. - First Floor
1,224 Sq. Ft. - Second Floor; 35,890 Cu. Ft.

● The charm of Early America is exemplified in this delightful design. Note the three areas which are highlighted by a fireplace. The three bedroom second floor is nicely planned. Make special note of the master bedroom's many fine features. Study the rest of this design's many fine qualities.

Design 12654

1,152 Sq. Ft. - First Floor
844 Sq. Ft. - Second Floor; 31,845 Cu. Ft.

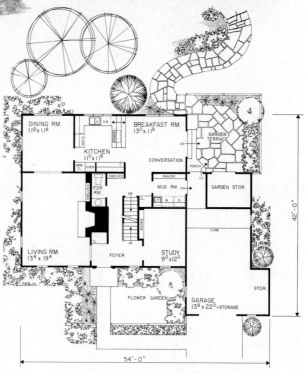

● This is certainly an authentic traditional salt-box. It features a symmetrical design with a center fireplace, a wide, paneled doorway and multi-paned, double-hung windows. Tucked behind the one-car garage is a garden shed which provides work and storage space. The breakfast room features French doors which open onto a flagstone terrace. The U-shaped kitchen has built-in counters which make efficient use of space. The upstairs plan houses three bedrooms.

Design 12320 *1,856 Sq. Ft. - First Floor; 1,171 Sq. Ft. - Second Floor; 46,699 Cu. Ft.*

● A charming Colonial adaptation with a Gambrel roof front exterior and a Salt Box rear. The focal point of family activities will be the spacious family kitchen with its beamed ceiling and fireplace. Blueprints include details for both three and four bedroom options. In addition to the family kitchen, note the family room with beamed ceiling and fireplace. Don't miss the study with built-in bookshelves and cabinets.

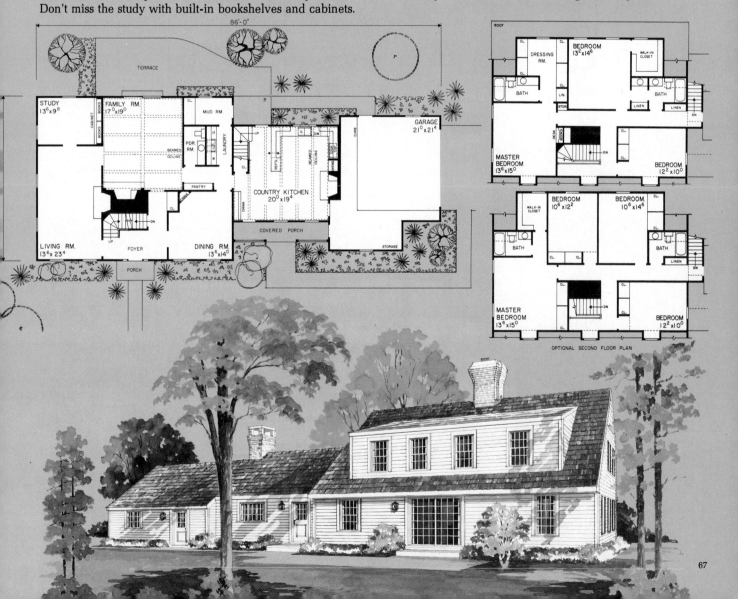

Design 12657 1,217 Sq. Ft. - First Floor
868 Sq. Ft. - Second Floor; 33,260 Cu. Ft.

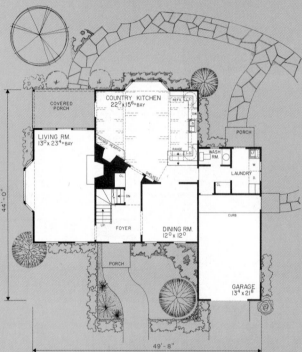

● Deriving its design from the traditional Cape Cod style, this facade features clapboard siding, small-paned windows and a transom-lit entrance flanked by carriage lamps. A central chimney services two fireplaces, one in the country-kitchen and the other in the formal living room which is removed from the disturbing flow of traffic. The master suite is located to the left of the upstairs landing. A full bathroom services two additional bedrooms.

Design 12658

1,218 Sq. Ft. - First Floor
764 Sq. Ft. - Second Floor; 29,690 Cu. Ft.

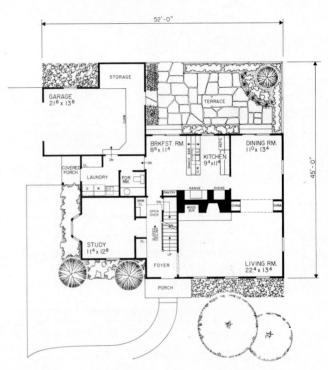

● Traditional charm of yesteryear is exemplified delightfully in this one-and-a-half story home. The garage has been conveniently tucked away in the rear of the house which makes this design ideal for a corner lot. Interior livability has been planned for efficient living. The front living room is large and features a fireplace with wood box. The laundry area is accessible by way of both the garage and a side covered porch. Enter the rear terrace from both eating areas, the formal dining room and the informal breakfast room.

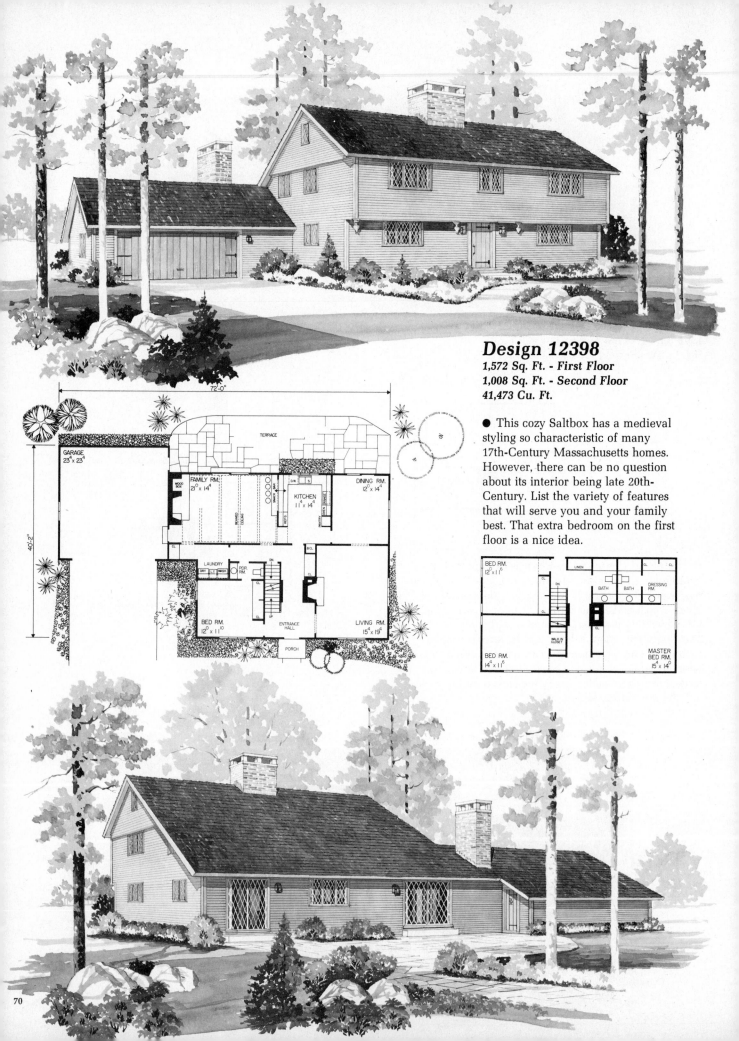

Design 12398

1,572 Sq. Ft. - *First Floor*
1,008 Sq. Ft. - *Second Floor*
41,473 Cu. Ft.

● This cozy Saltbox has a medieval styling so characteristic of many 17th-Century Massachusetts homes. However, there can be no question about its interior being late 20th-Century. List the variety of features that will serve you and your family best. That extra bedroom on the first floor is a nice idea.

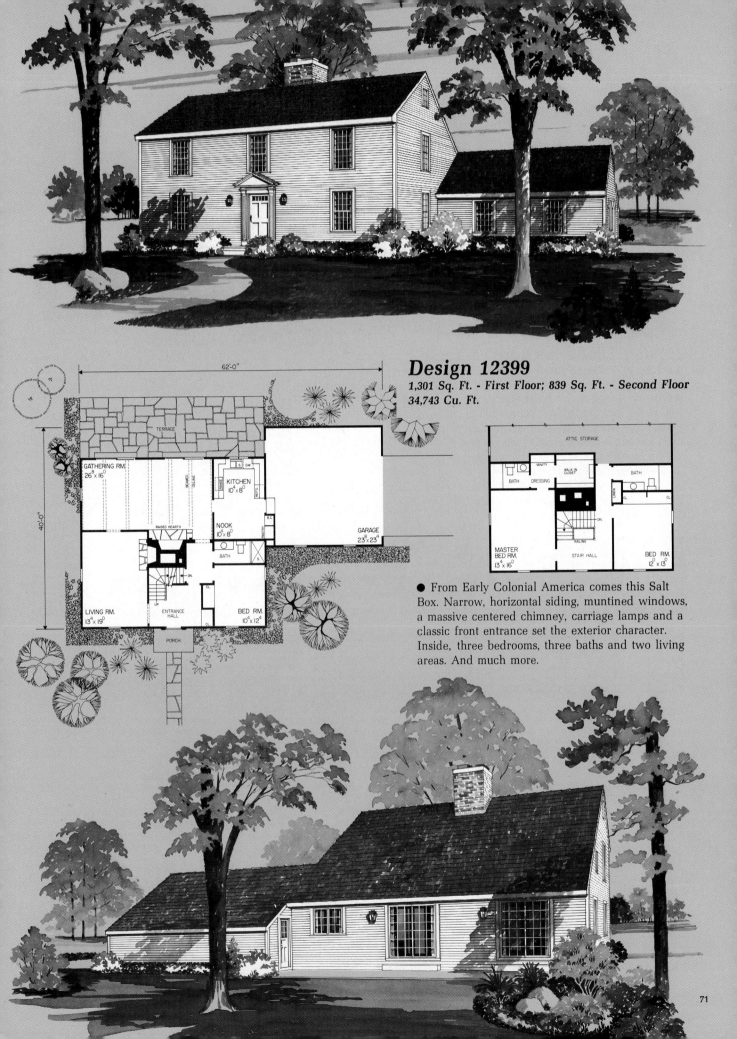

Design 12399

1,301 Sq. Ft. - First Floor; 839 Sq. Ft. - Second Floor
34,743 Cu. Ft.

62'-0"

40'-0"

TERRACE

GATHERING RM.
26⁸ x 16⁰
BEAMED CEILING

KITCHEN
10⁴ x 8⁰
RANGE D.W. REF'G.

RAISED HEARTH

NOOK
10⁴ x 8⁰
B.C.
PANTRY

LIVING RM.
13⁴ x 19⁰

ENTRANCE HALL
UP DN.
CL. CL.

BED RM.
10⁴ x 12⁴

BATH

GARAGE
23⁸ x 23⁴

PORCH

ATTIC STORAGE

BATH DRESSING VANITY WALK IN CLOSET BATH LINEN CL.

MASTER BED RM.
13⁴ x 16⁰

STAIR HALL
DN.
RAILING

BED RM.
12 x 13

● From Early Colonial America comes this Salt Box. Narrow, horizontal siding, muntined windows, a massive centered chimney, carriage lamps and a classic front entrance set the exterior character. Inside, three bedrooms, three baths and two living areas. And much more.

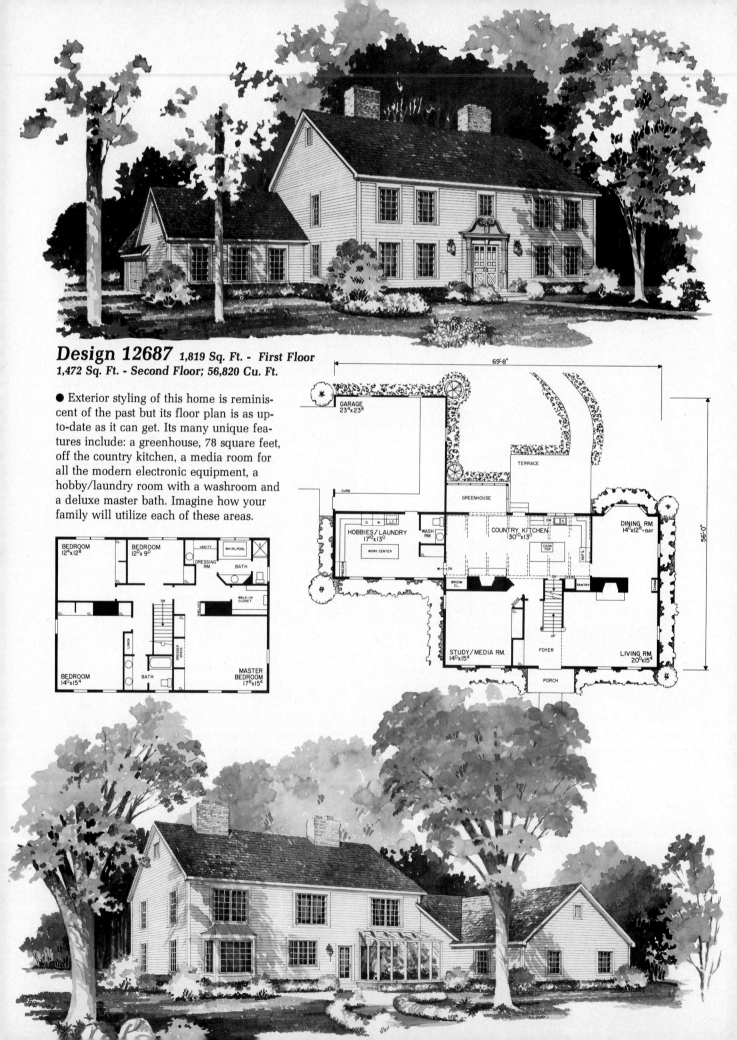

Design 12687 1,819 Sq. Ft. - First Floor
1,472 Sq. Ft. - Second Floor; 56,820 Cu. Ft.

● Exterior styling of this home is reminiscent of the past but its floor plan is as up-to-date as it can get. Its many unique features include: a greenhouse, 78 square feet, off the country kitchen, a media room for all the modern electronic equipment, a hobby/laundry room with a washroom and a deluxe master bath. Imagine how your family will utilize each of these areas.

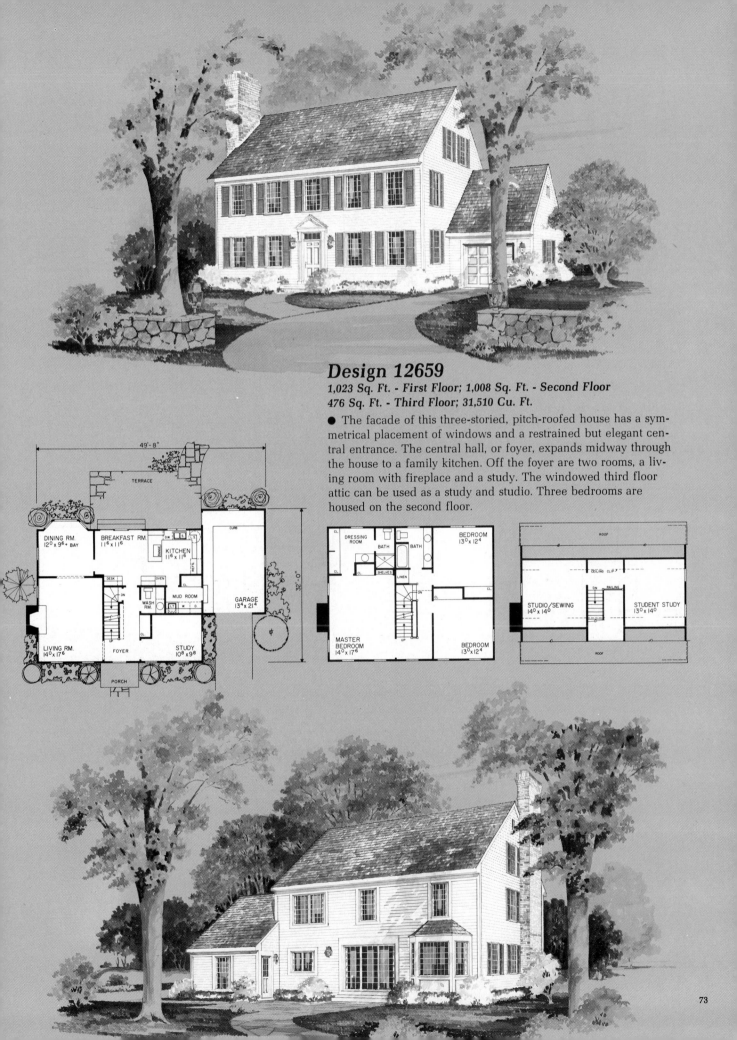

Design 12659

1,023 Sq. Ft. - First Floor; 1,008 Sq. Ft. - Second Floor
476 Sq. Ft. - Third Floor; 31,510 Cu. Ft.

● The facade of this three-storied, pitch-roofed house has a symmetrical placement of windows and a restrained but elegant central entrance. The central hall, or foyer, expands midway through the house to a family kitchen. Off the foyer are two rooms, a living room with fireplace and a study. The windowed third floor attic can be used as a study and studio. Three bedrooms are housed on the second floor.

49'-8"

TERRACE

DINING RM.
12⁰ x 9⁶ + BAY

BREAKFAST RM.
11⁶ x 11⁶

KITCHEN
11⁶ x 11⁶

RANGE

DW

CURB

GARAGE
13⁴ x 21⁴

DESK

OVEN

MUD ROOM

32'-0"

LIVING RM.
14⁰ x 17⁶

WASH. RM.

CL

FOYER

STUDY
10⁸ x 9⁸

PORCH

DN

UP

CL

DRESSING ROOM

BATH

BATH

BEDROOM
13⁰ x 12⁴

CL

CL

SHELVES

LINEN

DN

CL

CL

MASTER BEDROOM
14⁰ x 17⁶

UP

BEDROOM
13⁰ x 12⁴

ROOF

CEILING CLG'

DN

RAILING

STUDIO/SEWING
14⁰ x 14⁰

STUDENT STUDY
13⁰ x 14⁰

ROOF

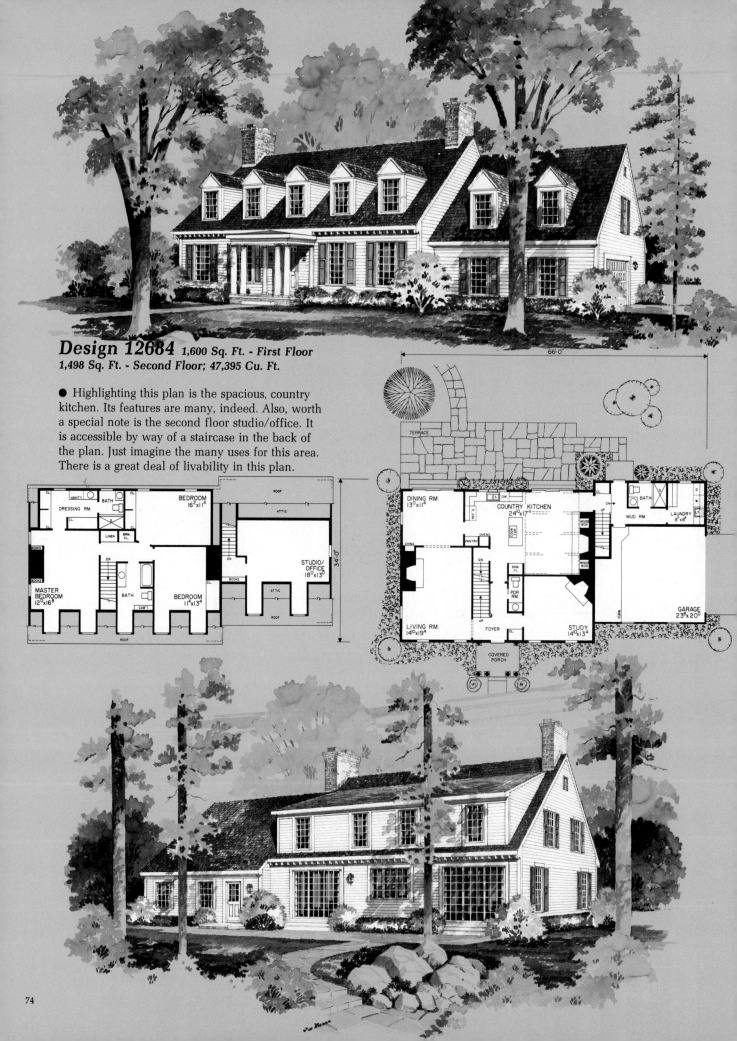

Design 12684 *1,600 Sq. Ft. - First Floor*
1,498 Sq. Ft. - Second Floor; 47,395 Cu. Ft.

● Highlighting this plan is the spacious, country kitchen. Its features are many, indeed. Also, worth a special note is the second floor studio/office. It is accessible by way of a staircase in the back of the plan. Just imagine the many uses for this area. There is a great deal of livability in this plan.

Design 12650

1,451 Sq. Ft. - First Floor
1,091 Sq. Ft. - Second Floor; 43,555 Cu. Ft.

● The rear view of this design is just as appealing as the front. The dormers and the covered porch with pillars is a charming way to introduce this house to the on-lookers. Inside, the appeal is also outstanding. Note the size (18 x 25) of the gathering room which is open to the dining room. Kitchen-nook area is very spacious and features an island range, built-in desk and more. It is a great convenience having the laundry in the service area which is close to the kitchen. Imagine, a fireplace in both the gathering room and the master bedroom! Make special note of the front and rear service entrances.

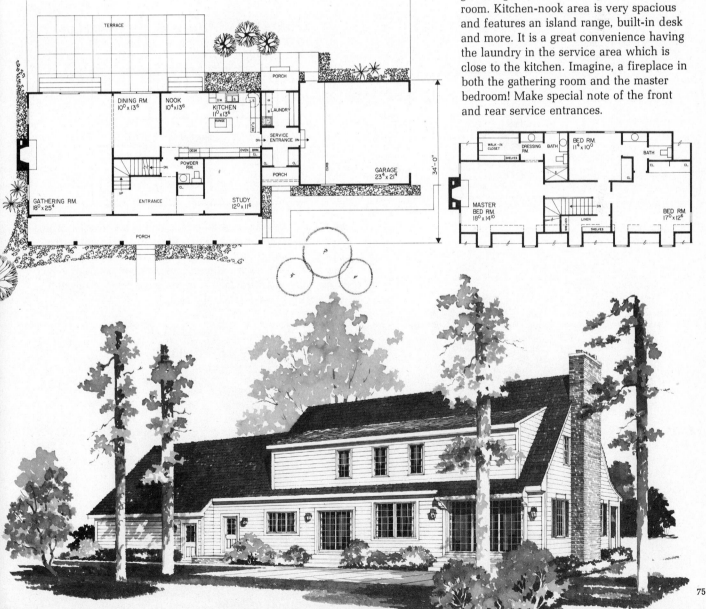

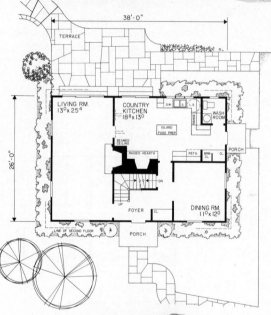

TERRACE

38'-0"

26'-0"

LIVING RM.
13⁰ x 25⁴

COUNTRY
KITCHEN
18⁸ x 13⁰

D.W. S L.S.

WASH
ROOM

RANGE

ISLAND
FOOD PREP.

BEAMED
CEILING

RAISED HEARTH

REF. BRM
CL

PORCH

UP DN.

FOYER CL

DINING RM.
11⁰ x 12⁰

LINE OF SECOND FLOOR

PORCH

Design 12666 988 Sq. Ft. - First Floor
1,147 Sq. Ft. - Second Floor; 35,490 Cu. Ft.

BEDROOM
11⁸ x 10⁰

WALK-IN
CLOSET

BATH

BEDROOM
12⁰ x 13⁴

PDR.
RM.

CL

LINEN CL CL

DN.

OPEN

MASTER
BEDROOM
14⁰ x 17⁸

BATH

SEAT.

S CL

BEDROOM
11⁰ x 12⁰

● A spacious country kitchen highlights the interior of this two-story. Its features include an island work center, fireplace, beamed ceiling and sliding glass doors leading to the rear terrace. A wash room and a side door are only steps away. A second fireplace is in the large living room. It, too, has sliding glass doors in the rear.

ENGLISH TUDOR HOUSES . . . .

have enjoyed a long and varied history in America. Recent years have seen a growth in popularity of this pleasing exterior style. From a purist standpoint, what is called Tudor today should really be referred to as Elizabethan. The many variations on the following pages are highlighted by simulated half-timber work, stucco, diamond-paned casement windows, massive sculptured chimneys, brick, stone and frame exterior walls, panelled doors, and varied roof planes. Note wavy siding and extra beam work. Of particular interest are the Cotswold Cottage/1½-story variations which project a low profile and retain a full measure of English charm.

Design 12356

1,969 Sq. Ft. - First Floor
1,702 Sq. Ft. - Second Floor
55,105 Cu. Ft.

● Here is truly an exquisite Tudor adaptation. The exterior, with its interesting roof lines, window treatment, stately chimney and its appealing use of brick and stucco, could hardly be more dramatic. Inside, the drama really begins to unfold as one envisions his family's living patterns. The delightfully large receiving hall has a two story ceiling and controls the flexible traffic patterns. The living and dining rooms, with the library nearby, will cater to the formal living pursuits. The guest room offers another haven for the enjoyment of peace and quiet. Observe the adjacent full bath. Just inside the entrance from the garage is the laundry room. For the family's informal activities there are the interactions of the family room - covered porch - nook - kitchen zone. Notice the raised hearth fireplace, the wood boxes, the sliding glass doors, built-in bar and the kitchen pass-thru. Adding to the charm of the family room is its high ceiling. From the second floor hall one can look down and observe the activities below.

Design 12586

984 Sq. Ft. - First Floor
1,003 Sq. Ft. - Second Floor; 30,080 Cu. Ft.

● A stately Tudor! With four large bedrooms. And lots of living space . . . formal living and dining rooms, a family room with a traditional fireplace, a spacious kitchen with nook.

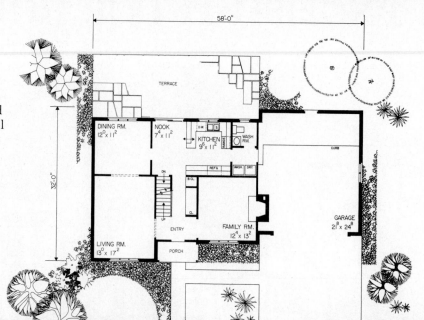

Design 12732

1,071 Sq. Ft. - First Floor
1,022 Sq. Ft. - Second Floor; 34,210 Cu. Ft.

● The two-story front entry hall will be dramatic indeed. Note the efficient kitchen adjacent to informal family room, formal dining room. Upstairs, three big bedrooms, two baths.

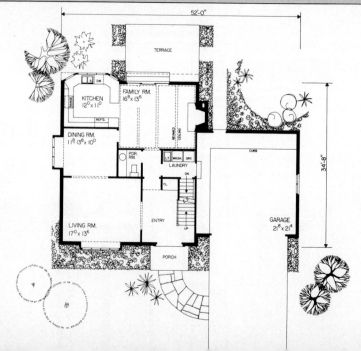

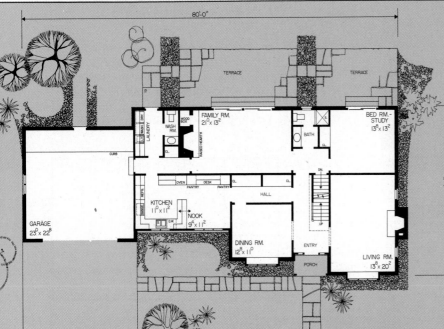

Design 12577

1,718 Sq. Ft. - First Floor
1,147 Sq. Ft. - Second Floor; 42,843 Cu. Ft.

● The exterior of this Tudor has interesting roof planes, delightful window treatment and recessed front entrance. The master suite with sitting room is one of the highlights of the interior.

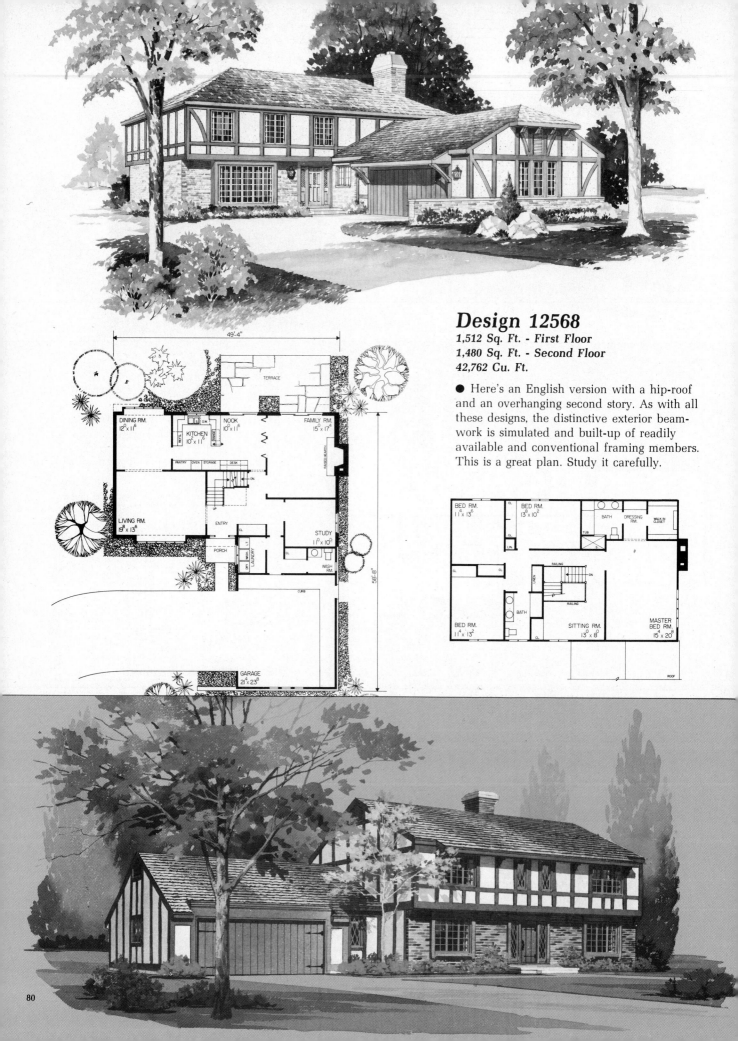

Design 12568

1,512 Sq. Ft. - First Floor
1,480 Sq. Ft. - Second Floor
42,762 Cu. Ft.

● Here's an English version with a hip-roof and an overhanging second story. As with all these designs, the distinctive exterior beam-work is simulated and built-up of readily available and conventional framing members. This is a great plan. Study it carefully.

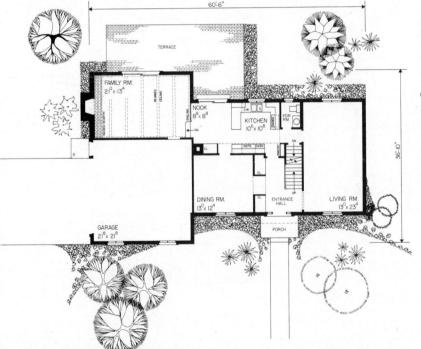

Design 12618
1,269 Sq. Ft. - First Floor
1,064 Sq. Ft. - Second Floor
33,079 Cu. Ft.

● This four bedroom Tudor design is the object of an outstanding investment for a lifetime of proud ownership and fine, family living facilities. Note that the family room is sunken and it, along with the nook, has sliding glass doors

Design 12637
1,308 Sq. Ft. - First Floor
1,063 Sq. Ft. - Second Floor; 34,250 Cu. Ft.

● A generous, centered entrance hall routes traffic efficiently to all areas. And what wonderfully spacious areas they are. Note living, dining, sleeping and bath facilities. Don't miss first floor laundry.

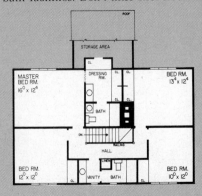

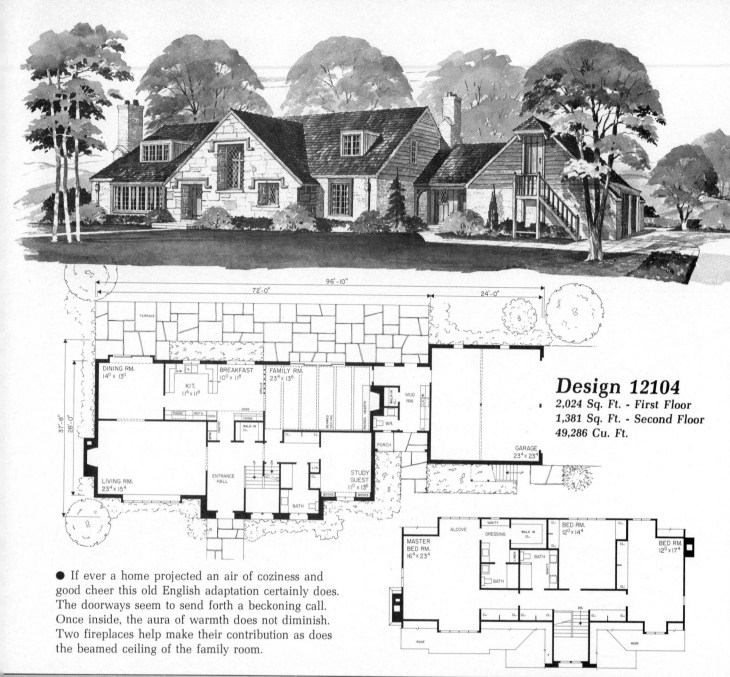

Design 12104

2,024 Sq. Ft. - First Floor
1,381 Sq. Ft. - Second Floor
49,286 Cu. Ft.

● If ever a home projected an air of coziness and good cheer this old English adaptation certainly does. The doorways seem to send forth a beckoning call. Once inside, the aura of warmth does not diminish. Two fireplaces help make their contribution as does the beamed ceiling of the family room.

Design 11991

1,262 Sq. Ft. - First Floor
1,108 Sq. Ft. - Second Floor; 31,073 Cu. Ft.

● Put yourself and your family in this English cottage adaptation and you'll all rejoice over your new home for many a year. The pride of owning and living in a home that is distinctive will be a constant source of satisfaction. Count the features that will serve your family well for years.

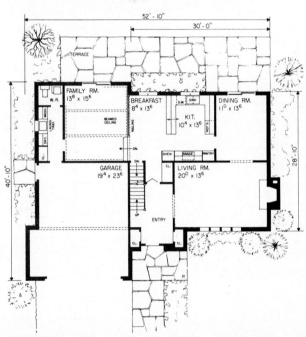

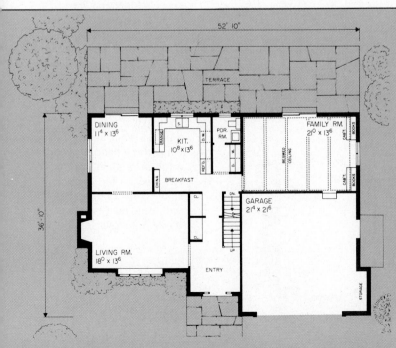

Design 12175 1,206 Sq. Ft. - First Floor

1,185 Sq. Ft. - Second Floor; 32,655 Cu. Ft.

● An English adaptation with all the amenities for gracious living. Note built-ins.

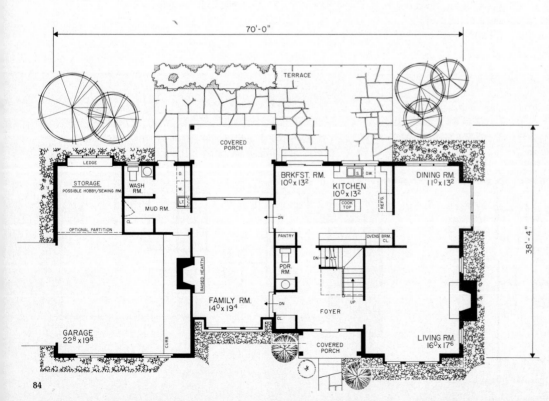

Design 12855

1,372 Sq. Ft. - First Floor
1,245 Sq. Ft. - Second Floor
44,495 Cu. Ft.

● This elegant Tudor house is perfect for the family who wants to move-up in living area, style and luxury. As you enter this home you will find a large living room with a fireplace on your right. Adjacent, the formal dining room has easy access to both the living room and the kitchen. The kitchen/breakfast room has an open plan and access to the rear terrace. Sunken a few steps, the spacious family room is highlighted with a fireplace and access to the rear, covered porch. Note the optional planning of the garage storage area. Plan this area according to the needs of your family. Upstairs, your family will enjoy three bedrooms and a full bath, along with a spacious master bedroom suite. Truly a house that will bring many years of pleasure to your family.

Design 11988

1,650 Sq. Ft. - First Floor
1,507 Sq. Ft. - Second Floor
49,474 Cu. Ft.

● A charming English Tudor
adaptation which retains all the
appeal of yesteryear, yet features
an outstanding and practical contemporary floor plan. With all
those rooms to serve a myriad of
functions, the active family will
lead a glorious existence. Imagine
a five bedroom second floor. Or,
make it a four bedroom, plus
study, upstairs. In addition to the
two full baths and fine closet
facilities, there is convenient access to the huge storage area over
the garage. Downstairs, flanking
the impressive, formal front entry
hall, there is space galore. The
twenty-six foot, end living room
will certainly be a favorite
feature. The family room is large
and will be lots of fun to furnish.
The excellent kitchen is strategically located between the formal
dining room and the informal
breakfast room. The mud room is
ideally located to receive traffic
from the garage as well as from
the rear yard. Don't miss the
wash room and the powder room.
Note pass-thru from kitchen to
family room and abundance of
storage available in garage.

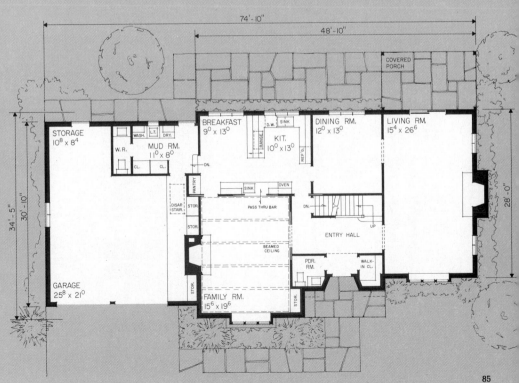

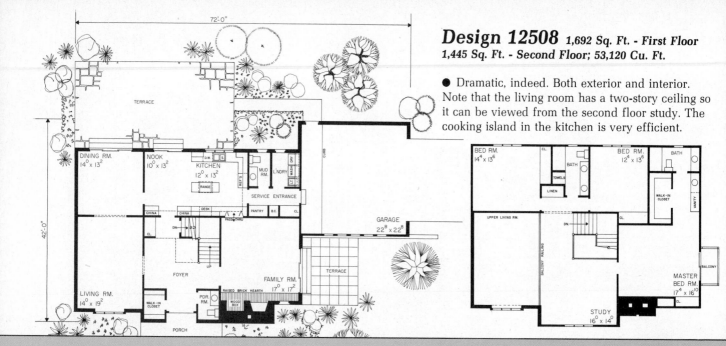

Design 12508 1,692 Sq. Ft. - First Floor
1,445 Sq. Ft. - Second Floor; 53,120 Cu. Ft.

● Dramatic, indeed. Both exterior and interior. Note that the living room has a two-story ceiling so it can be viewed from the second floor study. The cooking island in the kitchen is very efficient.

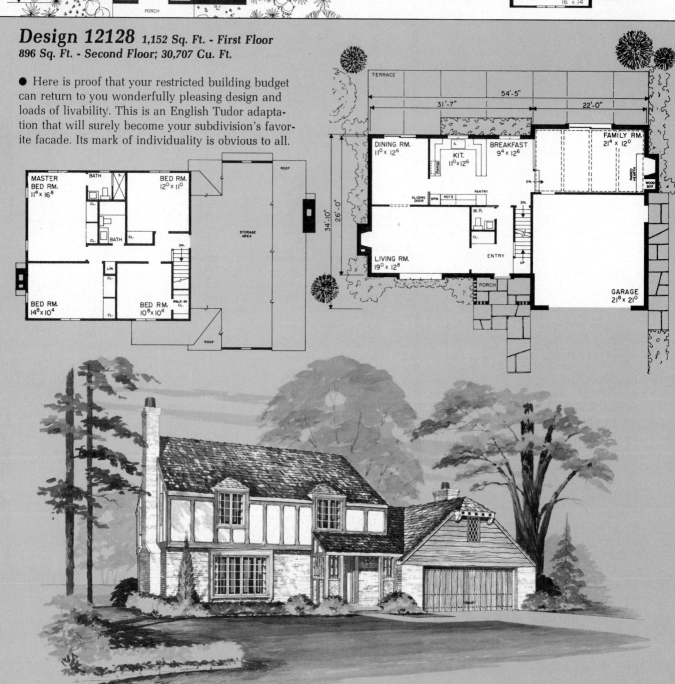

Design 12128 1,152 Sq. Ft. - First Floor
896 Sq. Ft. - Second Floor; 30,707 Cu. Ft.

● Here is proof that your restricted building budget can return to you wonderfully pleasing design and loads of livability. This is an English Tudor adaptation that will surely become your subdivision's favorite facade. Its mark of individuality is obvious to all.

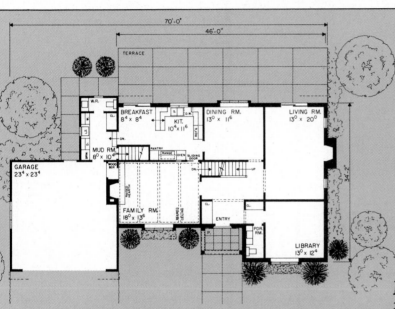

● Imagine, six bedrooms on the second floor. The first floor houses the living areas: family room, living room, dining areas plus a library. Not much more livability could be packed into this spaciously designed home.

Design 12141 1,490 Sq. Ft. - First Floor
1,474 Sq. Ft. - Second Floor; 50,711 Cu. Ft.

Design 12126 1,566 Sq. Ft. - First Floor
930 Sq. Ft. - Second Floor; 38,122 Cu. Ft.

● The configuration of this home is interesting. Its L-shape allows for flexible placement on your lot which makes it ideal for a corner lot. Exterior Tudor detailing is outstanding. Interior living potential is also excellent. Large formal and informal rooms are on the first floor along with the kitchen, dining room, laundry and spare bedroom or study. Three more bedrooms are on the second floor. Closets are plentiful throughout.

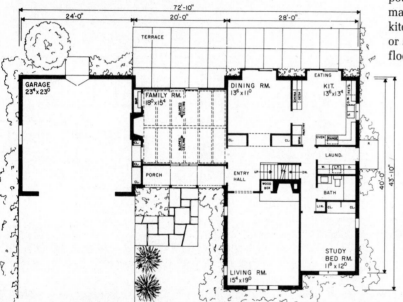

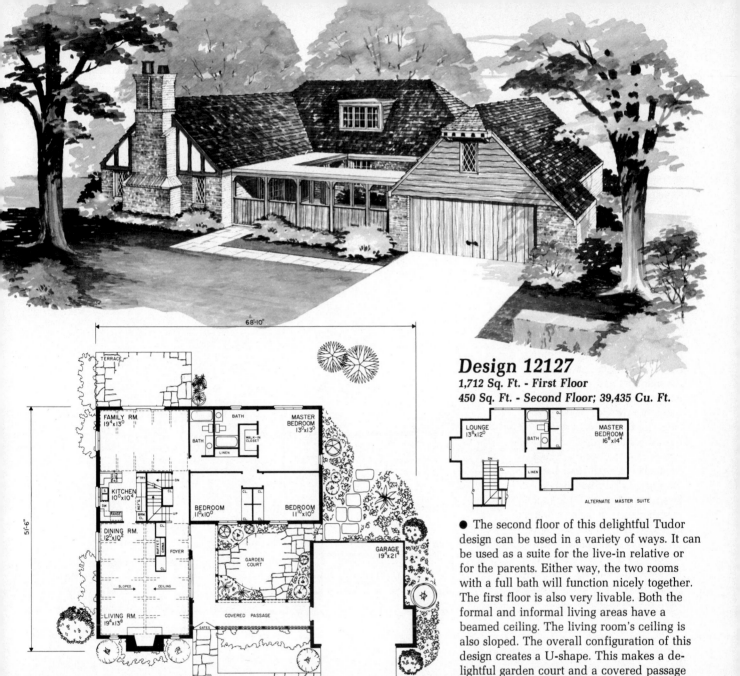

Design 12127
1,712 Sq. Ft. - First Floor
450 Sq. Ft. - Second Floor; 39,435 Cu. Ft.

ALTERNATE MASTER SUITE

● The second floor of this delightful Tudor design can be used in a variety of ways. It can be used as a suite for the live-in relative or for the parents. Either way, the two rooms with a full bath will function nicely together. The first floor is also very livable. Both the formal and informal living areas have a beamed ceiling. The living room's ceiling is also sloped. The overall configuration of this design creates a U-shape. This makes a delightful garden court and a covered passage from the garage.

Design 12190 1,221 Sq. Ft. - First Floor; 884 Sq. Ft. - Second Floor; 32,042 Cu. Ft.

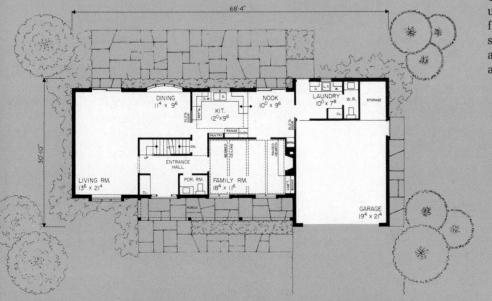

● Here is a Tudor adaptation with a popular floor plan. The open planning of the formal living - dining area results in a spacious atmosphere. Sliding glass doors and a bowed bay window foster an awareness of the rear yard.

Design 12794

1,680 Sq. Ft. - First Floor
1,165 Sq. Ft. - Second Floor
867 Sq. Ft. - Apartment
55,900 Cu. Ft.

● This exceptionally pleasing Tudor design has a great deal of interior livability to offer its occupants. Use the main entrance, enter into the foyer and begin your journey throughout this design. To the left of the foyer is the study, to the right, the formal living room. The living room leads to the rear, formal dining room. This room has access to the outdoors and is conveniently located adjacent to the kitchen. A snack bar divides the kitchen from the family room which also has access to outdoors plus it has a fireplace as does the living room. The second floor houses the family's four bedrooms. Down six steps from the mud room is the laundry and entrance to the garage, up six steps from this area is a complete apartment. This is an excellent room for a live-in relative. It is completely private by gaining access from the outdoor balcony.

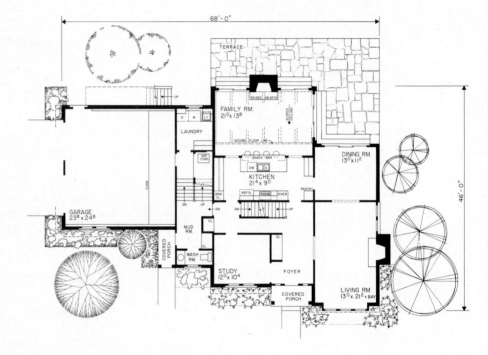

BED RM. 11⁰x14⁰ | BATH | BED RM. 12⁰x10⁴ | BED RM. 11⁰x14⁰
LINEN | CL. | LINEN
BATH | DRESSING RM. | CL. | CL. | DN. | LINEN
BED RM. 12⁸x10⁰ | BED RM. 14⁰x14⁰
MASTER BED RM. 18⁰x14⁶ | ROOF

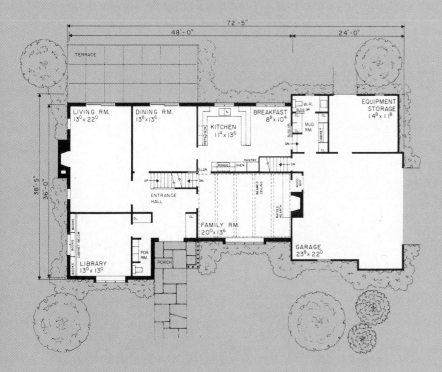

72'-5"
48'-0" | 24'-0"
TERRACE
LIVING RM. 13⁰x22⁰ | DINING RM. 13⁸x13⁶ | KITCHEN 11⁴x13⁶ | BREAKFAST 8⁸x10⁴ | W.R. | EQUIPMENT STORAGE 14⁸x11⁸
38'-5" | 36'-0"
UP | ENTRANCE HALL | RANGE | OVEN | PANTRY | BEAMED CEILING | RAISED HEARTH | MUD RM.
LIBRARY 13⁰x13⁰ | PDR. RM. | PORCH | FAMILY RM. 20⁰x13⁶ | GARAGE 23⁸x22⁰

Design 12148
1,656 Sq. Ft. - First Floor
1,565 Sq. Ft. - Second Floor
48,292 Cu. Ft.

● The charm of this Tudor adaptation could hardly be improved upon. Its fine proportion and exquisite use of materials result in a most distinctive home. However, the tremendous exterior appeal tells only half of the story. Inside there is a breathtaking array of highlights which will cater to the whims of the large family. Imagine six large bedrooms, two full baths and plenty of closets on the second floor! The first floor has a formal living zone made up of the big living room, the separate dining room and the sizeable library. A second zone is comprised of the U-shaped kitchen, the breakfast room and the family room — all contributing to fine informal family living patterns. Behind the garage is the mud room, washroom and the practical equipment storage room. Don't miss beamed ceiling, powder room, two fireplaces and two flights of stairs to the basement.

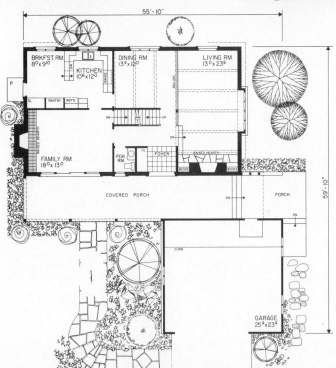

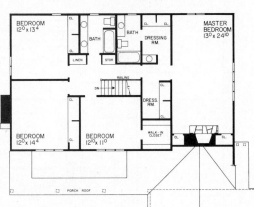

Design 12324 1,256 Sq. Ft. - *First Floor*
1,351 Sq. Ft. - *Second Floor; 37,603 Cu. Ft.*

● Dramatic, indeed! Both the interior and the exterior of these three Tudor designs deserve mention. Study each of them closely. The design featured here has a simple rectangular plan which will be relatively economical to build. This design is ideal for a corner lot.

Design 12274

1,941 Sq. Ft. - First Floor
1,392 Sq. Ft. - Second Floor
32,580 Cu. Ft.

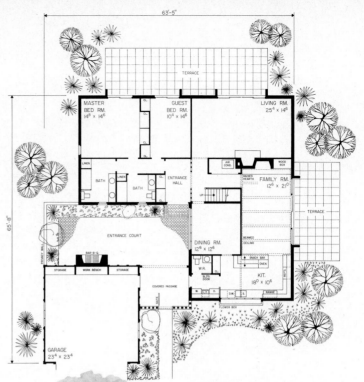

Design 12276

1,273 Sq. Ft. - First Floor
1,323 Sq. Ft. - Second Floor
40,450 Cu. Ft.

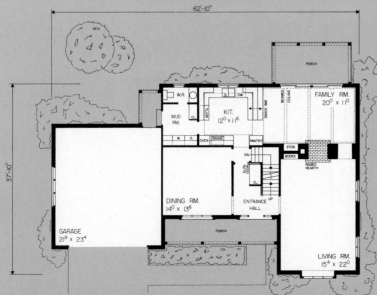

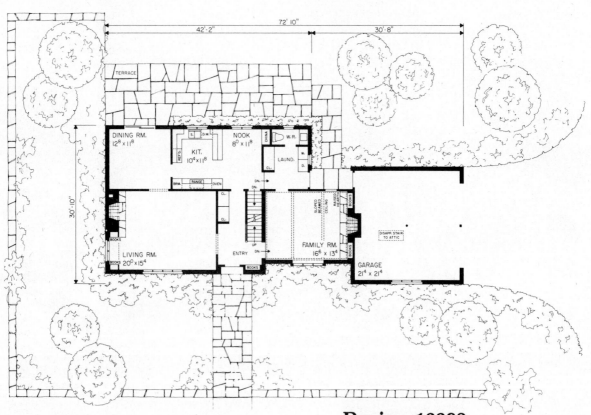

TERRACE

DINING RM.
12⁸ x 11⁶

KIT.
10⁴ x 11⁸

NOOK
8⁰ x 11⁸

CHINA

W.R.

LAUND.

RANGE   OVEN

CL.

DN.

UP

DN.

SLOPED BEAMED CEILING

RAISED HEARTH

BOOKS

DISAPP. STAIR TO ATTIC

BOOKS

LIVING RM.
20⁰ x 15⁴

ENTRY

FAMILY RM.
16⁶ x 13⁴

GARAGE
21⁴ x 21⁴

72' 10"

42' 2"

30' 8"

30' 10"

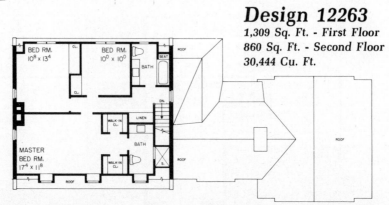

BED RM.
10⁸ x 13⁴

BED RM.
10⁰ x 10⁰

BATH

SEAT

ROOF

WALK-IN CL.

LINEN

DN.

BATH

MASTER BED RM.
17⁴ x 11⁸

WALK-IN CL.

ROOF

ROOF

ROOF

Design 12263

1,309 Sq. Ft. - First Floor
860 Sq. Ft. - Second Floor
30,444 Cu. Ft.

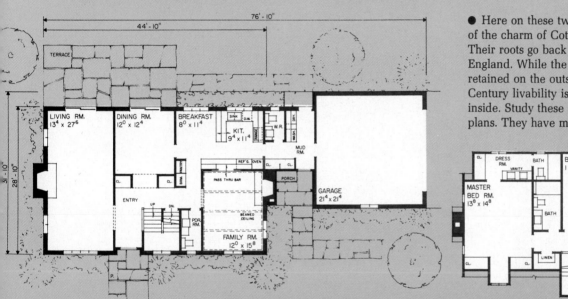

Here on these two pages are examples of the charm of Cotswold architecture. Their roots go back to 17th-Century England. While the old world appeal is retained on the outside, the late 20th-Century livability is readily apparent inside. Study these exteriors and floor plans. They have much to offer.

Design 11990 1,412 Sq. Ft. - First Floor; 1,064 Sq. Ft. - Second Floor; 37,282 Cu. Ft.

Design 12242

1,327 Sq. Ft. - First Floor
832 Sq. Ft. - Second Floor; 35,315 Cu. Ft.

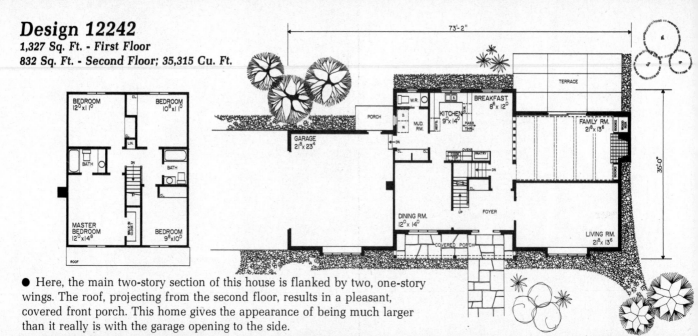

● Here, the main two-story section of this house is flanked by two, one-story wings. The roof, projecting from the second floor, results in a pleasant, covered front porch. This home gives the appearance of being much larger than it really is with the garage opening to the side.

● This is a most interesting home; both inside and out. Its L-shape with a covered porch and diamond lite windows is appealing. The floor plan features an extra bedroom, lounge and storage room. This is an exceptional design.

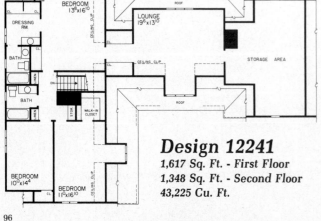

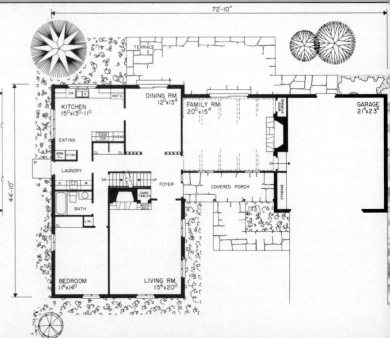

Design 12241

1,617 Sq. Ft. - First Floor
1,348 Sq. Ft. - Second Floor
43,225 Cu. Ft.

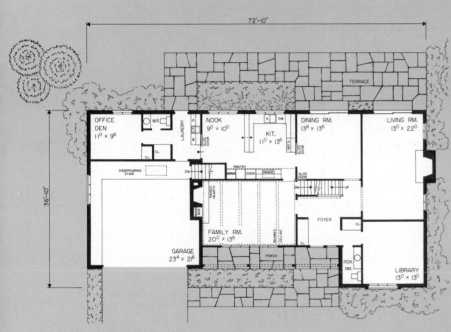

● Not only does the first floor of this plan contain formal and informal living areas, but it also houses a library and a rear office. Plus two washrooms and a first floor laundry. Now that is a lot of living space! Imagine a second floor with five bedrooms and a study. Or make it six bedrooms.

Design 12239

1,797 Sq. Ft. - First Floor
1,514 Sq. Ft. - Second Floor
44,371 Cu. Ft.

First floor labels: OFFICE DEN 11⁰ x 9⁶, LAUNDRY, W.R., NOOK 9⁰ x 10⁰, KIT. 11⁰ x 13⁶, DINING RM. 13⁸ x 13⁶, LIVING RM. 13⁰ x 22⁰, TERRACE, DISAPPEARING STAIR, PANTRY, BINS, OVEN, RANGE, RAISED HEARTH, BEAMED CEILING, FAMILY RM. 20⁰ x 13⁶, GARAGE 23⁴ x 21⁶, PORCH, FOYER, PDR. RM., LIBRARY 13⁰ x 13⁰. Dimensions 72'-10" and 36'-10".

Second floor labels: BED RM. 10⁸ x 13⁶, BED RM. 12⁰ x 10⁰, BATH, BED RM. 11⁴ x 13⁶, LINEN, BED RM. 14⁰ x 13⁶, BED RM. STUDY 13⁰ x 9⁶, DRESS. RM., BATH, MASTER BED RM. 17⁴ x 13⁰.

Design 12275 1,421 Sq. Ft. - First Floor; 1,456 Sq. Ft. - Second Floor; 45,330 Cu. Ft.

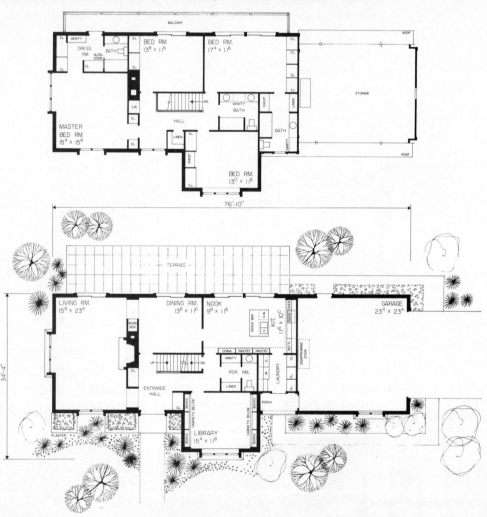

● This stately Tudor version is impressive, indeed. The fine proportion and architectural detailing give it a distinctive character all its own. Upon passing through the double front doors one is quickly aware of the excellent traffic circulation. No-tice how the entrance hall routes traffic to the various rooms. The end living room will enjoy the utmost in privacy. No unnecessary cross-room traffic here. The dining room is but a step or two from the hallway, the living room and the kitchen/nook area. The arrangement of the kitchen and its eating area will create a nostalgic country-kitchen atmosphere. The library can be called upon to serve a multitude of functions. Note powder room and laundry. Upstairs, four big bedrooms and three baths.

Design 12541
1,985 Sq. Ft. - First Floor
1,659 Sq. Ft. - Second Floor; 59,012 Cu. Ft.

● Here is English Tudor styling at its stately best. The massive stone work is complemented by stucco and massive beams. The diamond lite windows, the projecting bays, the carriage lamps and the twin chimneys add to the charm of this exterior. The spacious center entrance routes traffic effectively to all areas. Worthy of particular note is the formal living room with its fireplace, the adjacent family room overlooking the terrace, the quiet study with fireplace, two sizeable dining areas and an excellent master suite. Plus two more sizeable bedrooms.

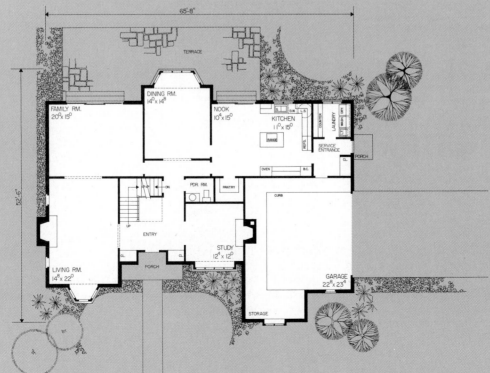

Design 12278 1,804 Sq. Ft. - First Floor; 939 Sq. Ft. - First Floor; 44,274 Cu. Ft.

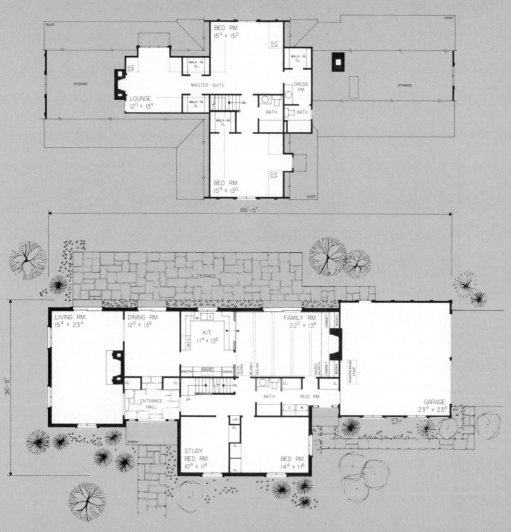

● This cozy Tudor adaptation is surely inviting. Its friendly demeanor seems to say, "welcome". Upon admittance to the formal front entrance hall, even the most casual of visitors will be filled with anticipation at the prospect of touring the house. And little wonder, too. Traffic patterns are efficient. Room relationships are excellent. A great feature is the location of the living, dining, kitchen and family rooms across the back of the house. Each enjoys a view of the rear yard and sliding glass doors provide direct access to the terrace. Another outstanding feature is the flexibility of the sleeping patterns. This may be a five bedroom house, or one with three bedrooms with study and lounge. Don't miss the three fireplaces and three baths.

Design 12373 1,160 Sq. Ft. - First Floor; 1,222 Sq. Ft. - Second Floor; 33,775 Cu. Ft.

● Finding more livability wrapped in such an attractive facade would be difficult, indeed. This charming Tudor adaptation will return big dividends per construction dollar. It is compact and efficient. And, of course, it will not require a big, expensive piece of property. The location of the two-car garage as an integral part of the structure has its convenience and economic advantages, too. The living room is sunken and is divided from the dining room by a railing which helps maintain the desirable spacious atmosphere. The family room with its beamed ceiling, attractive fireplace wall, built-in storage and snack bar functions well with both the kitchen and the outdoor terrace. Four bedrooms, two baths, plenty of closets and built-in vanities.

Design 12372 2,634 Sq. Ft. - First Floor; 819 Sq. Ft. - Second Floor; 47,867 Cu. Ft.

● What a wonderfully different and imposing two-story design this is! The Tudor styling and the varying roof planes, along with its U-shape, add to the air of distinction. From the driveway, steps lead past a big raised planter up to the enclosed entrance court. A wide overhanging roof shelters the massive patterned double doors flanked by diamond paned sidelites. The living room is outstanding. It is located a distance from other living areas and is quite spacious. The centered fireplace is the dominant feature, while sliding-glass doors open from each end onto outdoor terraces. The kitchen, too, is spacious and functions well. Two eating areas are nearby. It is worth noting that each of the major first floor rooms have direct access to the outdoor terraces. Note second floor suite which includes a lounge with built-in book cabinets.

Design 12391 *2,496 Sq. Ft. - First Floor; 958 Sq. Ft. - Second Floor; 59,461 Cu. Ft.*

● Here is a stately English adaptation that is impressive, indeed. The two-story octagonal foyer strikes a delightfully authentic design note. The entrance hall with open staircase and two-story ceiling is spacious. Clustered around the efficient kitchen are the formal living areas and those catering to informal activities. The family room with its beamed ceiling and raised hearth fireplace functions, like the formal living/dining zone, with the partially enclosed outdoor terrace. Three bedrooms with two baths comprise the first floor sleeping zone. Each room will enjoy its access to the terrace. Upstairs there are two more bedrooms and a study. Notice the sliding glass doors to the balcony and how the study looks down into the entrance hall. The three-car garage is great. Your own list of favorite features will surely be lengthy.

Design 12629

1,555 Sq. Ft. - First Floor
1,080 Sq. Ft. - Second Floor
38,479 Cu. Ft.

● This home will really be fun in which to live. In addition to the sizeable living, dining and family rooms, many extras will be found. There are two fireplaces one to serve each of the formal and the informal areas. The back porch is a delightful extra. It will be great to relax in after a long hard day. Note two half baths on the first floor and two full baths on the second floor to serve the three bedrooms. Count the number of closets in the spacious upstairs. The door from the bedroom leads to storage over garage.

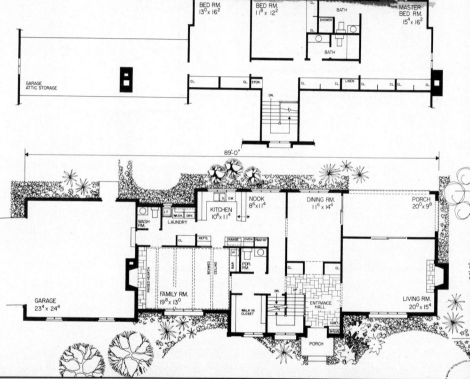

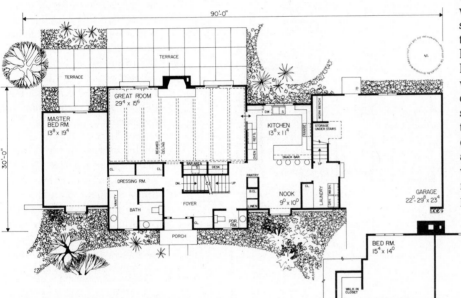

● This distinctive version of Tudor styling will foster many years of prideful ownership and unique, yet practical living patterns. The main portion of the facade is delightfully symmetrical. Inside, the family living will focus on the 29 foot great room with its dramatic fireplace and beamed ceiling. The kitchen is outstanding with snack bar and dining nook nearby. Note the three large bedrooms each having its own dressing room. Extra storage space is available above the garage or may be developed into another room. Oversized garage includes a built-in workbench. Study plan carefully. It has much to offer.

Design 12630 1,491 Sq. Ft. - First Floor
788 Sq. Ft. - Second Floor; 35,575 Cu. Ft.

Design 12674 1,922 Sq. Ft. - First Floor
890 Sq. Ft. - Second Floor; 37,411 Cu. Ft.

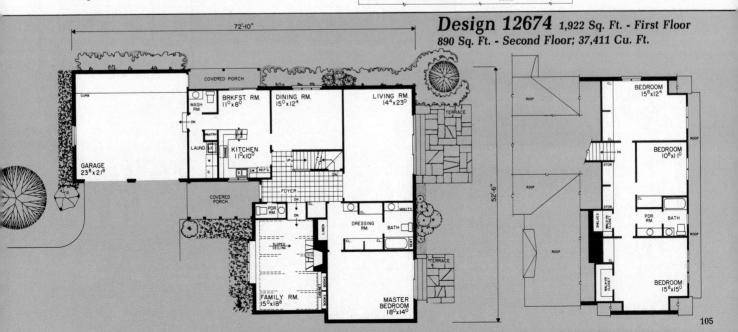

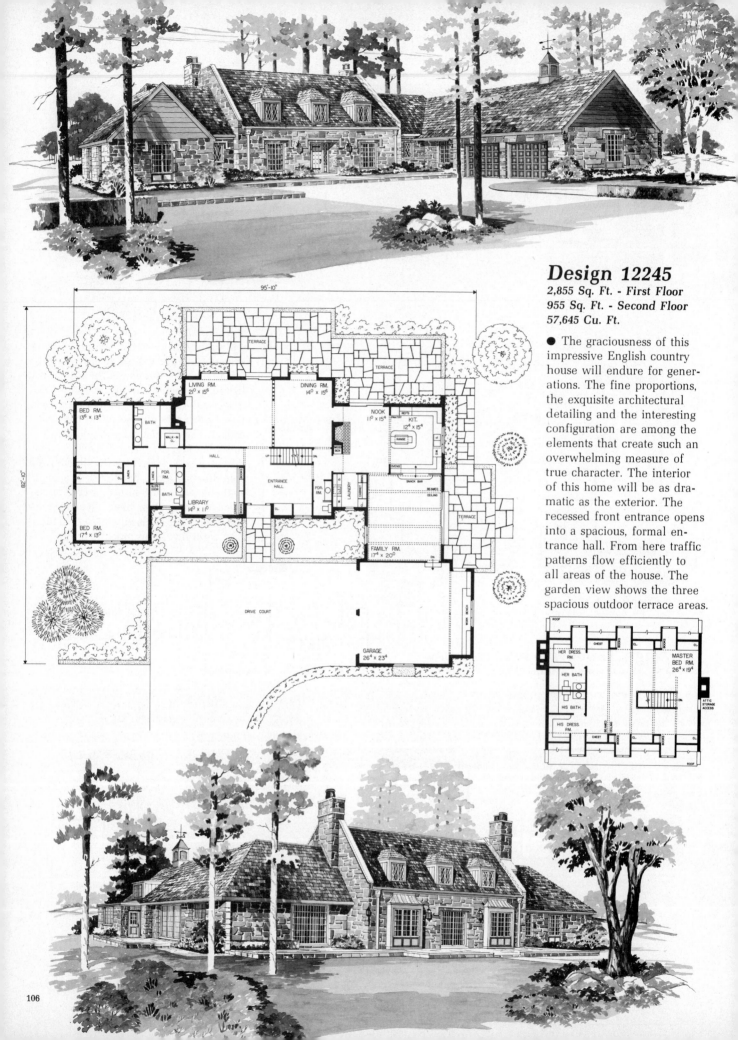

Design 12245

2,855 Sq. Ft. - First Floor
955 Sq. Ft. - Second Floor
57,645 Cu. Ft.

● The graciousness of this impressive English country house will endure for generations. The fine proportions, the exquisite architectural detailing and the interesting configuration are among the elements that create such an overwhelming measure of true character. The interior of this home will be as dramatic as the exterior. The recessed front entrance opens into a spacious, formal entrance hall. From here traffic patterns flow efficiently to all areas of the house. The garden view shows the three spacious outdoor terrace areas.

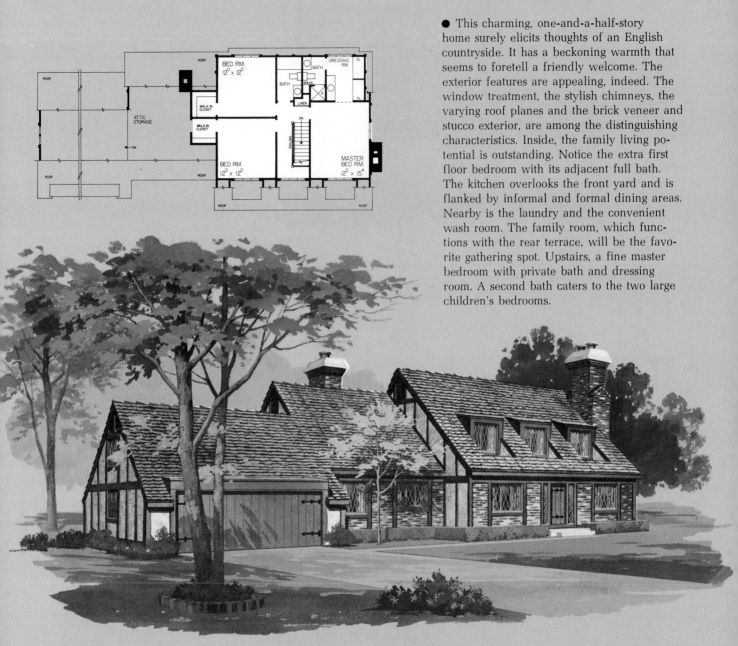

● This charming, one-and-a-half-story home surely elicits thoughts of an English countryside. It has a beckoning warmth that seems to foretell a friendly welcome. The exterior features are appealing, indeed. The window treatment, the stylish chimneys, the varying roof planes and the brick veneer and stucco exterior, are among the distinguishing characteristics. Inside, the family living potential is outstanding. Notice the extra first floor bedroom with its adjacent full bath. The kitchen overlooks the front yard and is flanked by informal and formal dining areas. Nearby is the laundry and the convenient wash room. The family room, which functions with the rear terrace, will be the favorite gathering spot. Upstairs, a fine master bedroom with private bath and dressing room. A second bath caters to the two large children's bedrooms.

Design 12626 1,420 Sq. Ft. - First Floor; 859 Sq. Ft. - Second Floor; 34,974 Cu. Ft.

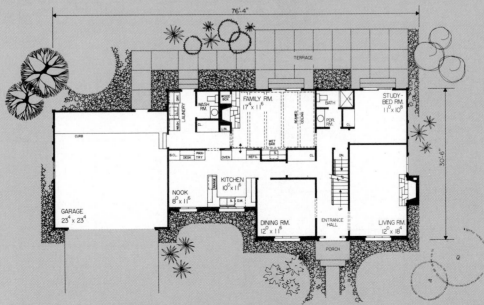

● This Tudor design has many fine features. The exterior is enhanced by front and side bay windows in the family and dining rooms. Along with an outstanding exterior, it also contains a modern and efficient floor plan within its modest proportions. Flanking the entrance foyer is a comfortable living room. The U-shaped kitchen is conveniently located between the dining and breakfast rooms.

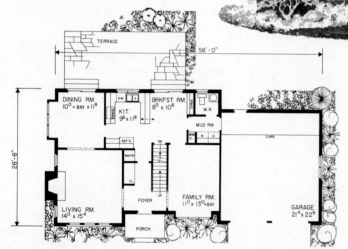

Design 12800 999 Sq. Ft. - First Floor
997 Sq. Ft. - Second Floor; 31,390 Cu. Ft.

● The charm of old England has been captured in this outstanding one-and-a-half story design. Interior livability will efficiently serve the various needs of all family members. The first floor offers both formal and informal areas along with the work centers. Features include: a wet-bar in the dining room, the kitchen's snack bar, first floor laundry and rear covered porch.

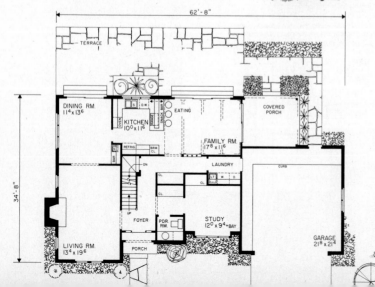

Design 12854 1,261 Sq. Ft. - First Floor
950 Sq. Ft. - Second Floor; 36,820 Cu. Ft.

FRENCH FACADES . . .

and the pleasing formality they successfully project, are featured in this section by a variety of adaptations. The Mansard roof lends itself to many floor plan configurations. The hip-roof is also highly identifiable with the French style. Brick quoins at the corners, dentils, casement windows, arched window openings and shutters, raised molding doors, carriage lamps, and wrought iron grillwork complete the picture. Center entrances, large foyers, formal living and dining rooms, family rooms and abundant second floor sleeping facilities are among the floor plan features of these French Facades. Don't miss the extra baths, studies, and first floor laundries.

Design 12543
2,345 Sq. Ft. - First Floor
1,687 Sq. Ft. - Second Floor; 76,000 Cu. Ft.

● Certainly a dramatic French adaptation highlighted by effective window treatment, delicate cornice detailing, appealing brick quoins and excellent proportion. Stepping through the double front doors the drama is heightened by the spacious entry hall with its two curving staircases to the second floor. The upper hall is open and looks down to the hall below. There is a study and a big gathering room which look out on the raised terrace. The work center is outstanding. The garage will accommodate three cars.

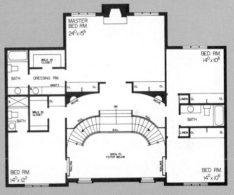

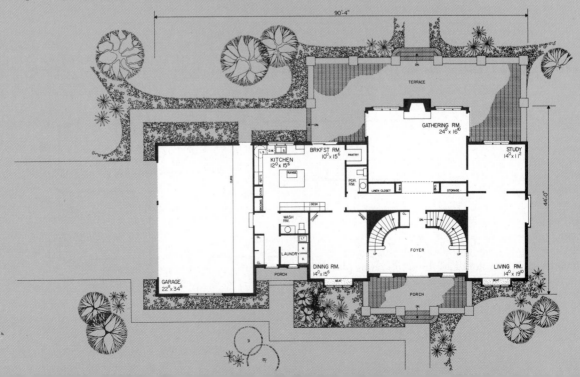

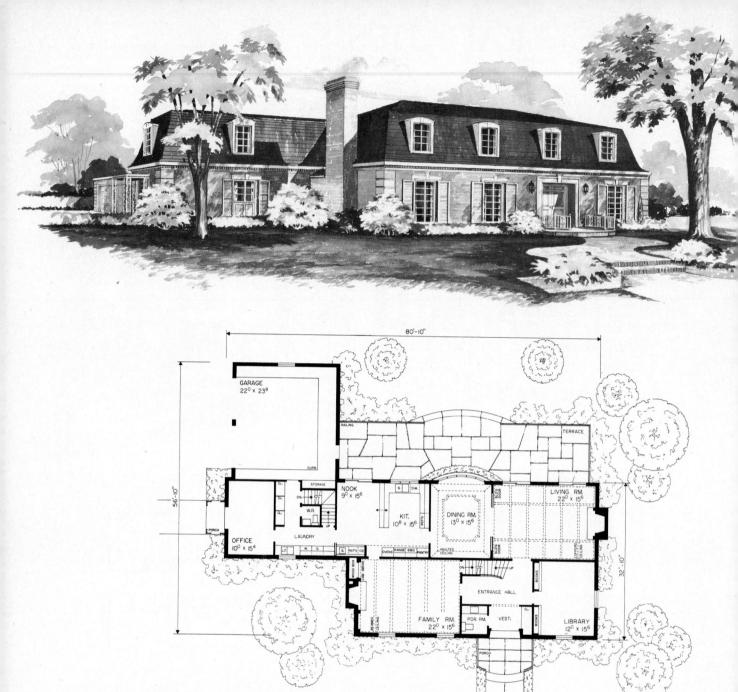

Design 11839 2,204 Sq. Ft. - First Floor; 1,486 Sq. Ft. - Second Floor; 330 Sq. Ft. - Maid's Area; 55,683 Cu. Ft.

● Imagine, five bedrooms, a quiet library, a home office (use it as a first floor hobby room if you prefer), a big family room, a first floor laundry, a maid's suite and three full baths plus an extra powder room and wash room! Note the large formal living and dining rooms which look out upon the raised terrace.

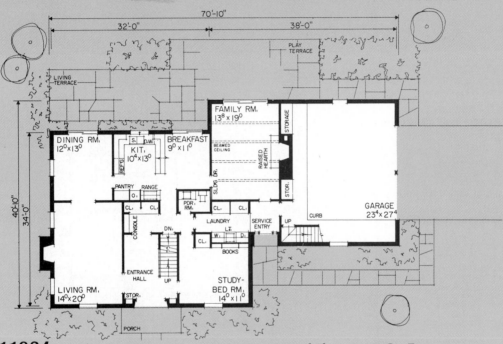

Design 11934 1,622 Sq. Ft. - First Floor; 2,002 Sq. Ft. - Second Floor; 51,758 Cu. Ft.

● The two-story French Mansard has become a favorite of many during the past few years. Its attractive proportion and pleasing formality have become familiar to most of us. Be sure to observe the fine architectural detailing such as the dentils at the cornice, the brick quoins at the corners, the recessed and paneled front entrance, the carriage lamps, etc. The interior of this home is even more outstanding. Here is a house that could function as a four, five or even a six bedroom home! And with plenty of space left over for formal and informal living and dining. For efficient housekeeping, there is the U-shaped kitchen and the separate first floor laundry. Observe the central location of powder room. Note hall storage facilities.

Design 12587
984 Sq. Ft. - First Floor
993 Sq. Ft. - Second Floor; 30,090 Cu. Ft.

● A traditional classic! A large living room and adjoining dining room . . . together they offer the correct setting for the most formal occasion. For casual times, a family room.

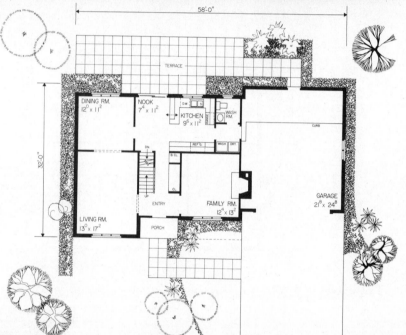

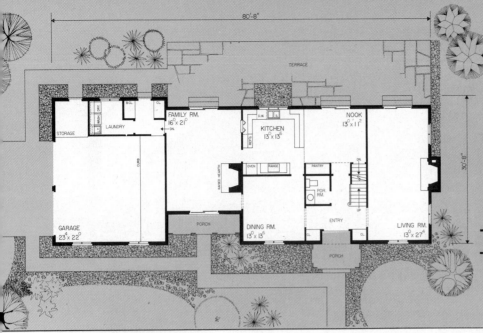

Design 12564
1,706 Sq. Ft. - First Floor
1,166 Sq. Ft. - Second Floor
48,640 Cu. Ft.

● French tone! Here's a home with Old World charm! But liveable in the American style. Formal and informal areas each have a fireplace. Three (optional four) bedrooms upstairs.

Design 12750
1,209 Sq. Ft. - First Floor
965 Sq. Ft. - Second Floor; 32,025 Cu. Ft.

● This four bedroom Mansard roof design is impressive, indeed. The covered front porch leads the way to an efficient floor plan. Includes a basement.

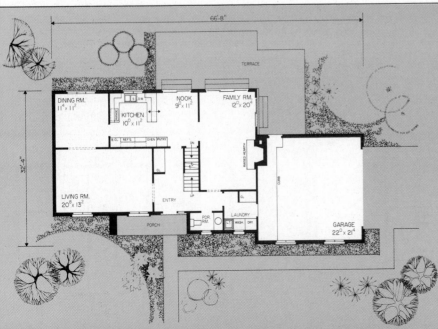

113

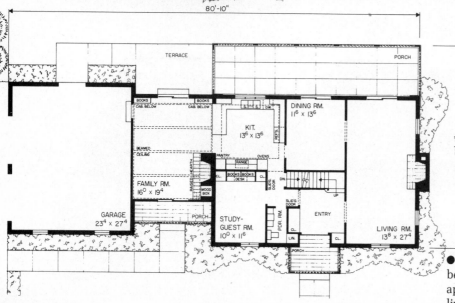

80'-10"

38'-5"

TERRACE
PORCH
BOOKS CAB. BELOW | BOOKS CAB. BELOW
KIT. 13⁶ x 13⁶
DINING RM. 11⁶ x 13⁶
BEAMED CEILING
FAMILY RM. 16⁰ x 19⁴
PANTRY
RANGE
OVENS
BOOKS DESK | BOOKS
WOOD BOX
GARAGE 23⁴ x 27⁴
PORCH
STUDY-GUEST RM. 10⁰ x 11⁶
SLDG DOOR
POR. RM.
ENTRY
UP
LIVING RM. 13⁸ x 27⁴
PORCH

BED. RM. 13⁶ x 13⁶
DRESS. RM.
MASTER BED RM. 17⁰ x 13⁶
BATH
CL. | CL.
DN
HALL
LINEN
BED RM. 10⁰ x 11²
BATH
PDR. RM.
CL.
BED RM. 13⁰ x 13⁶

Design 12222
1,485 Sq. Ft. - First Floor
1,175 Sq. Ft. - Second Floor
45,500 Cu. Ft.

● Gracious, formal living could hardly find a better backdrop than this two-story French adaptation. The exterior is truly exquisite. Inside, living patterns will be most enjoyable.

Design 12281
1,961 Sq. Ft. - First Floor
1,472 Sq. Ft. - Second Floor; 49,974 Cu. Ft.

● Regal in character, this French design is a fine example of excellent proportion and perfect symmetry. The distinctiveness of this home continues right through the front doors into the spacious entrance hall with its curving staircase.

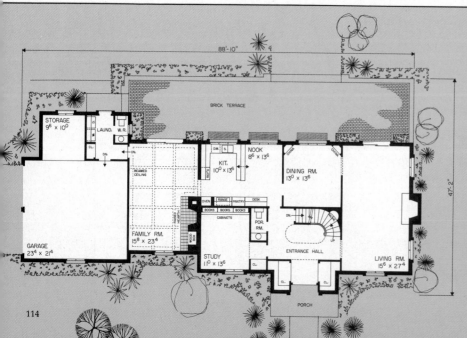

88'-10"

47'-2"

BRICK TERRACE
STORAGE 9⁶ x 10⁰
LAUND. W.R.
KIT. 10⁰ x 13⁶
NOOK 8⁶ x 13⁶
DINING RM. 13⁰ x 13⁶
BEAMED CEILING
RANGE OVEN PANTRY DESK
BOOKS BOOKS BOOKS
CABINETS
FAMILY RM. 15⁸ x 23⁴
GARAGE 23⁴ x 21⁴
STUDY 11⁰ x 13⁶
POR. RM.
ENTRANCE HALL
DN
LIVING RM. 15⁶ x 27⁴
PORCH

BED RM. 10⁴ x 13⁶
BATH
BED RM. 13⁰ x 11⁰
BATH
VANITY
DRESSING RM.
LINEN
OPEN STAIR WELL
RAILING
BED RM. 15⁰ x 11⁰
STAIR HALL
MASTER BED RM. 15⁴ x 17⁸

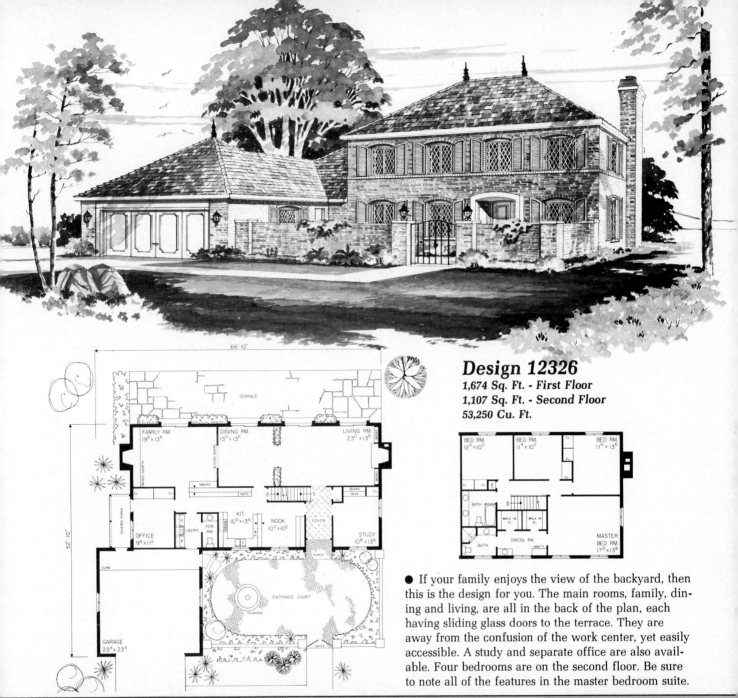

Design 12326
1,674 Sq. Ft. - First Floor
1,107 Sq. Ft. - Second Floor
53,250 Cu. Ft.

● If your family enjoys the view of the backyard, then this is the design for you. The main rooms, family, dining and living, are all in the back of the plan, each having sliding glass doors to the terrace. They are away from the confusion of the work center, yet easily accessible. A study and separate office are also available. Four bedrooms are on the second floor. Be sure to note all of the features in the master bedroom suite.

Design 11228 *2,583 Sq. Ft. - First Floor; 697 Sq. Ft. - Second Floor; 51,429 Cu. Ft.*

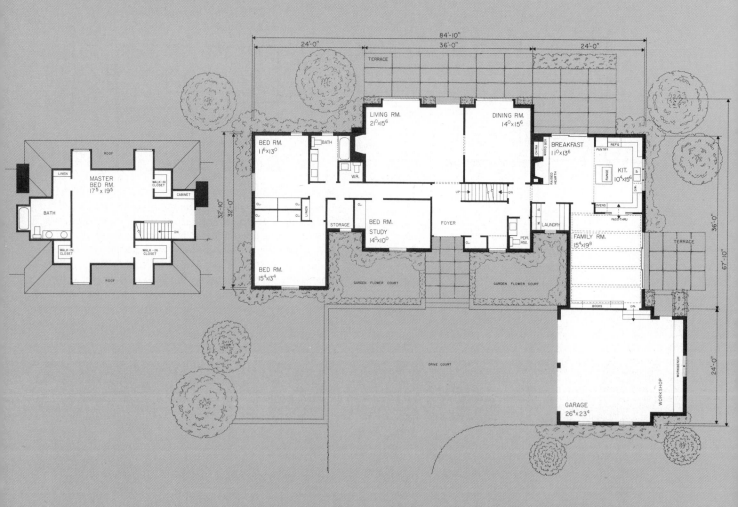

● This beautiful house has a wealth of detail taken from the rich traditions of French Regency design. The roof itself is a study in pleasant dormers and the hips and valleys of a big flowing area. A close examination of the plan shows the careful arrangement of space for privacy as well as good circulation of traffic. The spacious formal entrance hall sets the stage for good zoning. The informal living area is highlighted by the updated version of the old country kitchen. Observe the fireplace, and the barbecue. While there is a half-story devoted to the master bedroom suite, this home functions more as a one-story country estate design than as a 1½ story.

Design 12342

2,824 Sq. Ft. - First Floor
1,013 Sq. Ft. - Second Floor
59,882 Cu. Ft.

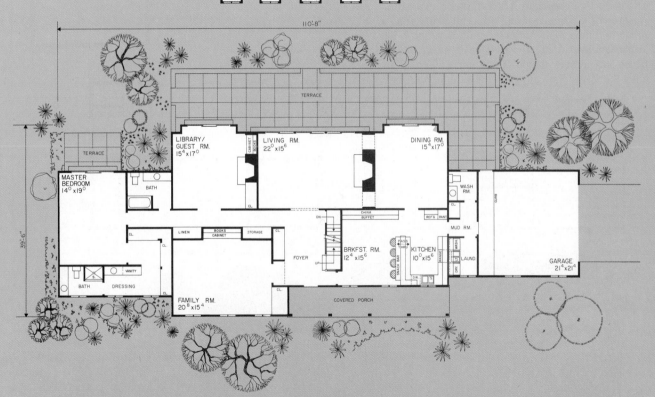

● A distinctive exterior characterized by varying roof planes, appealing window treatment, attractive chimneys and a covered front porch with prominent vertical columns. The main portion of the house is effectively balanced by the master bedroom wing on the one side and the garage wing on the other. As a buffer between house and garage is the mud room and the laundry. The kitchen is U-shaped, efficient and strategically located to serve the breakfast and dining rooms. Notice how the rooms at the rear function through sliding glass doors with the outdoor terrace areas. Fireplaces highlight both the spacious living room and the large library. The big family room features a built-in bookshelf and cabinet. Upstairs, two bedrooms and a study alcove will be found.

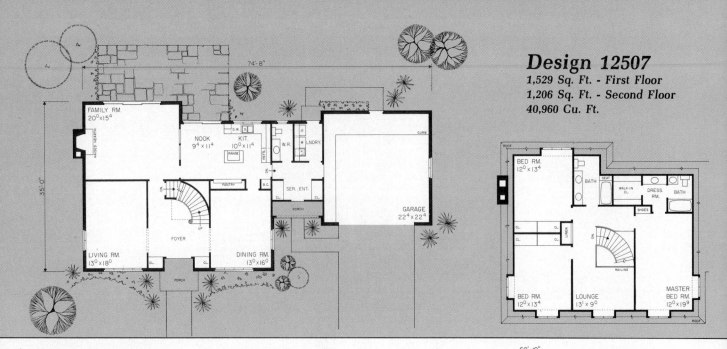

Design 12507
1,529 Sq. Ft. - First Floor
1,206 Sq. Ft. - Second Floor
40,960 Cu. Ft.

Design 11277 1,504 Sq. Ft. - First Floor
1,243 Sq. Ft. - Second Floor; 38,058 Cu. Ft.

● Exceptional livability under a distinctive, French Mansard roof. This is a house with enormous visual appeal. Massive brick chimneys are at each end of the house to add symmetry. The ability of this house to serve the large, active family is unquestioned. There are five bedrooms, two full baths, two extra washrooms, a formal and an informal living area, a separate dining room and a quiet library with built-in bookshelves. A covered passage connects the house and garage. Should you prefer, you could open the flat-roofed garage to the side of your lot.

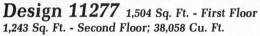

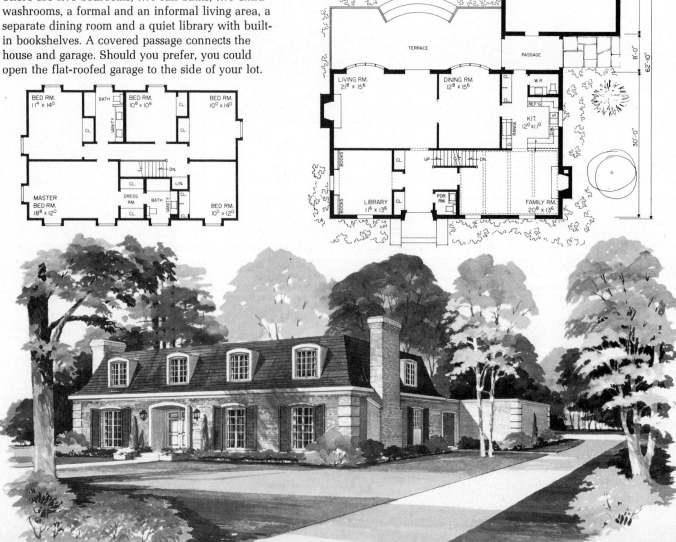

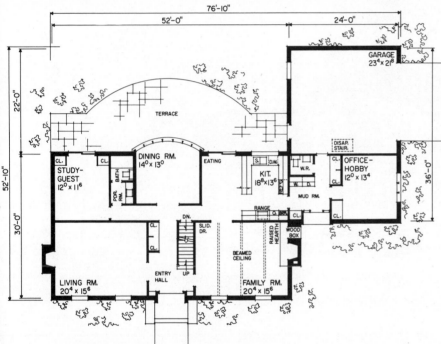

76'-10"

52'-0"

24'-0"

22'-0"

52'-10"

30'-0"

36'-0"

GARAGE
23⁴ x 21⁸

TERRACE

DINING RM.
14⁰ x 13⁰

EATING

KIT.
18⁸ x 13⁶

W.R.

OFFICE-
HOBBY
12⁰ x 13⁴

DISAP.
STAIR.

STUDY-
GUEST
12⁰ x 11⁶

CL.

CL.

BATH

PDR.
RM.

S. D.W.

W. D.

MUD RM.

CL.

RANGE

REF.

WOOD
BOX

RAISED
HEARTH

BEAMED
CEILING

DN.

SLID.
DR.

UP

ENTRY
HALL

CL.

CL.

LIVING RM.
20⁴ x 15⁶

FAMILY RM.
20⁴ x 15⁶

CL.

DRESS.
RM.

BATH

S.

BATH

CL.

BED RM.
16⁰ x 12⁶

VANITY VANITY

VANITY

LIN.

CL.

CL.

CL.

CL.

MASTER
BED RM.
18⁴ x 14⁸

DN.

BOOKS

CL.

CL.

CL.

CL.

BOOKS

BED RM.
16⁰ x 12⁶

● The home with a French Mansard roof is one of the most distinguished of all traditional styles. It has good proportion, delightful symmetry and a feeling of formality. The recessed, center entrance protects the double doors which lead into the entry hall, highlighted by the open staircase to the second floor. The traffic patterns of the plan are flexible and efficient.

Design 11733
1,944 Sq. Ft. - First Floor
1,308 Sq. Ft. - Second Floor; 61,152 Cu. Ft.

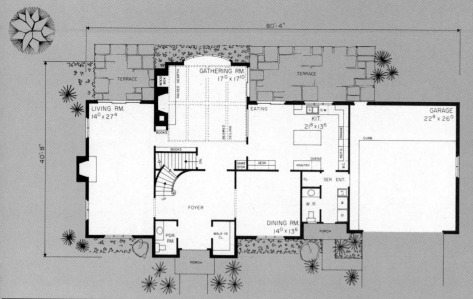

Design 12503
1,847 Sq. Ft. - First Floor
1,423 Sq. Ft. - Second Floor
50,671 Cu. Ft.

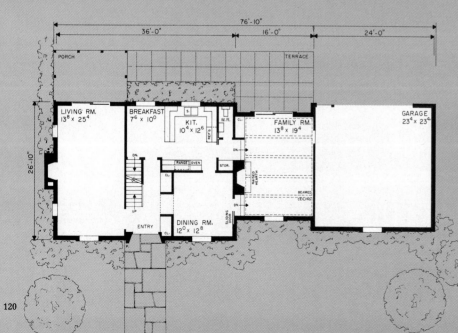

Design 11260
1,318 Sq. Ft. - First Floor
989 Sq. Ft. - Second Floor
31,787 Cu. Ft.

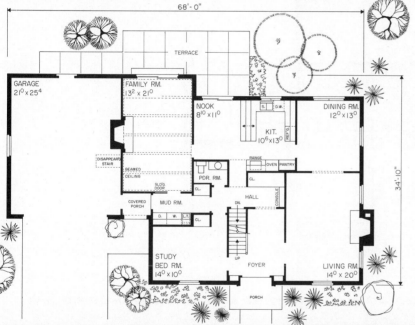

GARAGE 21⁰ x 25⁴

TERRACE

68'-0"

FAMILY RM. 13² x 21⁰

NOOK 8¹⁰ x 11⁰

DINING RM. 12⁰ x 13⁰

KIT. 10⁶ x 13⁰

DISAPPEARING STAIR

BEAMED CEILING

SLD'G DOOR

RANGE OVEN PANTRY

PDR. RM.

COVERED PORCH

MUD RM.

D. W. L.T.

STUDY BED RM. 14⁰ x 10⁰

HALL

DN. UP

FOYER

LIVING RM. 14⁰ x 20⁰

34'-10"

PORCH

Design 11774

1,574 Sq. Ft. - First Floor
1,124 Sq. Ft. - Second Floor
37,616 Cu. Ft.

BED RM. 15⁴ x 11⁴

BED RM. 15⁸ x 11⁴

CL. CL.
CL. CL.
CL.

LIN.

BATH

STORAGE

BATH

SEAT

DN.

BED RM. 12⁴ x 10⁰

CL.

MASTER BED RM. 17⁰ x 13⁰

121

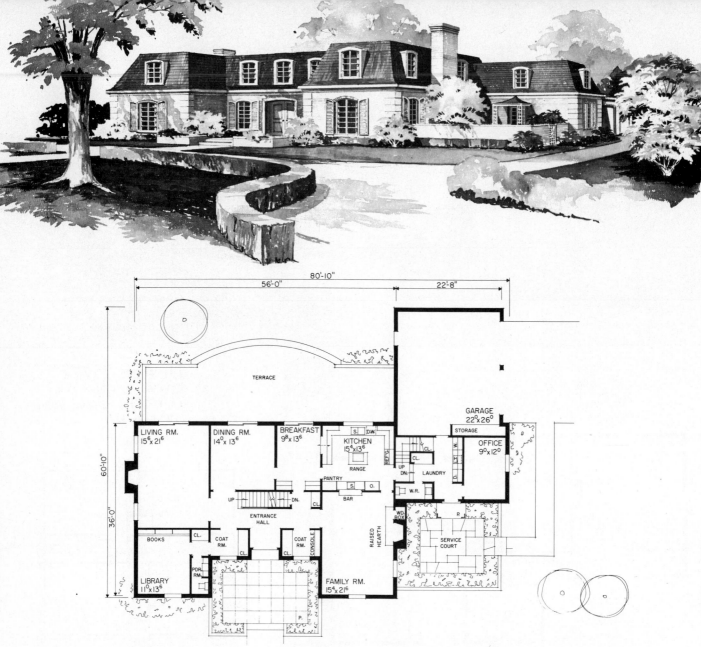

Design 11826 2,230 Sq. Ft. - First Floor; 1,576 Sq. Ft. - Second Floor; 308 Sq. Ft. - Maid's Area; 52,852 Cu. Ft.

● This dramatic French Mansard will provide all the livability the large, active family could possibly want. Its irregular shape results in truly captivating exterior lines. A front court and service court are the by-products of the recessed front and service entrances. A side drive leads to side-opening two-car garage. The interior features twelve (count them) major rooms. These include the quiet library, the isolated office and the private maid's room. In addition there are two coat rooms, a walk-in closet, a powder room, a wash room, a dressing room and three full baths. For family living there is the formal living room and the informal family room. For dining there is the separate dining room and breakfast room. For sleeping facilities there are four big bedrooms with plenty of closets. The first floor laundry is efficient. Three sets of sliding glass doors lead to the rear terrace.

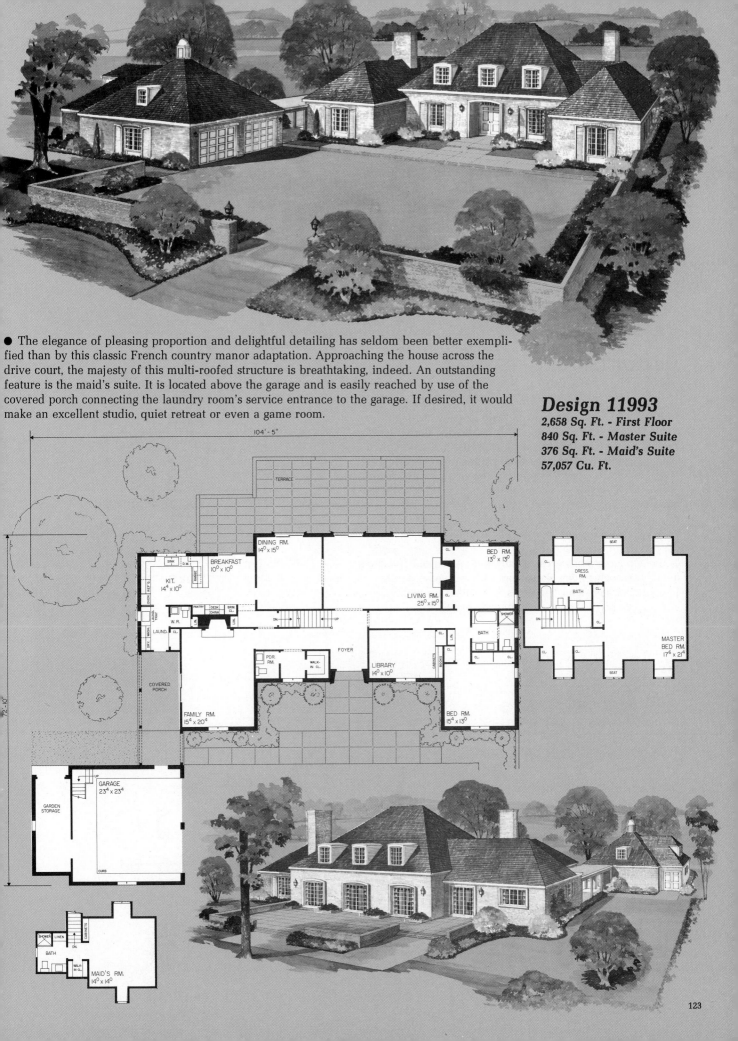

● The elegance of pleasing proportion and delightful detailing has seldom been better exemplified than by this classic French country manor adaptation. Approaching the house across the drive court, the majesty of this multi-roofed structure is breathtaking, indeed. An outstanding feature is the maid's suite. It is located above the garage and is easily reached by use of the covered porch connecting the laundry room's service entrance to the garage. If desired, it would make an excellent studio, quiet retreat or even a game room.

Design 11993

2,658 Sq. Ft. - First Floor
840 Sq. Ft. - Master Suite
376 Sq. Ft. - Maid's Suite
57,057 Cu. Ft.

Design 12376

1,422 Sq. Ft. - First Floor
1,020 Sq. Ft. - Second Floor; 38,134 Cu. Ft.

● Make your next home one that will be truly distinctive and a reflection of your good taste. This high styled design will surely catch the eye of even the most casual of passers-by. The appealing roof lines, the window treatment, the arched openings and the stucco exterior set the charming character of this two-story. The covered front porch provides sheltered entry to the spacious foyer. From this point traffic patterns flow efficiently to all areas. Notice how the family room/ laundry zone is sunken one step. The kitchen is flanked by the two eating areas and they overlook the rear yard. Each of the two large living areas feature a fireplace and functions directly through sliding glass doors with a covered porch. Upstairs there are four bedrooms, two baths and plenty of closets to serve the entire family adequately.

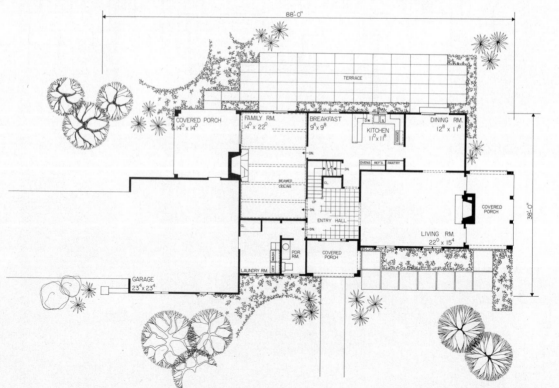

● The formality of French design is certainly impressive. This Mansard version has a notable hipped roof with a delicate nature. The exterior's architectural detailing is pleasing to behold. Double front doors are recessed and open to a center entrance hall. Note that the interior layout is practical and, indeed, efficient. The end living and dining rooms will foster formal living patterns, while the outstanding kitchen and family room with beamed ceiling will function together in a delightfully informal fashion. Both areas have the advantage to enjoy a fireplace. A woodbox is in the family room. Further, there is the quiet study or optional bedroom on the first floor. Upstairs, there are four excellent bedrooms, and two full baths.

Design 12249

1,417 Sq. Ft. - First Floor
1,171 Sq. Ft. - Second Floor
39,714 Cu. Ft.

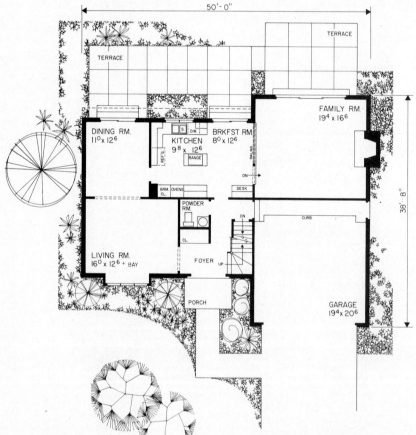

Design 12798

1,149 Sq. Ft. - First Floor
850 Sq. Ft. - Second Floor
28,450 Cu. Ft.

● An island range in the kitchen is a great feature of the work center in this two-story French designed home. The breakfast room has an open railing to the sunken family room so it can enjoy the view of the family room's fireplace.

Sliding glass doors in each of the major rear rooms, dining, breakfast and family rooms, lead to the terrace for outdoor enjoyment. The front, formal living room is highlighted by a bay window. A powder room is conven-

iently located on the first floor near all of the major areas. All of the sleeping facilities are housed on the second floor. Each of the four bedrooms will serve its occupants ideally. A relatively narrow lot can house this design.

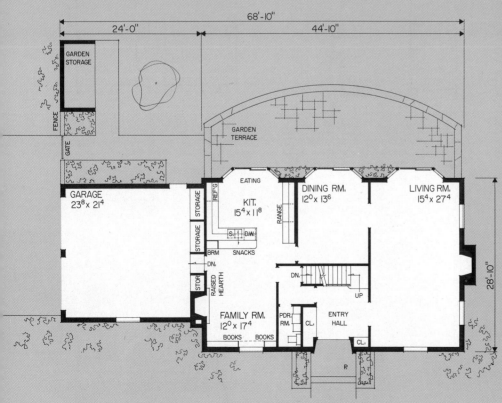

Design 11275

1,314 Sq. Ft. - First Floor
1,080 Sq. Ft. - Second Floor
33,656 Cu. Ft.

● Of French origin, the characteristic feature of this two story design is its Mansard roof. Also, enhancing the formality of its exterior are the beautifully proportioned windows, the recessed front entrance with double doors, the two stately chimneys and the attached two-car garage. The wonderfully efficient floor plan highlights a large end-living room with centered fireplace and a separate dining room. There is also a fine family room-kitchen arrangement with a pass-thru, raised hearth fireplace and strategically located powder room. Upstairs there are three family bedrooms, bath and glamorous master suite. The area over the garage may be utilized for bulk storage or developed as the fifth bedroom. Other bulk storage areas are to be found in the garage and the outdoor unit. Don't miss the sliding doors.

Design 11757

1,406 Sq. Ft. - First Floor
1,115 Sq. Ft. - Second Floor
36,204 Cu. Ft.

● The French Mansard style of a two-story is very popular with those seeking a design with gracious formality. Study this practical floor plan which has first floor laundry and four (optional five) bedrooms. Note two fireplaces.

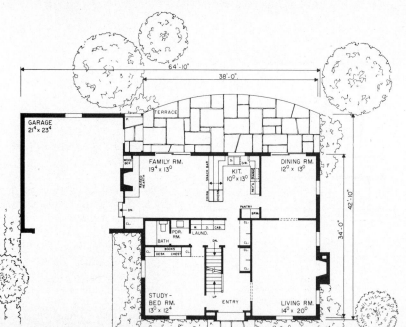

Design 11951
1,346 Sq. Ft. - First Floor
1,114 Sq. Ft. - Second Floor; 39,034 Cu. Ft.

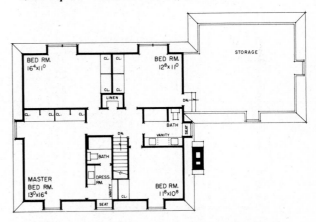

● This is surely a marvelous French home with its Mansard roof. It is equipped with all the necessary features including a large living room, dining room with access to the terrace, efficient kitchen and more.

Design 12152
1,317 Sq. Ft. - First Floor
1,111 Sq. Ft. - Second Floor; 37,198 Cu. Ft.

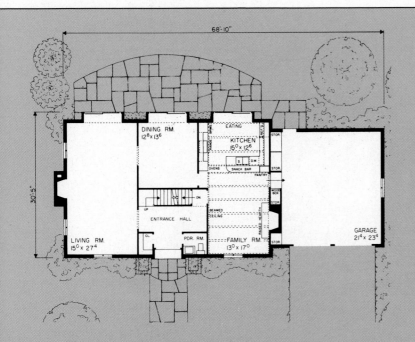

● Here is an interesting plan in which to think about living. Notice the zoning with the entrance hall and dining room dividing the formal and informal living areas. Upstairs there are four bedrooms and two full baths.

Design 12525
919 Sq. Ft. - First Floor
1,019 Sq. Ft. - Second Floor
29,200 Cu. Ft.

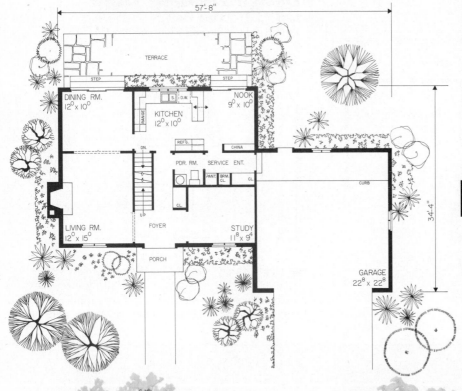

● Here is an economically built home that can be constructed with either of the two illustrated exteriors. Which is your favorite? The two study areas provide plenty of multi-purpose, informal living space.

EARLY COLONIAL DESIGNS . . . *as found in*

is section feature a wide variety of sizes and shapes with a myriad of charming exterior design details which recall our architectural heri-
ge. The Saltbox and Gambrel roofed structure has been an enduring and highly identifiable form. These houses, together with full two-
ory, are depicted here with a wide range of living potential for varying budgets and family sizes. Worthy of note are the fine traffic patterns
at emanate from the numerous center entry houses shown here. With the excellent sleeping, living and work area potential these are truly
omes for family living.

Design 12102 1,682 Sq. Ft. - First Floor; 1,344 Sq. Ft. - Second Floor; 42,960 Cu. Ft.

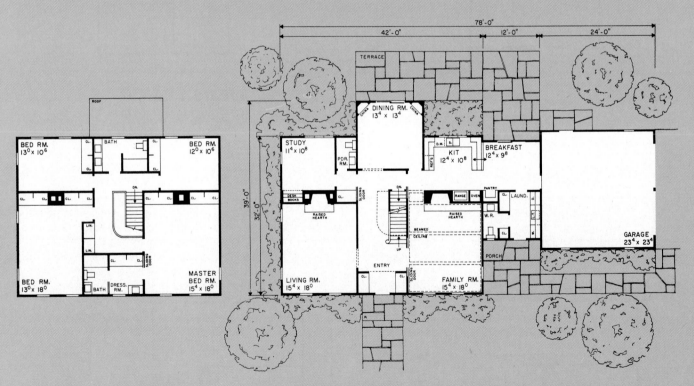

● This Early Colonial adaptation has its roots deep in the past. While it is long on history, it is equally long on 20th-Century livability features. The narrow horizontal siding, the appealing window treatment, the exquisite door detailing, the hip-roof, the mas-sive chimneys and the cupola are exterior architectural features which set the character. It would certainly be difficult by today's living standards to ask for more than what this floor plan offers. From the first floor laundry with its adjacent washroom to the study with its adjacent powder room, the interior is replete with con-venient living appointments. There is a wealth of "little" features such as the built-ins, the raised hearths, the pantry, the pass-thru to breakfast room and the beamed ceiling.

● Small house with big house features and livability. Some of the features include two full baths and extra storage upstairs; laundry, washroom and two fireplaces, each with a wood box on the first floor. Two sets of sliding glass doors lead to the terrace.

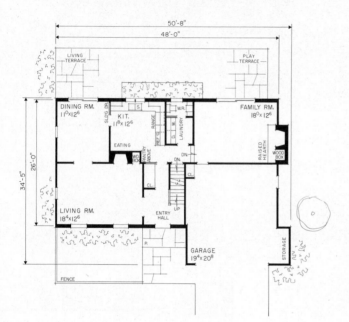

Design 11856
1,023 Sq. Ft. - First Floor
784 Sq. Ft. - Second Floor; 25,570 Cu. Ft.

● The appeal of this Colonial home will be virtually everlasting. It will improve with age and service the growing family well. Imagine your family living here. There are four bedrooms, 2½ baths, plus plenty of first floor living space.

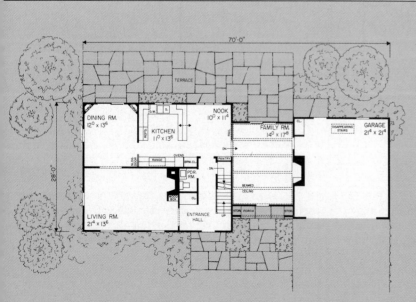

Design 12211
1,214 Sq. Ft. - First Floor
1,146 Sq. Ft. - Second Floor; 32,752 Cu. Ft.

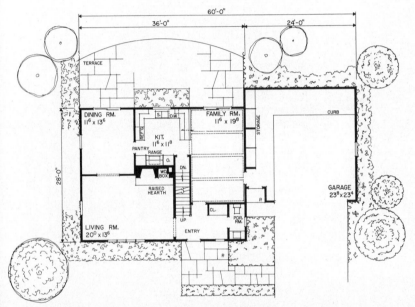

A Garrison type adaptation that projects all the romance of yesteryear. The narrow horizontal siding, the wide corner boards, the window detailing, the overhanging second floor and the massive, centered chimney help set this home apart.

Design 11849 1,008 Sq. Ft. - First Floor
1,080 Sq. Ft. - Second Floor; 31,153 Cu. Ft.

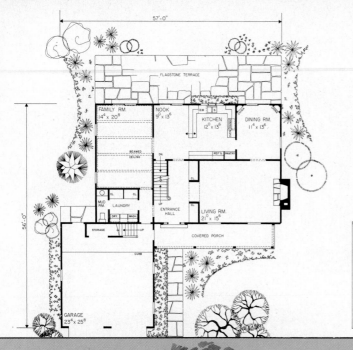

57'-0"

56'-0"

FLAGSTONE TERRACE

FAMILY RM.
14⁴ x 20⁸

NOOK
9⁰ x 13⁶

KITCHEN
12⁰ x 13⁶

DINING RM.
11⁴ x 13⁶

BEAMED CEILING

REF'G PANTRY

MUD RM.

LAUNDRY

DRY | WASH

STORAGE

ENTRANCE HALL

LIVING RM.
21⁴ x 15⁶

COVERED PORCH

CURB

GARAGE
23⁴ x 25⁸

● Efficiently planned, this two-story house will serve the family with ease. Four bedrooms are on the second floor, along with two full baths. Note the attic storage over the projecting garage.

ROOF

DRESSING | BATH | BATH | WALK-IN CLOSET

LINEN

CHEST

BED RM.
15⁴ x 10⁴

MASTER BED RM.
14⁴ x 12¹⁰

STAIR HALL

DN

CL

BED RM.
11⁶ x 10⁰

BED RM.
11⁶ x 11⁰

ROOF

DN

ATTIC STORAGE
17⁴ x 25⁸

ROOF

Design 12364
1,440 Sq. Ft. - First Floor
1,206 Sq. Ft. - Second Floor
38,044 Cu. Ft.

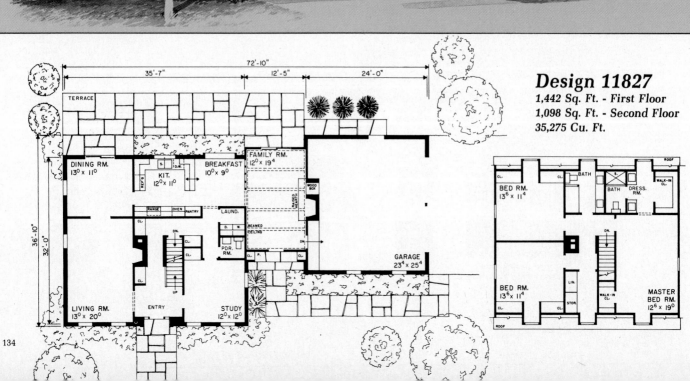

72'-10"

35'-7" | 12'-5" | 24'-0"

36'-10"

32'-0"

TERRACE

DINING RM.
13⁰ x 11⁰

REF'G

KIT.
12⁰ x 11⁰

D.W.

BREAKFAST
10⁰ x 9⁰

FAMILY RM.
12⁰ x 19⁴

WOOD BOX

RANGE | OVEN | PANTRY

LAUND.

D.W.

RAISED HEARTH

BEAMED CEILING

DN

CL

PDR. RM.

CL

CL

P.

GARAGE
23⁴ x 25⁴

LIVING RM.
13⁰ x 20⁰

ENTRY

UP

STUDY
12⁰ x 12⁰

Design 11827
1,442 Sq. Ft. - First Floor
1,098 Sq. Ft. - Second Floor
35,275 Cu. Ft.

ROOF

CL | CL | BATH

BED RM.
13⁶ x 11⁴

BATH | DRESS. RM. | WALK-IN CL.

DN

BED RM.
13⁶ x 11⁴

LIN.

WALK-IN CL.

STOR.

MASTER BED RM.
12⁶ x 19⁰

ROOF

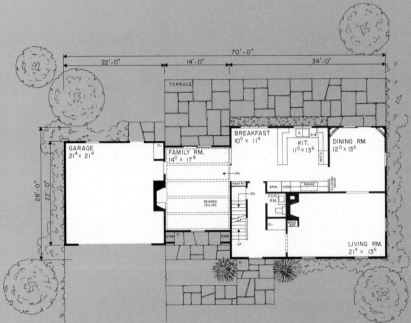

Design 12131

1,214 Sq. Ft. - First Floor
1,097 Sq. Ft. - Second Floor
30,743 Cu. Ft.

● The Gambrel-roof home is often the very embodiment of charm from the Early Colonial Period in American architectural history. Fine proportion and excellent detailing were the hallmarks of the era.

Design 12610 1,505 Sq. Ft. - First Floor; 1,344 Sq. Ft. - Second Floor; 45,028 Cu. Ft.

● This full two-story traditional will be worthy of note wherever built. It strongly recalls images of a New England of yesteryear. And well it might; for the window treatment is delightful. The front entrance detail is inviting. The narrow horizontal siding and the corner boards are appealing as are the two massive chimneys. The center entrance hall is large with a handy powder room nearby. The study has built-in bookshelves and offers a full measure of privacy. The interior kitchen has a pass-thru to the family room and enjoys all that natural light from the bay window of the nook. A beamed ceiling, fireplace and sliding glass doors are features of the family room. The mud room highlights a closet, laundry equipment and an extra wash room. Study the upstairs with those four bedrooms, two baths and plenty of closets. An excellent arrangement for all.

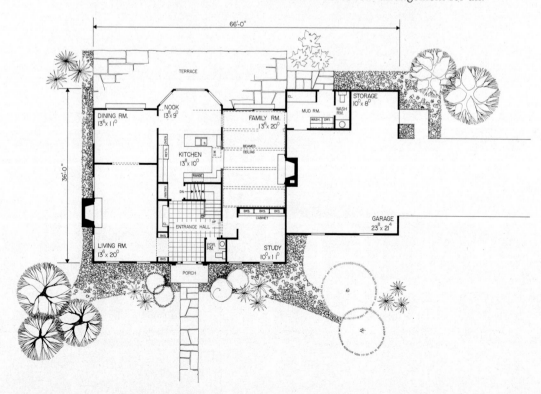

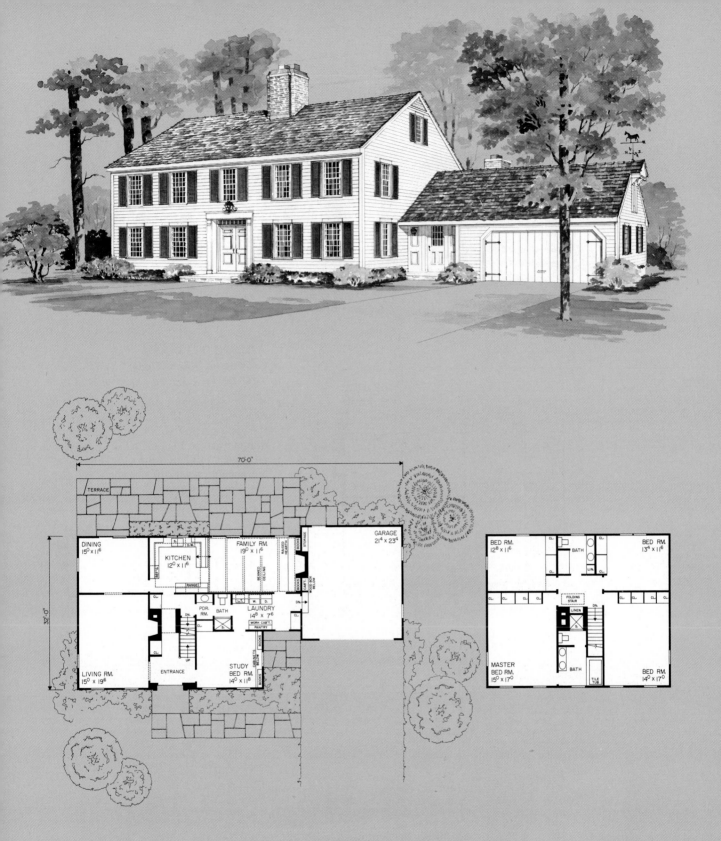

Design 12188
1,440 Sq. Ft. - First Floor; 1,280 Sq. Ft. - Second Floor; 40,924 Cu. Ft.

● This design is characteristic of early America and its presence will create an atmosphere of that time in our heritage. However, it will be right at home wherever located. Along with exterior charm, this design has outstanding livability to offer its occupants. Beginning with the first floor, there are formal and informal areas plus the work centers. Note the center bath which has direct access from three adjacent areas. Built-in book shelves are the feature of both the family room and the study/bedroom. Built-ins are also featured in the garage. Ascending up to the second floor, one will be in the private sleeping area. This area consists of the master suite, three bedrooms and full bath. Folding stairs are in the upstairs hall for easy access to the attic.

Design 12539

1,450 Sq. Ft. - First Floor
1,167 Sq. Ft. - Second Floor; 46,738 Cu. Ft.

● This appealingly proportioned Gambrel exudes an aura of coziness. The beauty of the main part of the house is delightfully symmetrical and is enhanced by the attached garage and laundry room. The center entrance routes traffic directly to all major zones of the house.

Design 12538
1,503 Sq. Ft. - First Floor
1,095 Sq. Ft. - Second Floor; 44,321 Cu. Ft.

● This Salt Box is charming, indeed. The livability it has to offer to the large and growing family is great. The entry is spacious and is open to the second floor balcony. For living areas, there is the study in addition to the living and family rooms.

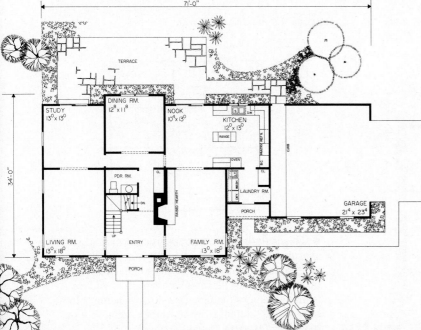

Design 12731
1,039 Sq. Ft. - First Floor
973 Sq. Ft. - Second Floor; 29,740 Cu. Ft.

● The multi-paned windows with shutters of this two-story highlight the exterior delightfully. Inside the livability is ideal. Formal and informal areas are sure to serve your family with ease. Note efficient U-shaped kitchen with handy first-floor laundry. Sleeping facilities on second floor.

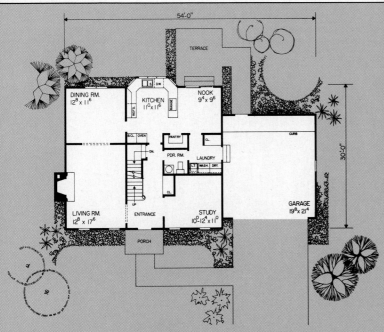

Design 12733 1,177 Sq. Ft. - First Floor; 1,003 Sq. Ft. - Second Floor; 32,040 Cu. Ft.

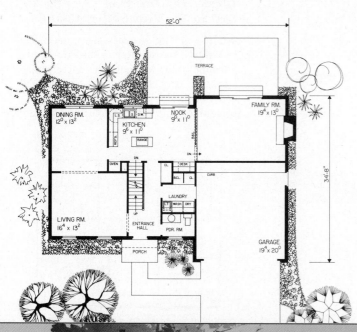

● This is definitely a four bedroom Colonial with charm galore. The kitchen features an island range and other built-ins. All will enjoy the sunken family room with fireplace, which has sliding glass doors leading to the terrace. Also a basement for recreational activities with laundry remaining on first floor for extra convenience.

Design 12598

1,016 Sq. Ft. - First Floor
890 Sq. Ft. - Second Floor; 30,000 Cu. Ft.

● An impressive, Early Colonial adaptation with a projecting two-car garage and front drive court. It will not demand a large, expensive piece of property. In days of high-cost building, this relatively modest-sized two-story will be a great investment. Note the huge living room. The basement lends itself to recreational facilities.

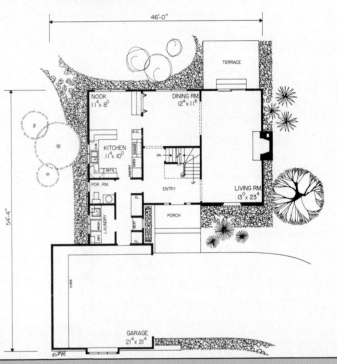

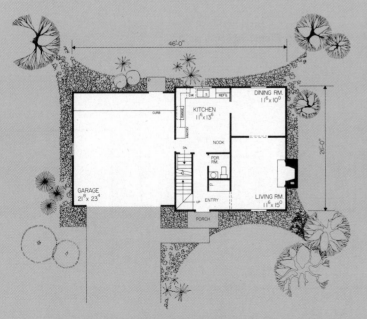

Design 12622

624 Sq. Ft. - First Floor
624 Sq. Ft. - Second Floor; 19,864 Cu. Ft.

● Appealing design can envelope little packages, too. Here is a charming, Early Colonial adaptation with an attached two-car garage to serve the young family with a modest building budget.

Design 12253 1,503 Sq. Ft. - First Floor; 1,291 Sq. Ft. - Second Floor; 44,260 Cu. Ft.

● The overhanging second floor sets the character of this Early American design. Study the features, both inside and out.

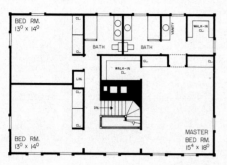

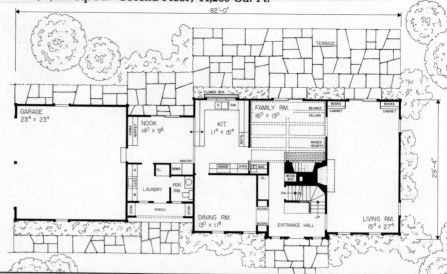

Design 11179 1,378 Sq. Ft. - First Floor; 1,040 Sq. Ft. - Second Floor; 35,022 Cu. Ft.

● Loads of livability. This home could be called upon to serve as a five bedroom design. It will function admirably however you choose.

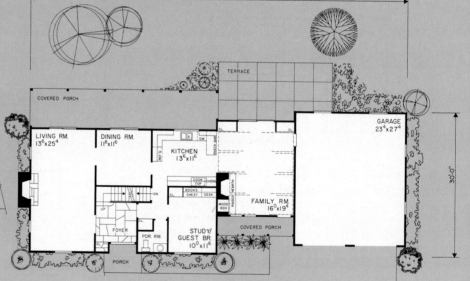

Design 11700 1,836 Sq. Ft. - First Floor; 1,232 Sq. Ft. - Second Floor; 44,660 Cu. Ft.

● Good zoning, fine traffic circulation, efficient work center, first floor laundry are among convenient living features.

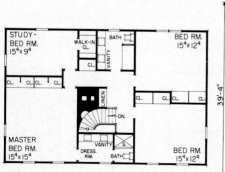

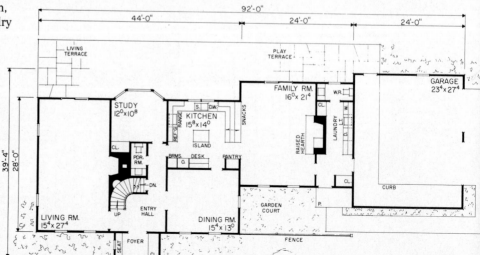

143

Design 12713

1,830 Sq. Ft. - First Floor
1,056 Sq. Ft. - Second Floor; 41,370 Cu. Ft.

● This home with its Gambrel roof and paned windows is sure to be a pleasure for the entire family. Along with the outside, the inside is a delight. The spacious family room creates an inviting atmosphere with sliding glass doors to the terrace, beamed ceiling and a raised hearth fireplace that includes a built-in wood box. A spectacular kitchen, too. Presenting a cooking island as well as a built-in oven, desk and storage pantry. A sunny breakfast nook, too, also with sliding glass doors leading to the terrace. A service entrance and laundry are adjacent. Note the size of the formal dining room and the fireplace in the living room. A first floor study/bedroom has a private terrace. Upstairs, there is the master suite and two more bedrooms and a bath.

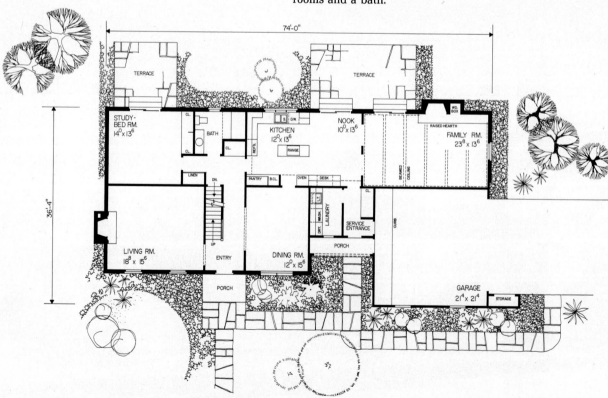

Design 12891

1,405 Sq. Ft. - First Floor
1,226 Sq. Ft. - Second Floor; 39,122 Cu. Ft.

● Here is a charming two-story house with a Gambrel roof that is very appealing. Entering this home, you will find a large dining room to the right which precedes an efficient kitchen. The adjacent breakfast room makes serving meals easy. The nice sized living room has a fireplace as does the family room. A wet bar and sliding glass doors are also in the family room. A powder room and laundry are on the first floor, too. Upstairs, you will find two bedrooms, a bath and a master bedroom suite with walk-in closet, tub and shower. Note that the second floor hall is open to the first floor.

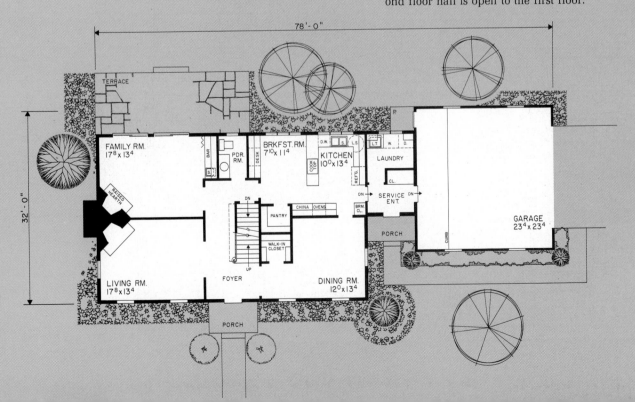

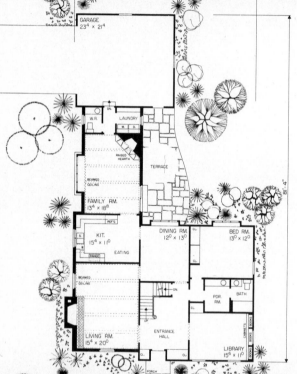

Design 12308

1,807 Sq. Ft. - First Floor
1,195 Sq. Ft. - Second Floor; 48,470 Cu. Ft.

● If yours is a corner lot you might want to give this attractive Colonial adaptation your consideration. Or, perhaps more significantly, if you have a large family this may be the design to solve your housing problem. Certainly you won't have to invest in a huge piece of property to enjoy the livability this home has to offer. In addition to the formal living room and informal family room, there is the separate dining room and kitchen eating space. Further, in addition to the three upstairs bedrooms, there is a fourth downstairs. The library could function as the fifth, if desired.

Design 12103

1,374 Sq. Ft. - First Floor
1,056 Sq. Ft. - Second Floor
36,672 Cu. Ft.

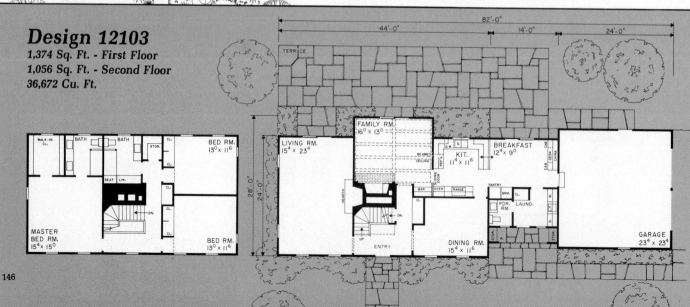

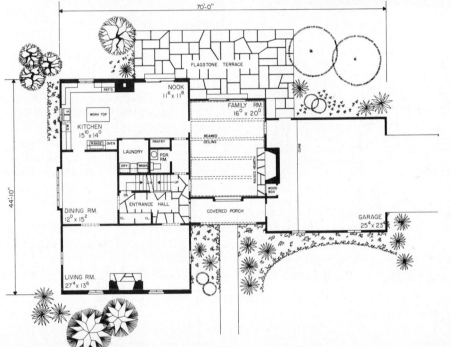

Design 12368

1,592 Sq. Ft. - First Floor
1,255 Sq. Ft. - Second Floor
54,516 Cu. Ft.

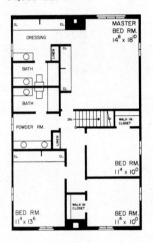

Design 12625
1,640 Sq. Ft. - First Floor
1,072 Sq. Ft. - Second Floor; 39,360 Cu. Ft.

● A 19th Century Farmhouse! So it might seem. But one with contemporary features . . . like the U-shaped kitchen with a built-in desk and appliances as well as a separate dining nook. Or the 20' by 13' family room. There, a beamed ceiling and raised-hearth fireplace add traditional warmth to a modern convention.

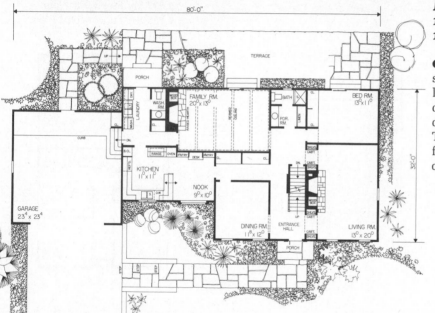

Design 11814 1,471 Sq. Ft. - First Floor
1,052 Sq. Ft. - Second Floor; 35,700 Cu. Ft.

● A Salt Box design that has all of the usual traditional exterior features. The interior shows what up-to-date floor planning can do inside the charm of yesteryear's exterior. A central entrance hall routes traffic directly to all major areas. The work area can be made to capture that cozy country kitchen atmosphere.

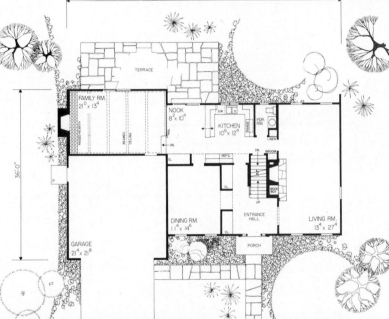

Design 12623
1,368 Sq. Ft. - First Floor
1,046 Sq. Ft. - Second Floor; 35,130 Cu. Ft.

● Take note of this four bedroom Salt Box design. Enter through the large entrance hall to enjoy this home. Imagine a living room 13 x 27 feet. Plus a family room. Both having a fireplace. Also, sliding glass doors in both the family room and nook leading to the rear terrace.

Design 12799 1,196 Sq. Ft. - First Floor
780 Sq. Ft. - Second Floor; 35,080 Cu. Ft.

● This two-story traditional design's facade with its narrow clapboards, punctuated by tall multi-paned windows, appears deceptively expansive. Yet the entire length of the house, including the garage, is 66 feet.

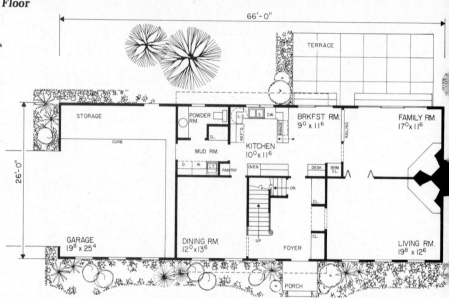

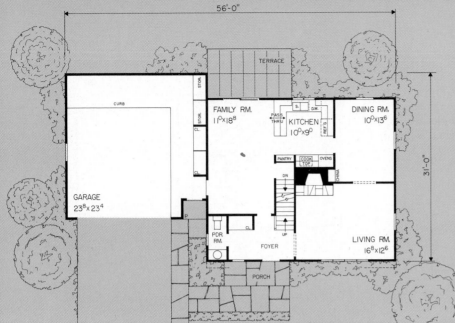

Design 11719 864 Sq. Ft. - First Floor
896 Sq. Ft. - Second Floor; 26,024 Cu. Ft.

● What an appealing low-cost Colonial adaptation. Most of the livability features generally found in the largest of homes are present to cater to family needs.

First floor labels: CURB, STOR., CL., STOR., CL., GARAGE 23⁸ x 23⁴, FAMILY RM. 11⁰ x 18⁸, TERRACE, KITCHEN 10⁰ x 9⁰, PASS THRU, S., D.W., REF'G., DINING RM. 10⁰ x 13⁶, PANTRY, COOK TOP, OVENS, CHINA, DN, P., PDR. RM., CL., UP, FOYER, LIVING RM. 16⁸ x 12⁶, PORCH

Dimensions: 56'-0", 31'-0"

Second floor labels: BEDROOM 11⁰ x 10⁰, CL., BATH, VANITY, BEDROOM 10⁰ x 11⁴, LINEN, WALK-IN CLOSET, LINEN, DN, CL., CL., BEDROOM 11⁰ x 13⁸, WALK-IN CLOSET, S., BATH, MASTER BEDROOM 13⁴ x 13⁴

Design 12870 900 Sq. Ft. - First Floor
467 Sq. Ft. - Second Floor Left Suite
493 Sq. Ft. - Second Floor Right Suite; 35,970 Cu. Ft.

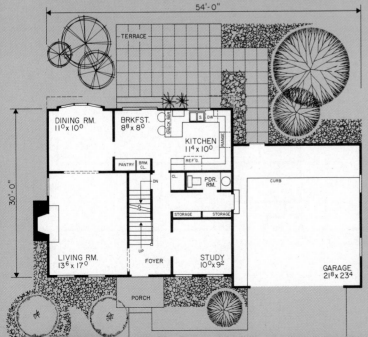

First floor labels: TERRACE, DINING RM. 11⁰ x 10⁰, BRKFST. 8⁸ x 8⁰, SNACK BAR, S., DW, KITCHEN 11⁴ x 10⁰, RANGE, PANTRY, BRM. CL., REF'G., DN, CL., PDR. RM., STORAGE, STORAGE, CURB, LIVING RM. 13⁶ x 17⁰, UP, FOYER, STUDY 10⁰ x 9², GARAGE 21⁸ x 23⁴, PORCH

Dimensions: 54'-0", 30'-0"

Second floor labels: BEDROOM 13² x 10⁴, CL., CL., BEDROOM 13² x 10⁴, CABINET, BOOKS, BOOKS, CABINET, LINEN, LINEN, BATH, SUITE ENT. HALL, BATH, STOR., STOR., CL., DN, CL., MASTER BEDROOM 11² x 13⁴, WALK-IN CLOSET, MASTER BEDROOM 11² x 13⁴, CL., SHELVES

● This colonial home was designed to provide comfortable living space for two families. The first floor is the common living area, with all of the necessary living areas; the second floor has two two-bedroom-one-bath suites. Built-ins are featured in the smaller bedroom.

Design 11986 896 Sq. Ft. - First Floor
1,148 Sq. Ft. - Second Floor; 28,840 Cu. Ft.

● This design with its distinctive Gambrel roof will spell charm wherever it may be situated - far out in the country, or on a busy thoroughfare. Compact and economical to build, it will be easy on the budget. Note the location of the family room. It is over the garage on the second floor.

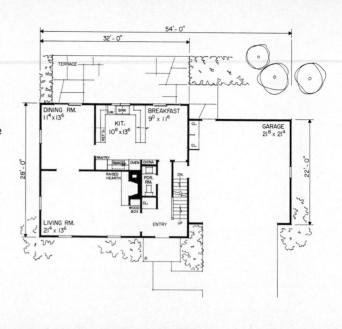

Design 11777 1,142 Sq. Ft. - First Floor
1,010 Sq. Ft. - Second Floor; 28,095 Cu. Ft.

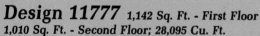

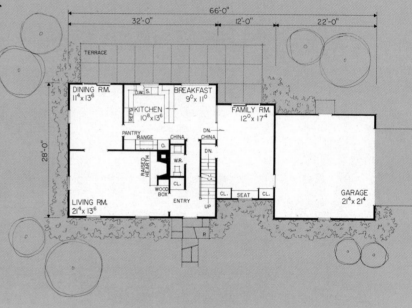

● If it's charm you are after, you'll find this design with a Gambrel roof difficult to top. Its distinctive air is enhanced by the attached family room unit and the two-car garage. The wide vertical siding delightfully contrasts with the narrow horizontal siding.

Design 12531 1,353 Sq. Ft. - First Floor
1,208 Sq. Ft. - Second Floor; 33,225 Cu. Ft.

● This design has its roots in the early history of New England. While its exterior is decidedly and purposely dated, the interior reflects an impressive 20th-Century floor plan. All of the elements are present to guarantee outstanding living patterns for today's large, active family.

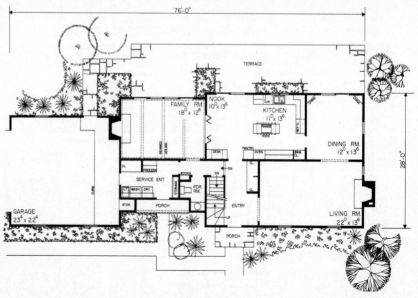

153

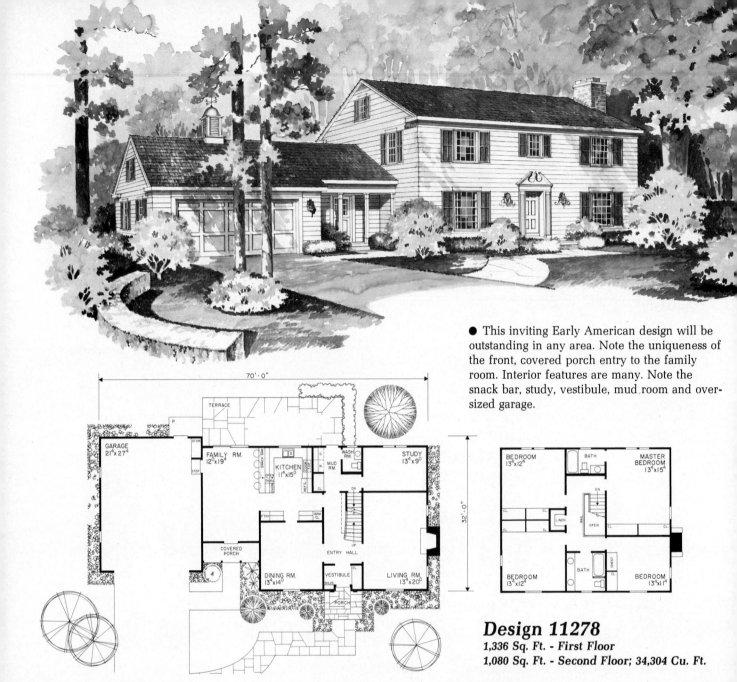

● This inviting Early American design will be outstanding in any area. Note the uniqueness of the front, covered porch entry to the family room. Interior features are many. Note the snack bar, study, vestibule, mud room and oversized garage.

Design 11278
1,336 Sq. Ft. - First Floor
1,080 Sq. Ft. - Second Floor; 34,304 Cu. Ft.

● Here is a design with all of the features a homeowner would want most in a new house. It abounds in exterior appeal and will be a neighborhood show place. Picture yourself relaxing on the front, covered porch after a hard day of work.

Design 11995
1,774 Sq. Ft. - First Floor
1,235 Sq. Ft. - Second Floor; 44,623 Cu. Ft.

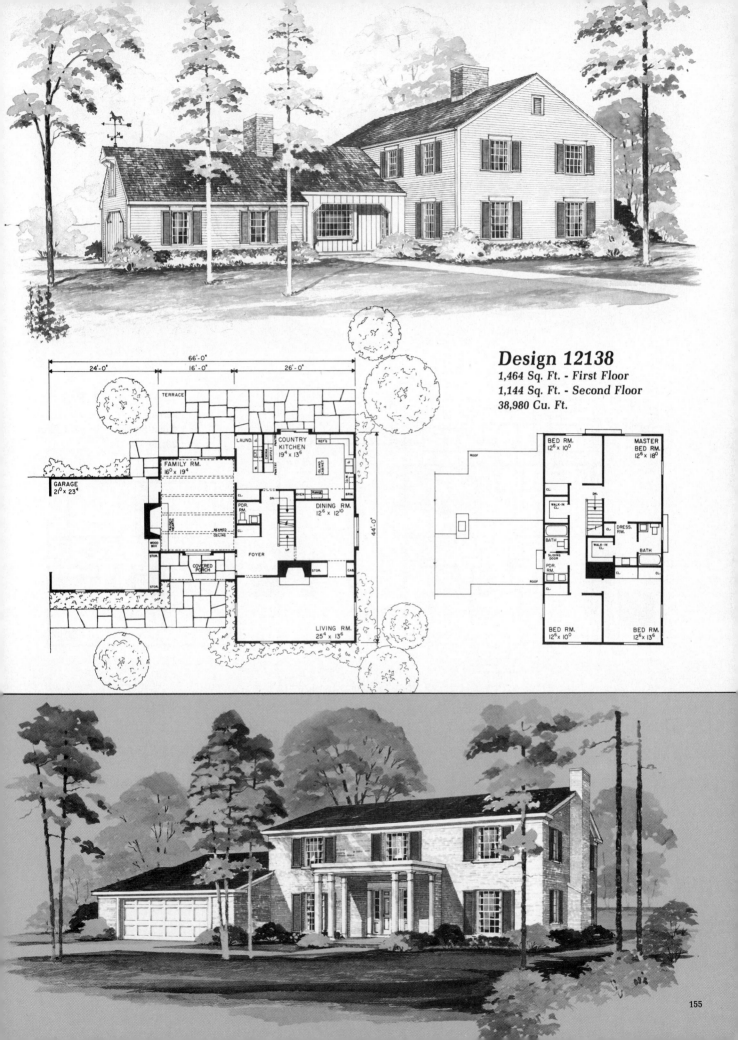

Design 12138

1,464 Sq. Ft. - First Floor
1,144 Sq. Ft. - Second Floor
38,980 Cu. Ft.

First Floor

TERRACE

GARAGE
21⁰ x 23⁴

FAMILY RM.
16⁰ x 19⁴

LAUND.

COUNTRY KITCHEN
19⁴ x 13⁶

REF'G

BEAMED CEILING

WOOD BOX

STOR.

PDR. RM.

CL.

CL.

OVEN   RANGE

ISLAND CABINET

COVERED PORCH

STOR.

FOYER

DN.

UP

DINING RM.
12⁶ x 12¹⁰

STOR.

CAB.

LIVING RM.
25⁴ x 13⁶

24'-0"   16'-0"   26'-0"

66'-0"

44'-0"

Second Floor

ROOF

BED RM.
12⁶ x 10⁰

MASTER BED RM.
12⁶ x 18⁰

CL.

WALK-IN CL.

BATH

DN.

DRESS. RM.

WALK-IN CL.

SLIDING DOOR

PDR. RM.

CL.

BATH

ROOF

CL.

BED RM.
12⁶ x 10⁰

BED RM.
12⁶ x 13⁶

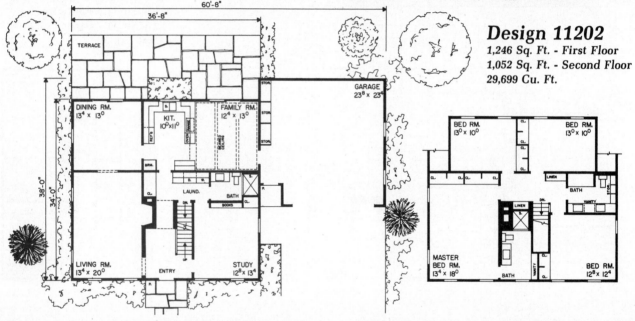

Design 11202
1,246 Sq. Ft. - First Floor
1,052 Sq. Ft. - Second Floor
29,699 Cu. Ft.

First Floor (Design 11202):

60'-8"
36'-8"
38'-0"
34'-0"

TERRACE
DINING RM. 13⁴ x 13⁰
KIT. 10⁰ x 11⁰
FAMILY RM. 12⁴ x 13⁰
GARAGE 23⁸ x 23⁴
STOR.
BRM.
LAUND.
BATH
BOOKS
CL.
LIVING RM. 13⁴ x 20⁰
ENTRY
STUDY 12⁸ x 13⁴

Second Floor (Design 11202):

BED RM. 13⁰ x 10⁰
BED RM. 13⁰ x 10⁰
CL.
LINEN
BATH
LINEN
DN.
VANITY
MASTER BED RM. 13⁴ x 18⁰
BATH
BED RM. 12⁸ x 12⁴

Design 11266
1,374 Sq. Ft. - First Floor
1,094 Sq. Ft. - Second Floor
31,969 Cu. Ft.

Second Floor (Design 11266):

BED RM. 12⁸ x 10⁰
BED RM. 12⁸ x 10⁰
CL. CL. CL. CL.
LINEN
BATH
VANITY
LINEN
DN.
BATH
MASTER BED RM. 13⁴ x 18⁸
VANITY
BED RM. 12⁸ x 13⁴

First Floor (Design 11266):

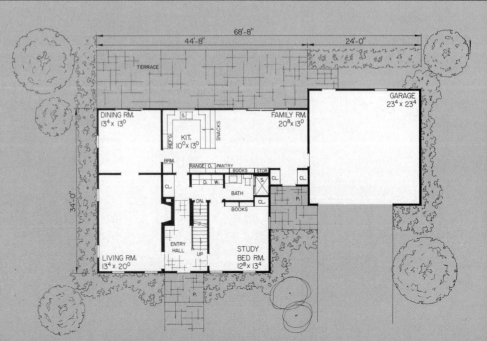

68'-8"
44'-8"
24'-0"
34'-0"

TERRACE
DINING RM. 13⁴ x 13⁰
KIT. 10⁰ x 13⁰
SNACKS
FAMILY RM. 20⁸ x 13⁰
GARAGE 23⁴ x 23⁴
BRM.
RANGE O. PANTRY
BOOKS
STOR.
CL.
BATH
BOOKS
LIVING RM. 13⁴ x 20⁰
ENTRY HALL
UP
STUDY BED RM. 12⁸ x 13⁴

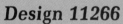

Design 11142 1,525 Sq. Ft. - First Floor
952 Sq. Ft. - Second Floor (1,053 Sq. Ft. - Four Bedroom Option); 32,980 Cu. Ft.

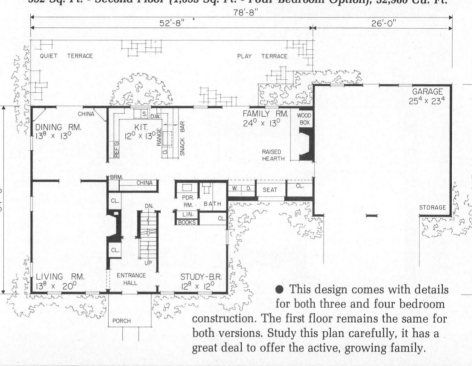

Second Floor (Three Bedroom):

BED RM. 13⁸ x 10⁰
CL.
CL.
CL.
LIN.
BATH
DN.
CL. CL.
VANITY
WALK IN CL.
BATH
S.
MASTER BED RM. 13⁸ x 20⁰
BED RM. 12⁸ x 14⁶

Second Floor (Four Bedroom):

BED RM. 12⁸ x 10⁰
CL.
BED RM. 12⁸ x 10⁰
CL.
CL.
CL. CL. CL. CL.
LINEN
BATH
STORAGE
LIN.
DN.
S.
VANITY
UP
MASTER BED RM. 13⁴ x 18⁰
BATH
VANITY
CL.
BED RM. 12⁸ x 12⁴

First Floor:

78'-8"
52'-8"
26'-0"
34'-0"
38'-0"

QUIET TERRACE
PLAY TERRACE
DINING RM. 13⁸ x 13⁰
CHINA
KIT. 12⁰ x 13⁰
S.
D.W.
RANGE
REF. G.
SNACK BAR
FAMILY RM. 24⁰ x 13⁰
WOOD BOX
RAISED HEARTH
GARAGE 25⁴ x 23⁴
BRM.
CHINA
CL.
PDR. RM.
BATH
W. D.
SEAT
CL.
STORAGE
DN.
LIN.
BOOKS
UP
CL.
LIVING RM. 13⁸ x 20⁰
ENTRANCE HALL
STUDY-B.R. 12⁸ x 12⁰
PORCH

● This design comes with details for both three and four bedroom construction. The first floor remains the same for both versions. Study this plan carefully, it has a great deal to offer the active, growing family.

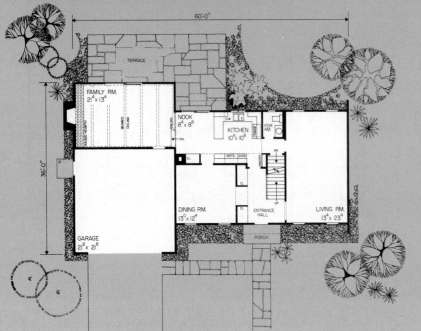

Design 12617

1,223 Sq. Ft. - First Floor
1,018 Sq. Ft. - Second Floor; 30,784 Cu. Ft.

● Another Gambrel roof version just loaded with charm. Notice the delightful symmetry of the window treatment. Inside, the large family will enjoy all the features that assure convenient living. The end-living room will have excellent privacy.

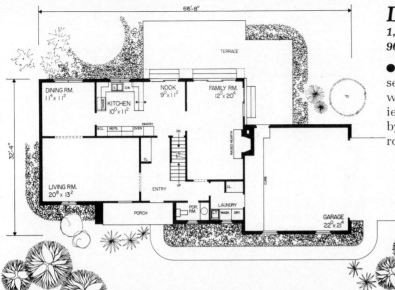

Design 12751

1,202 Sq. Ft. - First Floor
964 Sq. Ft. - Second Floor; 33,830 Cu. Ft.

● This Gambrel roof version of a Colonial is sure to serve your family efficiently. The U-shaped kitchen with pass-thru to breakfast nook will be very convenient to the busy homemaker. The terrace is accessible by way of sliding glass doors in the nook and family room.

Design 12189

1,134 Sq. Ft. - First Floor
1,063 Sq. Ft. - Second Floor; 31,734 Cu. Ft.

● Imagine this Colonial adaptation on your new building site! The recessed entrances add an extra measure of appeal. While each family member will probably have his own favorite set of highlights, all will surely agree that the living patterns will be just great.

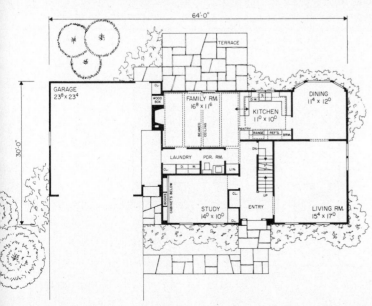

159

Design 11712 1,618 Sq. Ft. - First Floor
1,074 Sq. Ft. - Second Floor; 37,349 Cu. Ft.

● The Connecticut Gambrel roof design is a fine embodiment of old New England. Here, the center entrance hall leads directly through the house to the rear terrace. There will be no annoying cross-room traffic in the living room and the dining room may be completely bypassed whenever desired.

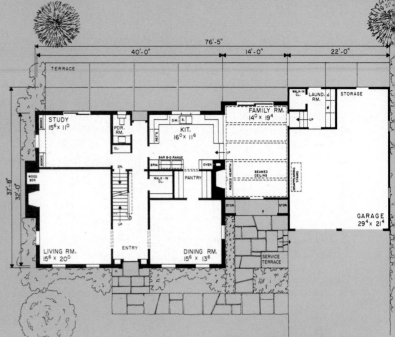

Design 11141 1,360 Sq. Ft. - First Floor
939 Sq. Ft. - Second Floor; 33,180 Cu. Ft.

● A 27 foot end living room, a fireplace in the breakfast room and master bedroom and a generous area over the garage for possible future development are highlights of this design. Don't overlook the many other features which include the family room, extra washroom, dining room, etc.

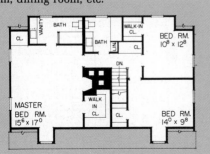

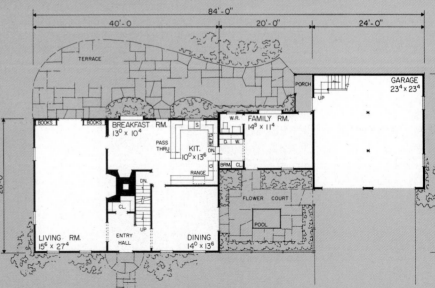

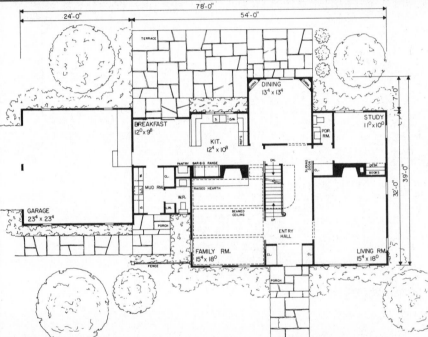

● The heritage of the New England seacoast shows in this house with its Gambrel roof widow's walk and high chimney pots. As if all that livability on the first and second floors was not enough, there is the third floor which may be developed to suit your requirements.

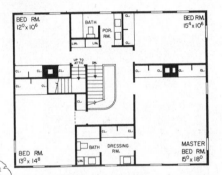

Design 12100
1,682 Sq. Ft. - First Floor
1,344 Sq. Ft. - Second Floor; 39,563 Cu. Ft.

Design 12295

1,947 Sq. Ft. - First Floor
1,092 Sq. Ft. - Second Floor
43,795 Cu. Ft.

● This L-shaped two-story will make efficient use of your building site. The floor plan and how it functions is extremely interesting and practical. Study it carefully.

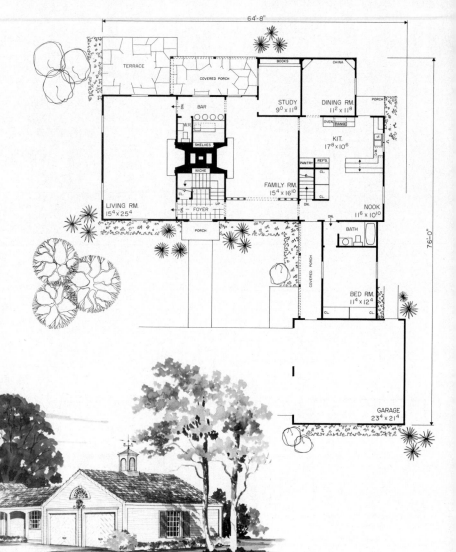

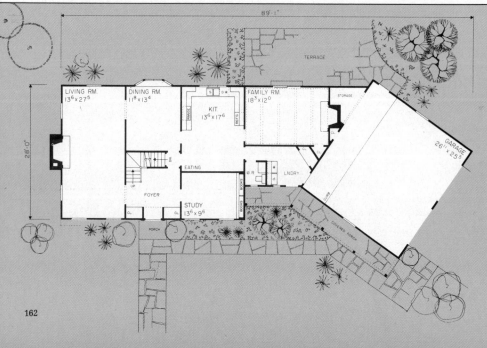

● Angular in its configuration, this inviting home offers loads of livability. There are five bedrooms, study, family room and a 27 foot long living room.

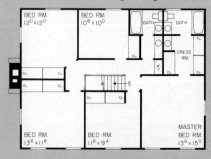

Design 12322

1,480 Sq. Ft. - First Floor
1,172 Sq. Ft. - Second Floor
41,112 Cu. Ft.

Design 12346

1,510 Sq. Ft. - First Floor
1,009 Sq. Ft. - Second Floor
36,482 Cu. Ft.

● A fine mixture of exterior materials, window treatment, and roof planes help set the character here. Envision your family enjoying all that this design has to offer.

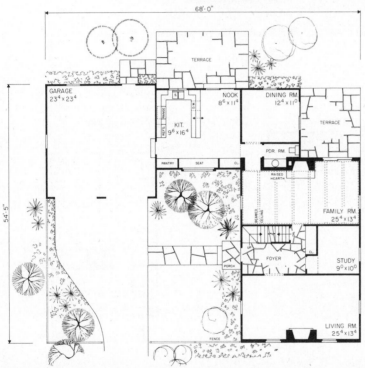

Design 11914 *1,470 Sq. Ft. - First Floor; 888 Sq. Ft. - Second Floor; 30,354 Cu. Ft.*

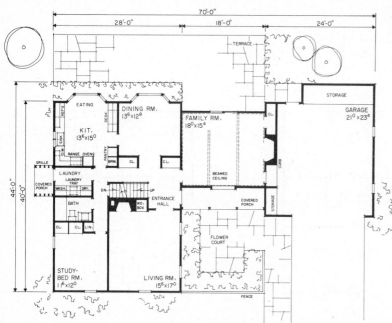

● What an interesting facade for passers-by to enjoy. Here, the delightful configuration of the Gambrel roof is fully visible from the road. The interior has all the features to help assure living convenience at its best. What are your favorite features?

Design 11745 1,440 Sq. Ft. - First Floor; 1,124 Sq. Ft. - Second Floor; 34,148 Cu. Ft.

● A picture of charm. For sheer exterior appeal this house would be difficult to top. And inside there is an abundance of livability. Imagine, four bedrooms, three baths, guest room, family room, separate dining room and first floor laundry.

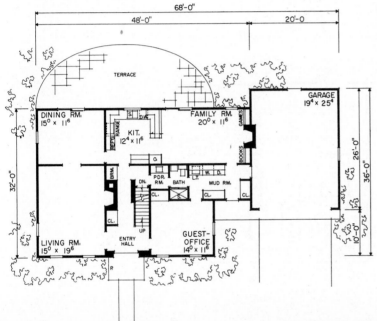

Design 12224
1,567 Sq. Ft. - First Floor
1,070 Sq. Ft. - Second Floor; 37,970 Cu. Ft.

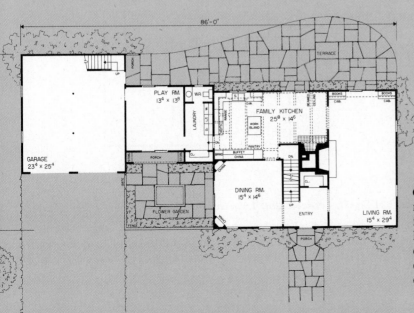

● Certainly reminiscent of the charm of rural New England. The focal point of the first floor is easily the spacious family-kitchen. Formerly referred to as the country-kitchen, this area with its beamed ceiling and fireplace will have a warm and cozy atmosphere, indeed.

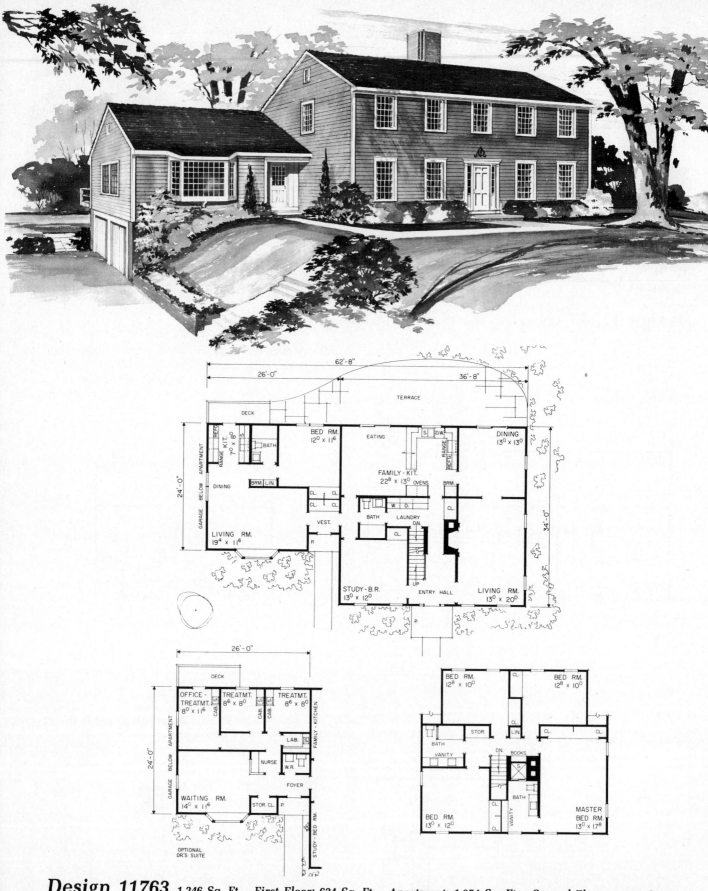

Design 11763 *1,246 Sq. Ft. - First Floor; 624 Sq. Ft. - Apartment; 1,054 Sq. Ft. - Second Floor; 42,260 Cu. Ft.*

● A charming New England Salt Box designed to satisfy the needs of the large family, plus provide facilities for a live-in relative! Many houses can be a problem in adapting to the living requirements of an in-residence relative. But, not this one. Your family will have all the space it needs, while your relative will enjoy all his or her privacy and independence. This apartment area may also be adapted to function as a doctor's suite.

SOUTHERN COLONIAL VERSIONS...

and more Georgian adaptations are featured in this section. In addition, a few reminders of New Orleans with its wrought iron work are included. Stately Greek Revival columns supporting projecting pediment gables have become symbols of gracious living. Other variations of this theme are hardly less dramatic as evidenced by winged two-story houses. The formal Georgian designs are enhanced by the massive twin chimneys, symmetrical window arrangement and appealing front entrance detailing. Brick quoins, dentils, carriage lamps, recessed entrances, and cupolas are among the other attractive features.

Design 12889
2,529 Sq. Ft. - First Floor
1,872 Sq. Ft. - Second Floor
80,670 Cu. Ft.

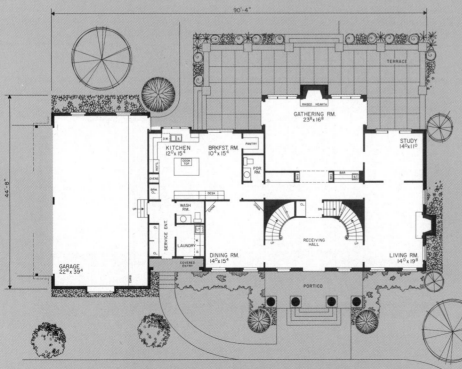

● This is truly classical, Georgian design at its best. Some of the exterior highlights of this two-story include the pediment gable with cornice work and dentils, the beautifully proportioned columns, the front door detailing and the window treatment. These are just some of the features which make this design so unique and appealing. Behind the facade of this design is an equally elegant interior. Imagine greeting your guests in the large receiving hall. It is graced by two curving staircases and opens to the formal living and dining rooms. Beyond the living room is the study. It has access to the rear terrace. Those large, informal occasions for family get-togethers or entertaining will be enjoyed in the spacious gathering room. It has a centered fireplace flanked by windows on each side, access to the terrace and a wet bar. Your appreciation for this room will be never-ending. The work center is efficient: the kitchen with island cook top, breakfast room, washroom, laundry and service entrance. The second floor also is outstanding. Three family bedrooms and two full baths are joined by the feature-filled master bedroom suite. Study this area carefully. If you like this basic floor plan but would prefer a French exterior, see Design 12543 on page 109.

Design 12673

1,895 Sq. Ft. - First Floor
1,661 Sq. Ft. - Second Floor; 59,114 Cu. Ft.

● A two-story pillared entrance portico and tall multi-paned windows, flanking the double front doors, together accentuate the facade of this Southern Colonial design. This brick home is stately and classic in its exterior appeal. The three-car garage opens to the side so it does not disturb the street view. This is definitely a charming home that will stand strong for many years into the future. Not only is the exterior something to talk about, but so is the interior. Enter into the extremely spacious foyer and begin to discover what this home has to offer in the way of livability. Front, living and dining rooms are at each end of this foyer. The living room is complimented by a music room, or close it off and make it a bedroom. A full bath is nearby. The formal dining room will be easily served by the kitchen as will the breakfast room and snack bar. The family room is spacious and features a built-in wet bar which can be closed off by doors. An open, staircase leads to the second floor, four bedroom sleeping area.

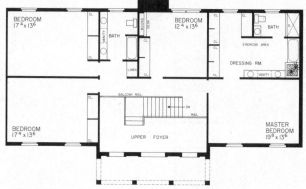

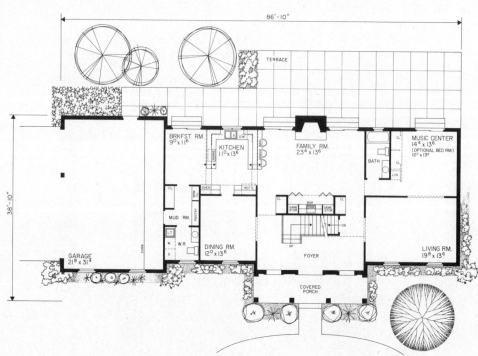

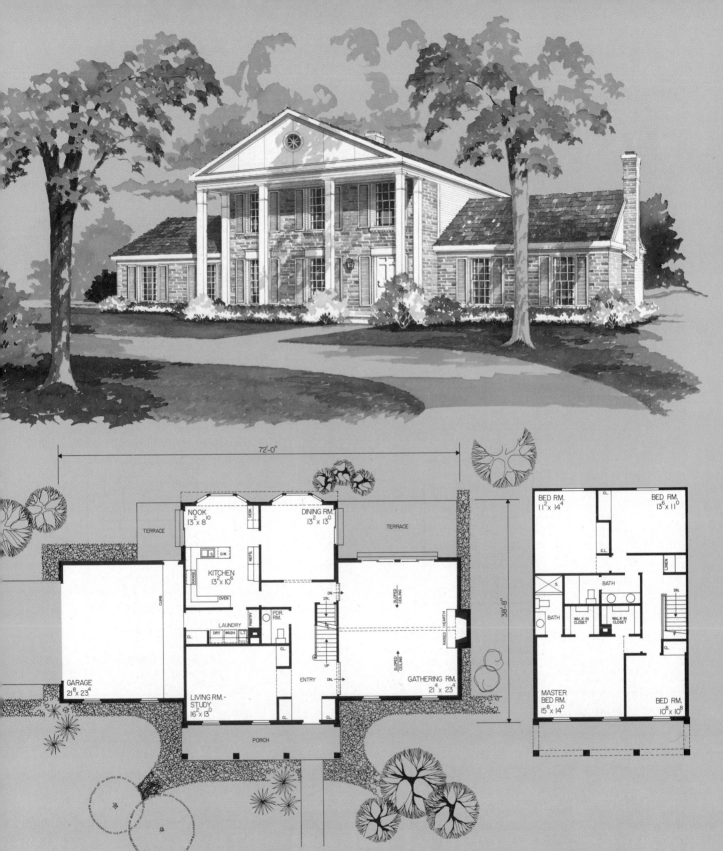

Design 12700 1,640 Sq. Ft. - First Floor; 1,129 Sq. Ft. - Second Floor; 42,200 Cu. Ft.

● Southern Colonial grace! And much more. An elegant gathering room, more than 21' by 23' large. . . with sloped ceilings and a raised-hearth fireplace. Plus two sets of sliding glass doors that open onto the terrace. Correctly appointed formal rooms! A living room with full length paned windows. And a formal dining room that features a large bay window. Plus a contemporary kitchen. A separate dining nook that includes another bay window. Charming and sunny! Around the corner, a first floor laundry offers more modern conveniences. Four large bedrooms! Including a master suite with two walk-in closets and private bath. This home offers all the conveniences that make life easy! And its eminently suited to a family with traditional tastes. List your favorite features.

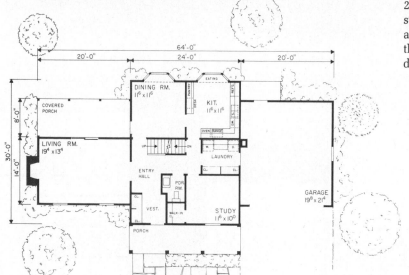

A Southern Colonial adaptation under 2,000 square feet. The two projecting, one-story wings are devoted to the living room and garage. The two-story portion houses three bedrooms, 2½ baths, study, laundry, dining room and kitchen with eating area.

Design 12107
1,020 Sq. Ft. - First Floor
720 Sq. Ft. - Second Floor
25,245 Cu. Ft.

Design 11773

1,546 Sq. Ft. - First Floor
1,040 Sq. Ft. - Second Floor
33,755 Cu. Ft.

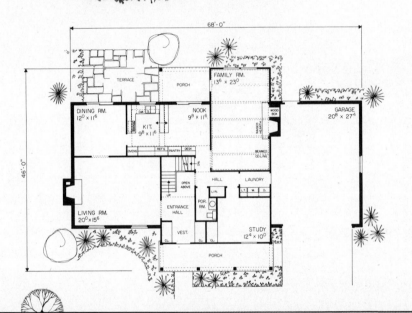

Design 11208

1,170 Sq. Ft. - First Floor
768 Sq. Ft. - Second Floor
26,451 Cu. Ft.

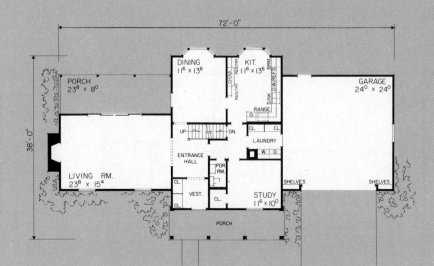

● A Georgian Colonial adaptation on the grand scale. The authentic front entrance is delightfully detailed. Two massive end chimneys, housing four fireplaces, are in keeping with the architecture of its day.

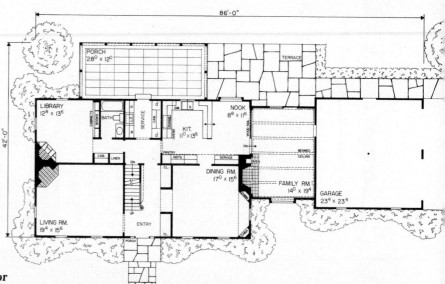

Design 12221 1,726 Sq. Ft. - First Floor
1,440 Sq. Ft. - Second Floor; 50,204 Cu. Ft.

Design 11852 1,802 Sq. Ft. - First Floor
1,603 Sq. Ft. - Second Floor; 51,361 Cu. Ft.

● This is an impressive Georgian adaptation. The front entrance detailing, the window treatment and the masses of brick help put this house in a class of its own.

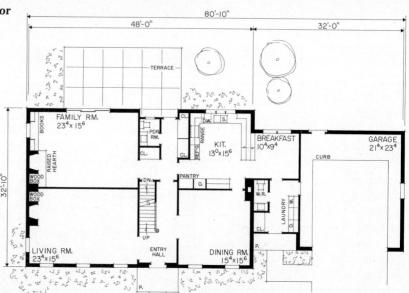

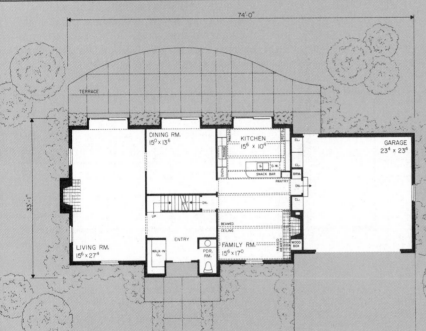

This stately home, whose roots go back to an earlier period in American architecture, will forever retain its aura of distinction. The spacious front entry effectively separates the formal and informal living zones. Four bedrooms on second floor.

Design 12250
1,442 Sq. Ft. - First Floor
1,404 Sq. Ft. - Second Floor; 46,326 Cu. Ft.

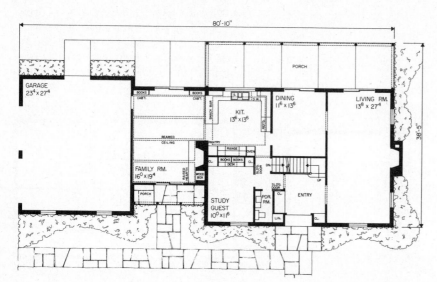

● A big, end living room featuring a fireplace and sliding glass doors is the focal point of this Georgian design. Adjacent is the formal dining room strategically located but a couple of steps from the efficient kitchen. Functioning closely with the kitchen is the family room.

Design 12176

1,485 Sq. Ft. - First Floor
1,175 Sq. Ft. - Second Floor; 41,646 Cu. Ft.

Design 11767

1,510 Sq. Ft. - First Floor
1,406 Sq. Ft. - Second Floor
42,070 Cu. Ft.

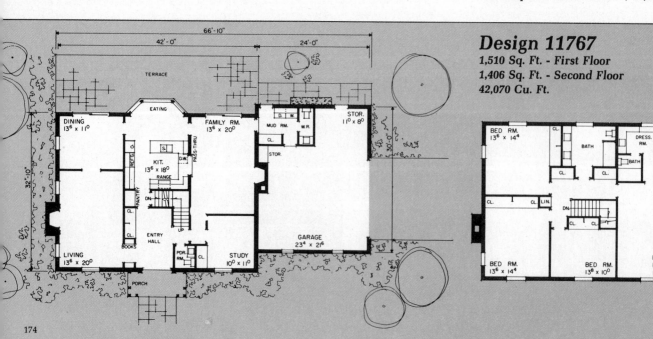

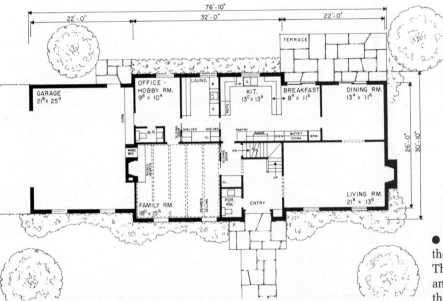

Design 12139

1,581 Sq. Ft. - First Floor
991 Sq. Ft. - Second Floor
36,757 Cu. Ft.

● Four bedrooms and two baths make-up the second floor of this two-story design. The first floor has all of the living areas and work center. Note the convenience of the powder room at the entry.

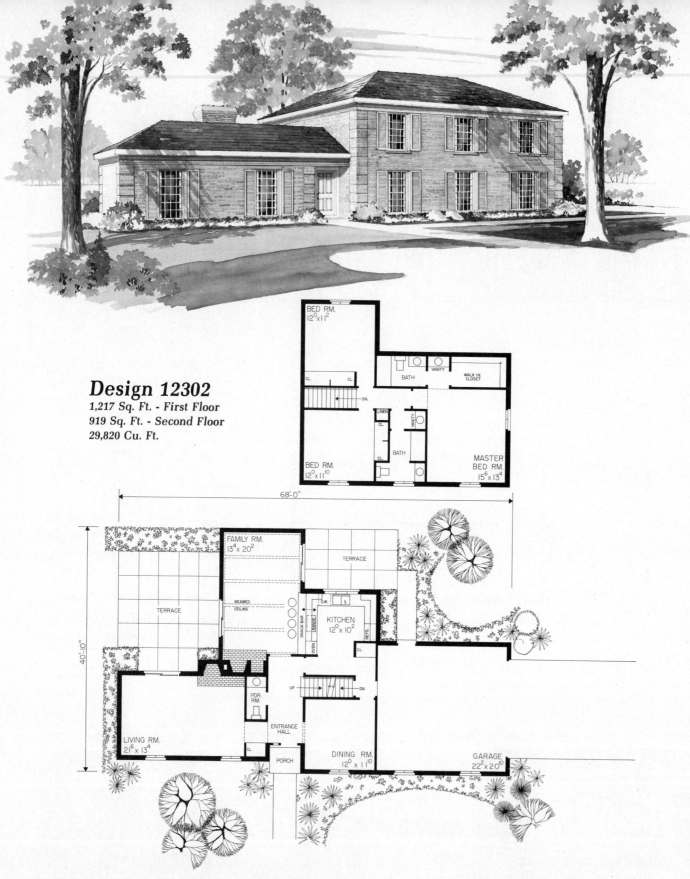

Design 12302

1,217 Sq. Ft. - First Floor
919 Sq. Ft. - Second Floor
29,820 Cu. Ft.

BED RM.
12⁰ x 11²

BATH

VANITY

WALK-IN
CLOSET

CL.   CL.

DN.

LINEN
CL.

VANITY

BED RM.
12⁰ x 11¹⁰

CL.

BATH

MASTER
BED RM.
15⁶ x 13⁴

68'-0"

40'-10"

FAMILY RM.
13⁴ x 20²

TERRACE

TERRACE

BEAMED
CEILING

SNACK BAR

D.W.   S.

KITCHEN
12⁰ x 10²

REFG.

OVEN   RANGE

CL.

UP   DN.

PDR.
RM.

ENTRANCE
HALL

LIVING RM.
21⁶ x 13⁴

CL.

PORCH

DINING RM.
12⁰ x 11¹⁰

GARAGE
22² x 20⁰

● This formal Georgian adaptation with its brick masses, its corner quoins, the delightful window treatment, the recessed front entrance, and the cornice detail, has a most interesting and efficient interior. It is most interesting to note that the two car garage is part of the main house structure. The projecting wings are the living and family rooms. Each has direct access to private outdoor terraces. Adjacent fireplaces serve each of these living areas. There will be no cross-room traffic through the kitchen. It will be easy to work in and be but an arms reach from the family room snack bar. Off the entrance hall is the formal dining room with its handy access to the kitchen. Three bedrooms and two baths comprise the second floor. Note the two built-in vanities.

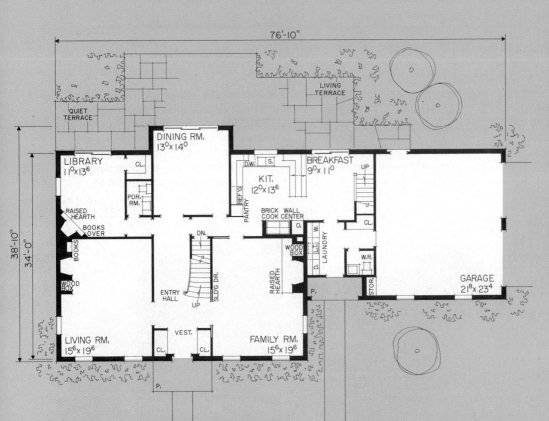

Design 11858

1,794 Sq. Ft. - First Floor
1,474 Sq. Ft. - Second Floor
424 Sq. Ft. - Studio
54,878 Cu. Ft.

● You'll never regret your choice of this Georgian design. Its stately facade seems to foretell all of the exceptional features to be found inside. From the delightful spacious front entry hall, to the studio or maid's room over the garage, this home is unique all along the way. Imagine four fireplaces, three full baths, two extra washrooms, a family room, plus a quiet library. Don't miss the first floor laundry. Note the separate set of stairs to the studio, or maid's room. The center entrance leads to the vestibule and the wonderfully spacious entry hall. All the major areas are but a step or two from this formal hall. The kitchen is well-planned and strategically located between the separate dining room and the breakfast room. Sliding glass doors permit easy access to the functional rear terraces.

Design 12839 1,565 Sq. Ft. - First Floor; 1,120 Sq. Ft. - Second Floor; 58,925 Cu. Ft.

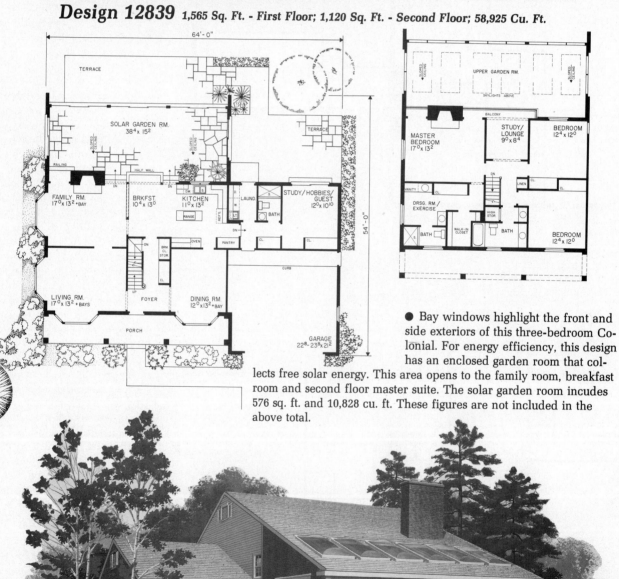

● Bay windows highlight the front and side exteriors of this three-bedroom Colonial. For energy efficiency, this design has an enclosed garden room that collects free solar energy. This area opens to the family room, breakfast room and second floor master suite. The solar garden room incudes 576 sq. ft. and 10,828 cu. ft. These figures are not included in the above total.

Design 12840 1,529 Sq. Ft. - First Floor; 1,344 Sq. Ft. - Second Floor; 44,504 Cu. Ft.

● This traditional two-story design will keep you warm because it is super-insulated to shut out the cold. It is designed for cold climates and is so well insulated that it can be built facing any direction - even north. The key behind its energy efficiency is its double exterior walls separated by R-33 insulation and a raised roof truss that insures ceiling insulation will extend to the outer wall. Front and rear air locks and triple-glazed, underscaled (24" wide) windows also contribute to the energy savings. The interior floor planning has a great deal to recommend it, too. Formal and informal living areas, plus a study! The interior kitchen area will be hard to beat. It has pass-thrus to the formal dining room and the family room. All of the sleeping facilities, four bedrooms and two baths, are on the second floor. The section at right describes the technical characteristics of this super-insulated house.

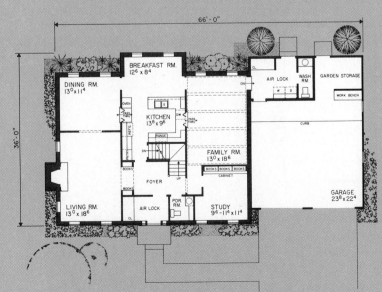

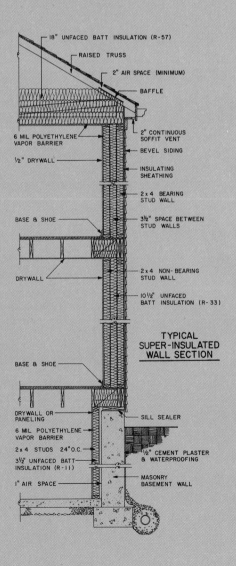

TYPICAL SUPER-INSULATED WALL SECTION

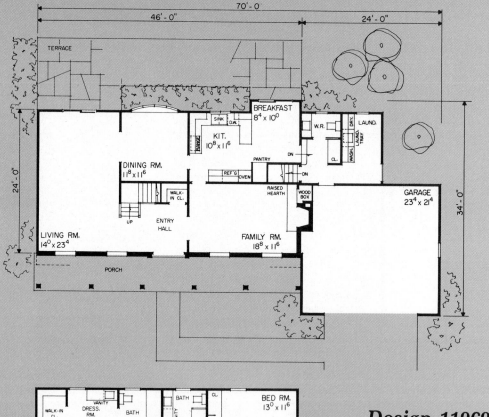

TERRACE

BREAKFAST
8⁴ x 10⁰

W.R. | DRY. | LAUND.

SINK | D.W.

RANGE

KIT.
10⁸ x 11⁶

WASH. | LAUND. | TRAY

DINING RM.
11⁸ x 11⁶

PANTRY

REF'G | OVEN

CL.

DN

WALK-IN CL.

RAISED HEARTH

DN

UP

ENTRY HALL

WOOD BOX

GARAGE
23⁴ x 21⁴

LIVING RM.
14⁰ x 23⁴

FAMILY RM.
18⁸ x 11⁶

PORCH

WALK-IN CL. | VANITY | DRESS. RM. | BATH | BATH | CL. | CL. | BED RM.
13⁰ x 11⁶

CL. | VANITY | LIN. | VANITY

MASTER BED RM.
14⁰ x 17⁰

DN

WALK-IN CL.

BOOKS | DESK

LIN. | CL.

BED RM.
15⁰ x 10⁰

CL.

BED RM.
13⁰ x 13⁶

Design 11969
1,329 Sq. Ft. - First Floor
1,196 Sq. Ft. - Second Floor
35,000 Cu. Ft.

● Stately, indeed. For sheer dramatic effect it will be difficult to beat the impact of the six towering columns of this Southern Colonial adaptation. In addition to the projecting roof which forms the porch, the second floor extends out over the first floor close to two feet. This in itself is an interesting feature. The four large bedrooms upstairs are complemented by good storage and two full baths. Study the many features that this plan has to offer.

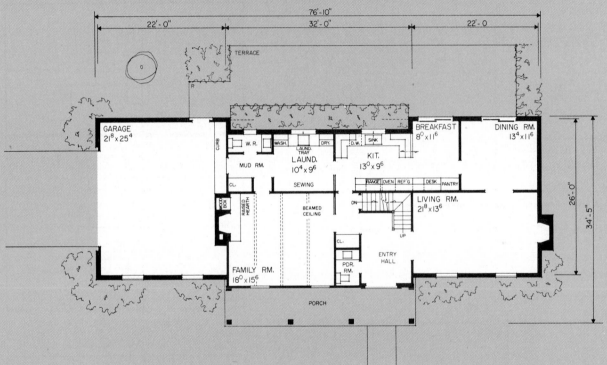

Design 11954

1,448 Sq. Ft. - First Floor
896 Sq. Ft. - Second Floor
38,096 Cu. Ft.

● Graceful porch columns of this house are reminiscent of Southern plantation homes. The first floor plan is well zoned with informal and formal living spaces definitely separated. Bedrooms are tucked away on the second floor. Added attractions are two fireplaces, a laundry with sufficient space for a sewing nook, beamed ceiling in family room, two powder rooms and two full baths. Note breakfast and dining rooms, both have access to the rear terrace.

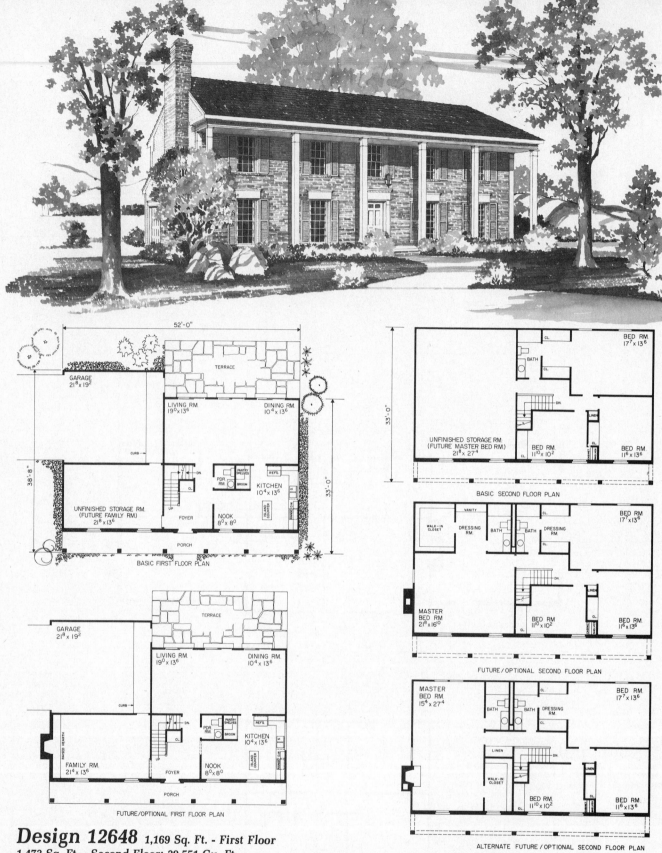

BASIC FIRST FLOOR PLAN

FUTURE/OPTIONAL FIRST FLOOR PLAN

BASIC SECOND FLOOR PLAN

FUTURE/OPTIONAL SECOND FLOOR PLAN

ALTERNATE FUTURE/OPTIONAL SECOND FLOOR PLAN

Design 12648 1,169 Sq. Ft. - First Floor
1,473 Sq. Ft. - Second Floor; 39,551 Cu. Ft.

● If you are looking for a house to fit your present family, but also need one when it is full grown, then this is the design for you. This house appears large, but until the two unfinished rooms (one upstairs and one on the first floor), are completed it is an economical house. Later development of these rooms conserves initial construction expense. A major economy has been realized because the basic structural work is already standing. From the outside, onlookers will never know that there are unfinished rooms inside. The exterior appeal is outstanding with its two-story pillars extending from the overhanging roof and its rows of windows which cover the length of the facade. The rear elevation features three sets of sliding glass doors.

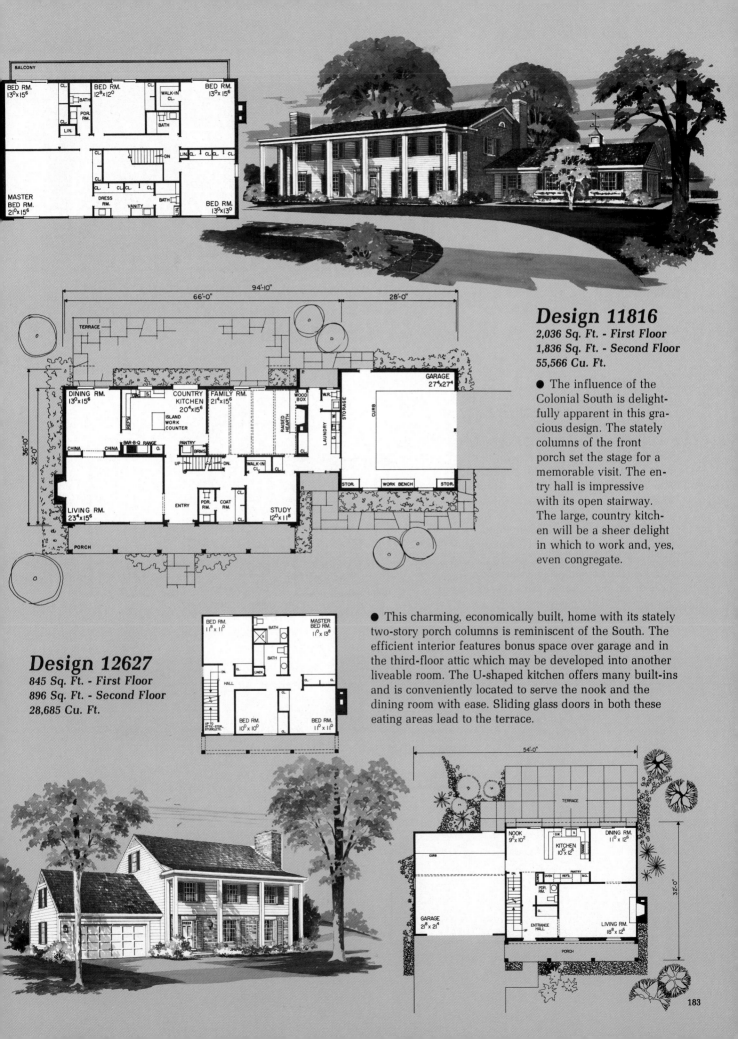

Floor Plan Labels — Top Left

BALCONY

BED RM. 13⁰x15⁶ CL. BED RM. 12⁸x12⁰ CL. WALK-IN CL. BED RM. 13⁰x15⁶

BATH PDR. RM. CL. BATH

LIN.

CL. LIN. CL. CL. CL. CL. DN

CL.

MASTER BED RM. 21⁰x15⁶ CL. CL. CL. DRESS RM. BATH BED RM. 13⁰x13⁰ VANITY LIN.

Design 11816 Floor Plan

94'-10"
66'-0" 28'-0"

TERRACE

DINING RM. 13⁰x15⁶ COUNTRY KITCHEN 20⁴x15⁶ FAMILY RM. 21⁰x15⁶ WOOD BOX W.R. STORAGE CURB GARAGE 27⁴x27⁴

ISLAND WORK COUNTER RAISED HEARTH LAUNDRY

CHINA CHINA BAR-B-Q RANGE O. PANTRY CL. 32'-0" 36'-0"

UP BRMS DN WALK-IN CL. CL.

LIVING RM. 23⁴x15⁶ ENTRY PDR. RM. COAT RM. CL. STUDY 12⁰x11⁸ STOR. WORK BENCH STOR.

PORCH

Design 11816
2,036 Sq. Ft. - First Floor
1,836 Sq. Ft. - Second Floor
55,566 Cu. Ft.

● The influence of the Colonial South is delightfully apparent in this gracious design. The stately columns of the front porch set the stage for a memorable visit. The entry hall is impressive with its open stairway. The large, country kitchen will be a sheer delight in which to work and, yes, even congregate.

Design 12627 Floor Plan

BED RM. 11⁸x11⁰ BATH MASTER BED RM. 11⁰x13⁸

BATH LINEN

DN HALL CL. CL.

UP TO ATTIC-STOR-STUDIO,ETC. BED RM. 10⁰x10⁰ CL. BED RM. 11⁰x11⁴

Design 12627
845 Sq. Ft. - First Floor
896 Sq. Ft. - Second Floor
28,685 Cu. Ft.

● This charming, economically built, home with its stately two-story porch columns is reminiscent of the South. The efficient interior features bonus space over garage and in the third-floor attic which may be developed into another liveable room. The U-shaped kitchen offers many built-ins and is conveniently located to serve the nook and the dining room with ease. Sliding glass doors in both these eating areas lead to the terrace.

54'-0"

TERRACE

CURB NOOK 9²x10² KITCHEN 10⁰x9⁰ D.W. DINING RM. 11⁰x12⁶ 32'-0"

PANTRY OVEN REF. B.Q.

GARAGE 21⁸x21⁴ PDR. RM. DN CL.

ENTRANCE HALL LIVING RM. 18⁸x12⁶

PORCH

Design 12553

2,065 Sq. Ft. - First Floor
1,612 Sq. Ft. - Second Floor; 65,772 Cu. Ft.

● A stately Southern Colonial that could hardly be more impressive, or offer more pleasureable livability. The massive columns and the pediment gable are dramatic. No less so, is the open ceiling of the large gathering room. The second floor lounge area looks down on this favorite family living area. The two-story front entrance has its special appeal, also. Observe the quiet living room and its adjacent study. The bedroom bath arrangement of the second floor is particularly noteworthy. The oversized garage will accommodate three cars.

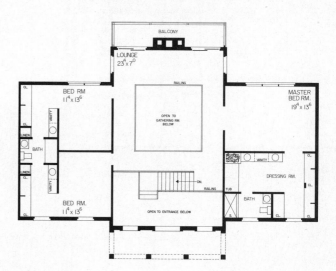

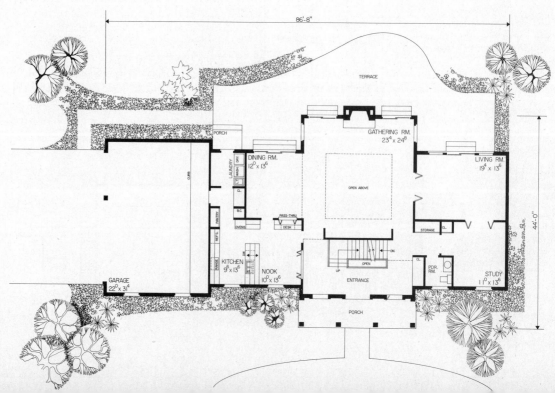

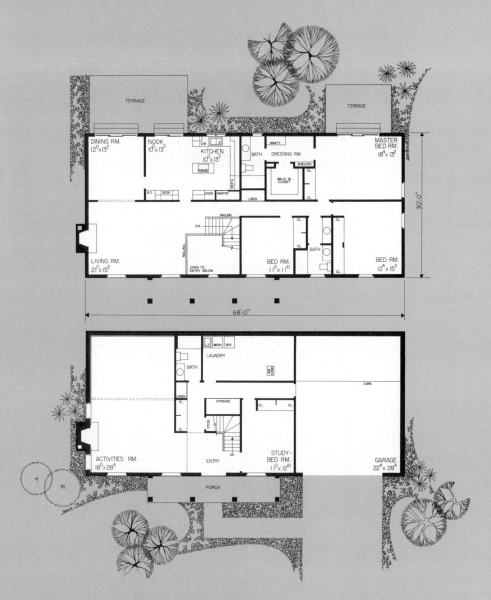

Design 12547

1,340 Sq. Ft. - *First Floor*
1,946 Sq. Ft. - *Second Floor*
40,166 Cu. Ft.

● Here are living patterns that are decidedly different for two-story living. In fact, since it is built into a sloping site, it may also be characterized as a bi-level adaptation. It is the exposure of the first floor in the front that creates that two story effect. With the activities room and the study (or fourth bedroom) there is significant livability on this level. Of course, upstairs there is the complete living unit. Its access to outdoor living is through sliding glass doors to the rear yard terraces. The master bedroom with all that space and storage, is outstanding. The living room is spacious and enjoys the open view of the high ceilinged entry. There are two fireplaces, three full baths and a fine laundry room. Note garage storage space.

Design 12572

1,258 Sq. Ft. - First Floor
1,251 Sq. Ft. - Second Floor; 42,160 Cu. Ft.

● This home offers great livability. Four bedrooms and two baths (each with a vanity) upstairs. And the first floor has features galore. Note the barbecue in the kitchen. Two fireplaces for added charm.

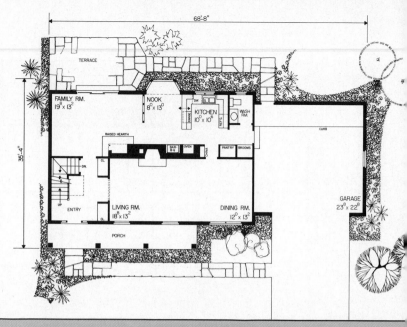

Design 12762

2,345 Sq. Ft. - First Floor
1,016 Sq. Ft. - Second Floor; 53,740 Cu. Ft.

● This home features a full apartment to the side to accommodate a live-in relative. The main house has all the features to ensure happiness for years to come. The three-car garage is sure to come in handy.

Design 12575

2,207 Sq. Ft. - First Floor
1,611 Sq. Ft. - Second Floor; 71,750 Cu. Ft.

● What a fine home this will make. Note the large entry with circular staircase. Three separate terraces. Lounge upstairs overlooking the gathering room. Extra storage space in three-car garage.

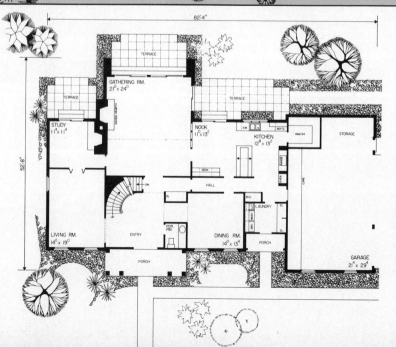

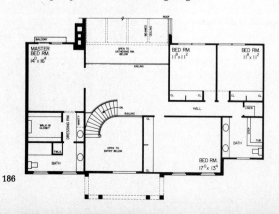

187

Design 12140 1,822 Sq. Ft. - First Floor; 1,638 Sq. Ft. - Second Floor; 52,107 Cu. Ft.

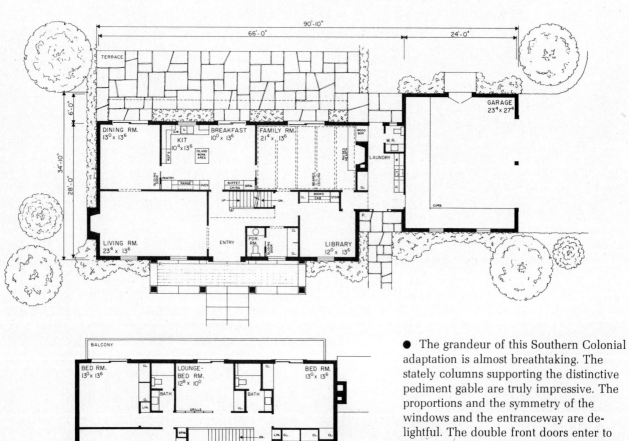

● The grandeur of this Southern Colonial adaptation is almost breathtaking. The stately columns supporting the distinctive pediment gable are truly impressive. The proportions and the symmetry of the windows and the entranceway are delightful. The double front doors enter to a spacious hall. Among the noteworthy features are the library, the powder room and the spacious kitchen area. Also, the second floor has three baths and a lounge or fifth bedroom. An outdoor balcony is accessible from each of the three rear bedrooms. What other features does your family like? Why not make a list?

● This Southern Colonial adaptation is certainly one of a kind. It will forever foster the feeling of distinctiveness as well as individuality. The second floor porches provide the shelter for the porticos. The solidly proportioned pillars of the porticos are delightful, indeed. The center entry introduces one to a very orderly and formal interior, which is planned to assure each room its full measure of privacy. If desired, however, the family room may easily be opened up to function directly with the kitchen-nook area. The library will be a favorite spot for retreat. Four large bedrooms and three full baths are the highlights of the upstairs. Notice the complete accessibility of the two porches. The garage is attached and has a generous bulk storage area. Ideal for garden, lawn equipment.

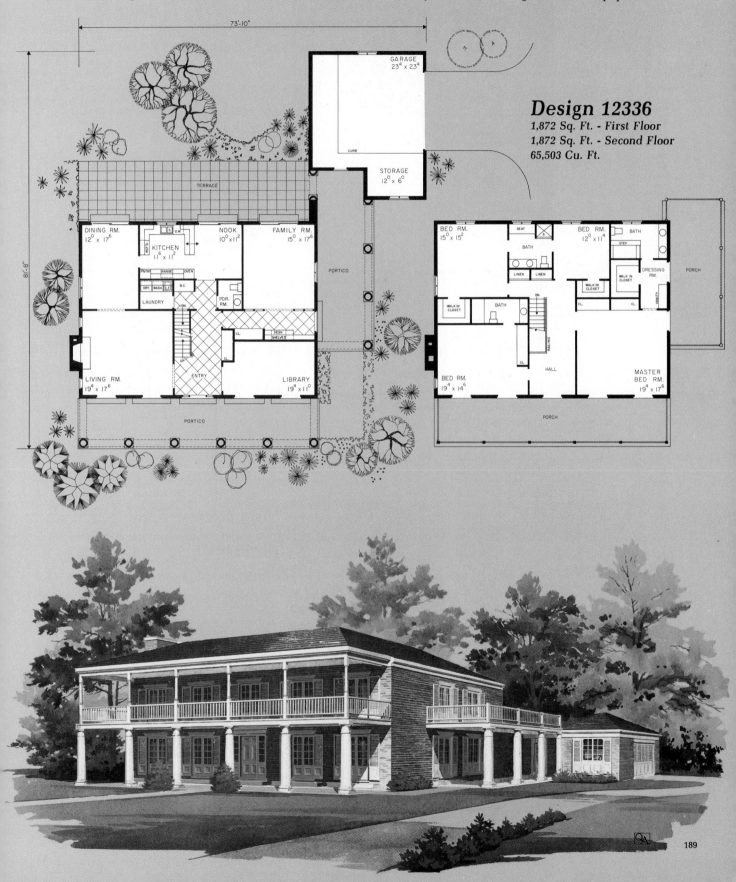

Design 12336
1,872 Sq. Ft. - First Floor
1,872 Sq. Ft. - Second Floor
65,503 Cu. Ft.

Design 12555
1,701 Sq. Ft. - First Floor
1,240 Sq. Ft. - Second Floor
44,025 Cu. Ft.

● Here is an interesting and delight-ful use of contrasting exterior materials. A curving, open stairway leads to the second floor with its dra-matic balcony effect over the vestibule. Imagine, a 22 foot square gathering room!

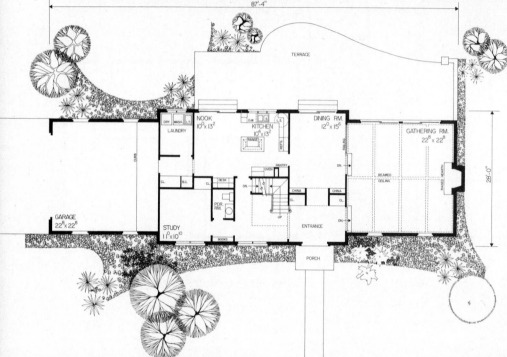

Design 12524
994 Sq. Ft. - First Floor
994 Sq. Ft. - Second Floor; 32,937 Cu. Ft.

● This small two-story, with a modest investment, will result in an impres-sive exterior and an outstanding in-terior which will provide exceptional livability. Your list of features will be long and surely impressive.

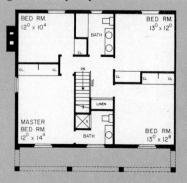

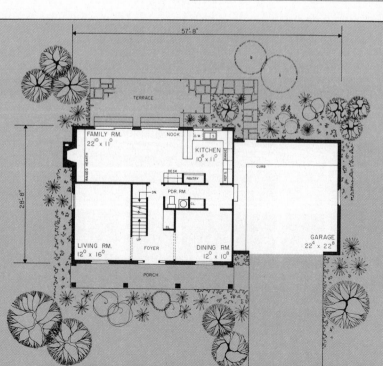

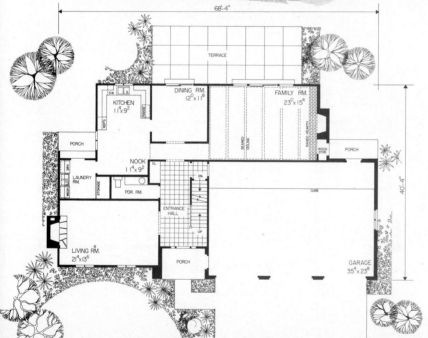

Design 12388
1,441 Sq. Ft. - First Floor
1,187 Sq. Ft. - Second Floor; 36,466 Cu. Ft.

● It isn't very often that you see an attached three-car garage. But, this isn't the only practical feature of this design. There are many others. Don't miss sun deck, laundry room, two fireplaces and sliding doors to terrace.

Design 11860 1,828 Sq. Ft. - First Floor; 1,456 Sq. Ft. - Second Floor; 51,210 Cu. Ft.

● This gracious adaptation is reminiscent of New Orleans. While the projecting second floor balcony sets the character, the dramatic bay windows, flanking the double doors of the front entrance, add a full measure of charm. The spacious center entry hall establishes efficient traffic patterns. The traffic will flow conveniently to all areas of the house.

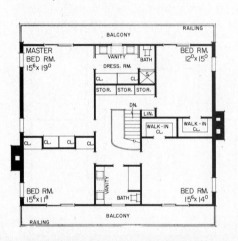

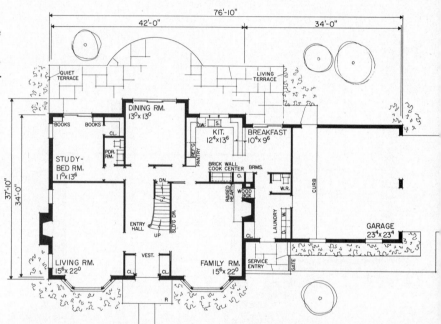

Design 11843 1,384 Sq. Ft. - First Floor; 1,320 Sq. Ft. - Second Floor; 38,183 Cu. Ft.

● New Orleans revisited. This adaptation is positively captivating. The recessed portion of the front exterior is highlighted by the second floor balcony with delightful wrought iron railing and posts, plus its two sets of French doors. The front entry is further recessed and features gracious double doors which are flanked by appealing carriage lamps. Inside, there is space galore.

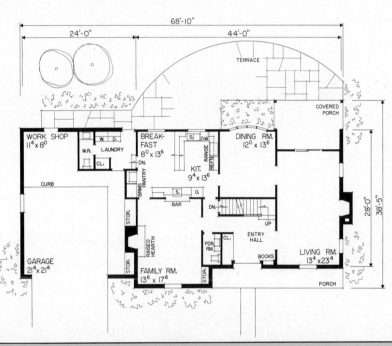

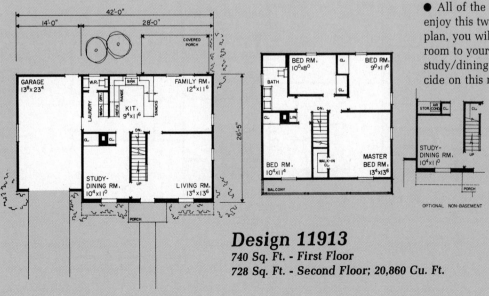

Design 11913
740 Sq. Ft. - First Floor
728 Sq. Ft. - Second Floor; 20,860 Cu. Ft.

● All of the members in your family will enjoy this two-story home. Entering this plan, you will find a nice-sized living room to your right. To your left, is a study/dining room. You family will decide on this room's use. A few steps away is the efficient kitchen and family room - an ideal place to entertain friends. Take note of the first floor laundry and washroom. Upstairs, you will be served by three bedrooms and a full bath. A master bedroom with a walk-in closet also is on this floor. With or without a basement, this will be a great low-cost two-story home for your family.

Design 12133 *3,024 Sq. Ft. - First Floor; 826 Sq. Ft. - Second Floor; 54,883 Cu. Ft.*

● A country-estate home which will command all the attention it truly deserves. The projecting pediment gable supported by the finely proportioned columns lends an aura of elegance. The window treatment, the front door detailing, the massive, capped chimney, the cupola, the brick veneer exterior and the varying roof planes complete the characterization of an impressive home. Inside, there are 3,024 square feet on the first floor. In addition, there is a two bedroom second floor should its development be necessary. However, whether called upon to function as one, or 1-1/2 story home it will provide a lifetime of gracious living. Don't overlook the compartment baths, the big library, the coat room, the beamed ceiling family room, the two fireplaces, the breakfast room and the efficient kitchen. Note pass-thru to breakfast room.

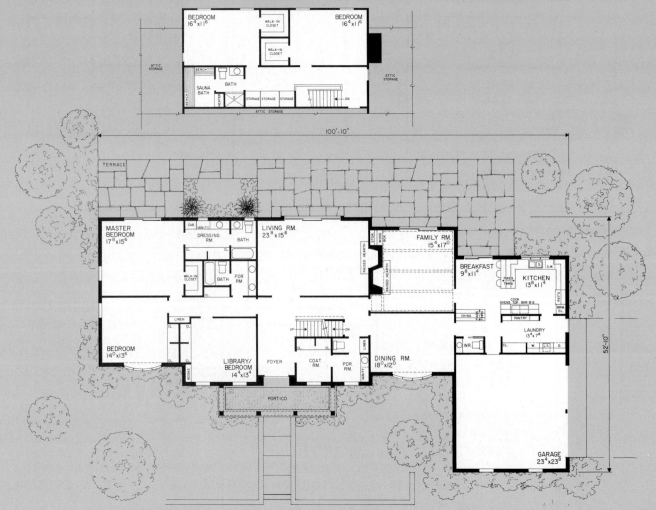

First Floor Plan

LOWER FLOWER COURT

TERRACE

PORCH

MASTER BED RM. 13⁰ x 15⁶

LIVING RM. 22⁰ x 15⁶

FAMILY RM. 23⁸ x 13⁶

PORCH

BATH

DRESSING RM.

BATH

LINEN

CL.

CL.

ENTRANCE HALL

BREAKFAST

KIT. 17⁰ x 16⁶

BED RM. 13⁴ x 11⁶

BED RM. 14⁰ x 11⁶

VESTIBULE

COAT RM.

PDR. RM.

DINING 16⁰ x 11⁶

LAUNDRY

W.R.

PORCH

GARAGE 23⁴ x 27⁴

Second Floor Plan

FLAT ROOF

ROOF

BED RM. 17⁰ x 18⁸

BED RM. 14⁰ x 11⁶

FLAT ROOF

ROOF

ROOF

CEILING CLG.

WALK IN CL.

RAILING

WALK-IN CL.

WALK-IN CL.

BATH

WALK-IN CL.

STOR. LINEN STOR.

ROOF

Design 11711 2,580 Sq. Ft. - First Floor; 938 Sq. Ft. - Second Floor; 46,788 Cu. Ft.

● If the gracious charm of the Colonial South appeals to you, this may be just the house you've been waiting for. There is something solid and dependable in its well-balanced facade and wide, pillared front porch. Much of the interest generated by this design comes from its interesting expanses of roof and angular projection of its kitchen and garage. The feeling of elegance is further experienced upon stepping inside, through double doors, to the spacious entrance hall where there is the separate coat room. Adjacent to this is the powder room, also convenient to the living areas. The work area of the kitchen and laundry room is truly outstanding. Designed as a five bedroom house, each is large. Storage and bath facilities are excellent.

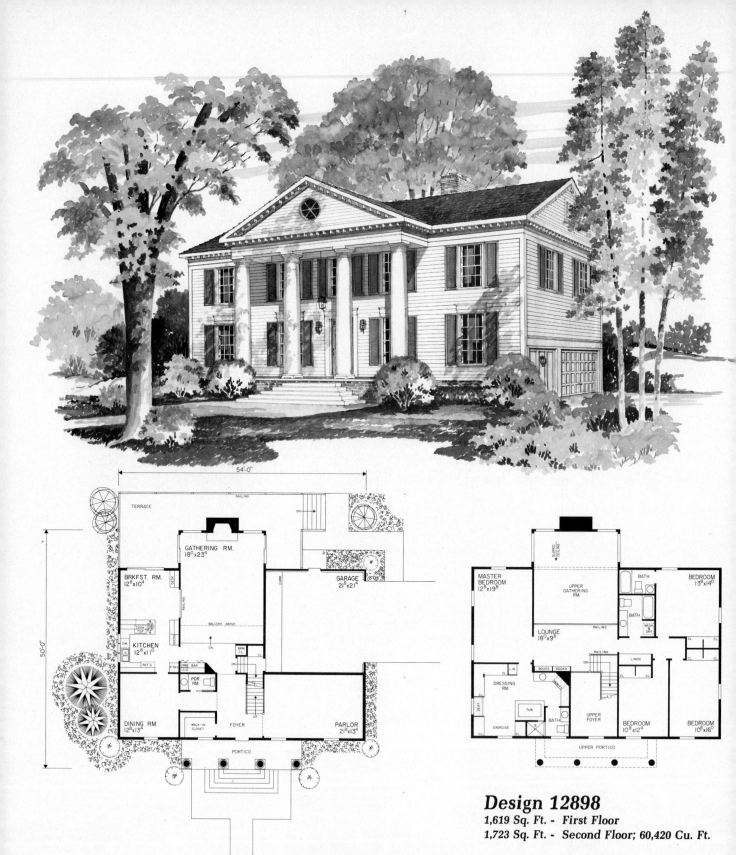

Design 12898
1,619 Sq. Ft. - First Floor
1,723 Sq. Ft. - Second Floor; 60,420 Cu. Ft.

● Four soaring Doric columns highlight the exterior of this Greek Revival dwelling. The elevation reflects a balanced design that incorporates four bedrooms and a two-car garage in one central unit. The stylish heart of this dwelling is a two-story gathering room. A balcony lounge on the second floor offers a quiet aerie overlooking this living area. Both of these areas will have sunlight streaming through the high windows. A second living area is the parlor. It could serve as the formal area whereas the gathering room could be considered informal. Entrance to all of these areas will be through the foyer. It has an adjacent powder room and spacious walk-in closet. The U-shaped kitchen will conveniently serve the breakfast and dining rooms. Second floor livability is outstanding. Study all of the features in the master bedroom: dressing room, tub and shower, large vanity and exercise area. Three more bedrooms, another has a private bath which would make it an ideal guest room.

THE FARMHOUSE THEME . . .

is one that can be found in abundance throughout the country. It can take many forms and project a limitless variety of faces. It can be a full two-story or feature a partial half-story second floor. It can feature an exterior of wood, stone, brick or a combination of all three materials. Perhaps its most predominant feature is the front porch. And, of course, this can be executed in numerous ways. The wrap-around porch is once again becoming the favorite of many. Understandably, the farmhouse was known for its abundance of bedrooms. Accordingly, four, five and even six bedroom examples are featured here.

Design 12223 1,266 Sq. Ft. - First Floor; 1,232 Sq. Ft. - Second Floor; 34,286 Cu. Ft.

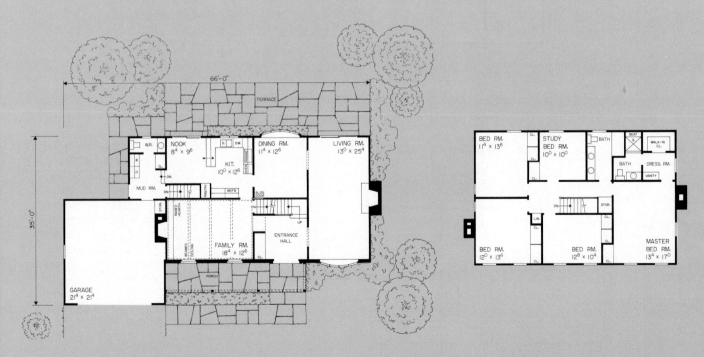

● The appealing double front doors of this home open wide to fine livability for the large, growing family. The spacious entrance hall is flanked by the formal, end living room and the all-purpose, beamed ceiling family room. Both rooms have a commanding fire-place. The U-shaped kitchen overlooks the rear yard and is but a step, or two, from the breakfast nook and the formal dining room. The mud room controls the flows of traffic during the inclement weather. Observe the laundry equipment and the wash room. Five bedrooms, two full baths, and plenty of closets are what make the second floor truly outstanding. There are a number of other convenient living features that make this design distinctive. How many of these can you list?

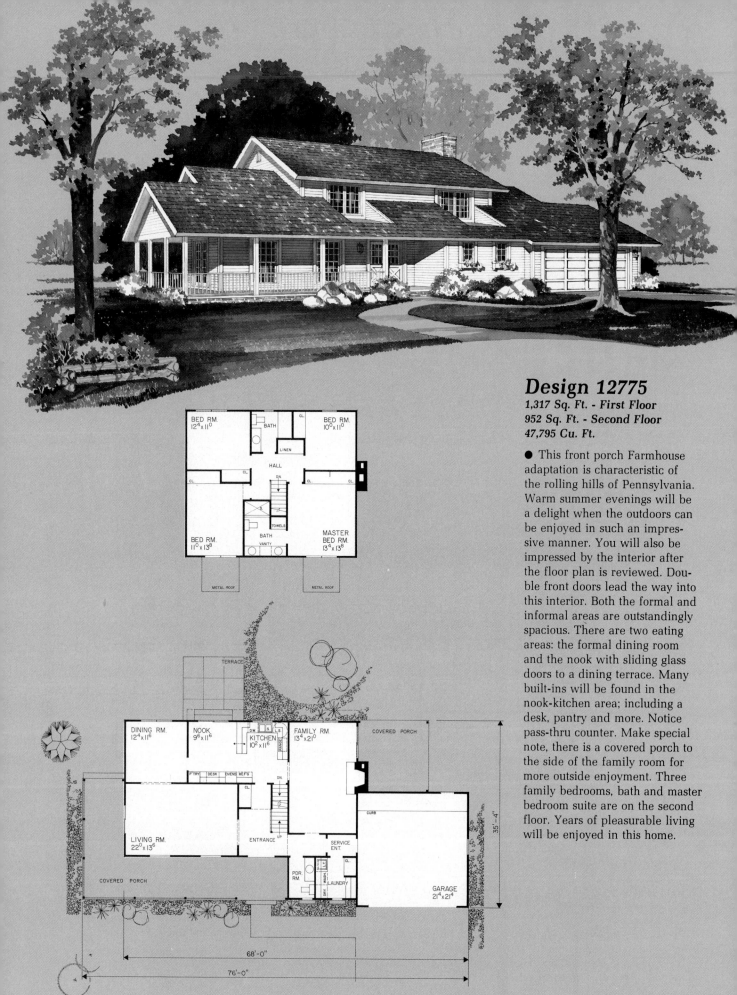

Design 12775

1,317 Sq. Ft. - First Floor
952 Sq. Ft. - Second Floor
47,795 Cu. Ft.

● This front porch Farmhouse adaptation is characteristic of the rolling hills of Pennsylvania. Warm summer evenings will be a delight when the outdoors can be enjoyed in such an impressive manner. You will also be impressed by the interior after the floor plan is reviewed. Double front doors lead the way into this interior. Both the formal and informal areas are outstandingly spacious. There are two eating areas: the formal dining room and the nook with sliding glass doors to a dining terrace. Many built-ins will be found in the nook-kitchen area; including a desk, pantry and more. Notice pass-thru counter. Make special note, there is a covered porch to the side of the family room for more outside enjoyment. Three family bedrooms, bath and master bedroom suite are on the second floor. Years of pleasurable living will be enjoyed in this home.

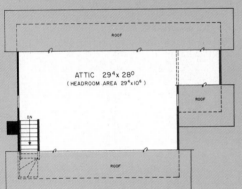

ATTIC 29⁴ x 28⁰
(HEADROOM AREA 29⁴ x 10⁶)

BED RM.
STUDY
11⁰ x 13²

BATH DRESSING RM.

MASTER
BED RM.
13⁰ x 13²

BATH

BED RM.
10⁰ x 10⁶

BED RM.
13⁰ x 10⁶

Design 12774

1,370 Sq. Ft. - First Floor
969 Sq. Ft. - Second Floor
38,305 Cu. Ft.

● Another Farmhouse adaptation with all the most up-to-date features expected in a new home. Beginning with the formal areas, this design offers pleasures for the entire family. There is the quiet corner living room which has an opening to the sizeable dining room. This room will enjoy plenty of natural light from the delightful bay window overlooking the rear yard. It is also conveniently located with the efficient U-shaped kitchen just a step away. The kitchen features many built-ins with pass-thru to the beamed ceiling nook. Sliding glass doors to the terrace are fine attractions in both the sunken family room and nook. The service entrance to the garage has a storage closet on each side, plus there is a secondary entrance through the laundry area. Recreational activities and hobbies can be pursued in the basement area. Four bedrooms, two baths upstairs.

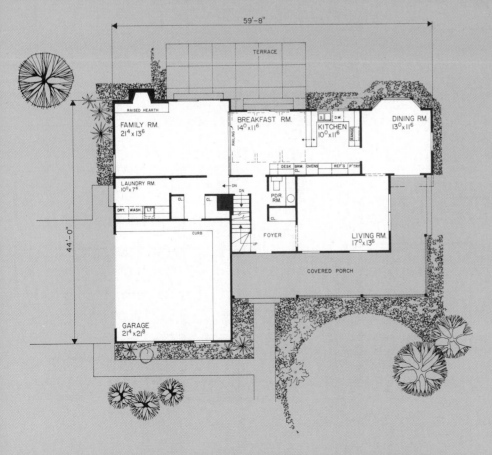

59'-8"

TERRACE

RAISED HEARTH

FAMILY RM.
21⁴ x 13⁶

BREAKFAST RM.
14⁰ x 11⁶

KITCHEN
10⁰ x 11⁶

DINING RM.
13⁰ x 11⁶

LAUNDRY RM.
10⁰ x 7⁶

DESK OVENS REF'G P'TRY

DRY. WASH.

44'-0"

CURB

PDR.
RM.

FOYER

LIVING RM.
17⁰ x 13⁶

GARAGE
21⁴ x 21⁸

COVERED PORCH

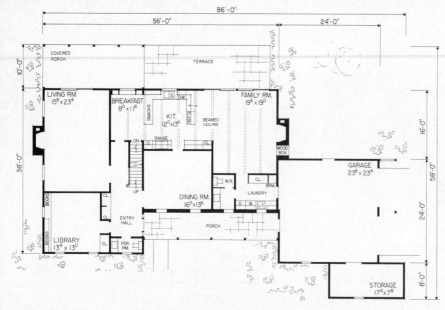
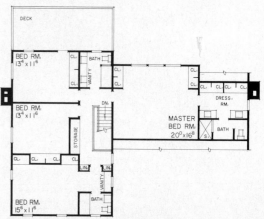

Design 11239
1,822 Sq. Ft. - First Floor
1,419 Sq. Ft. - Second Floor; 41,650 Cu. Ft.

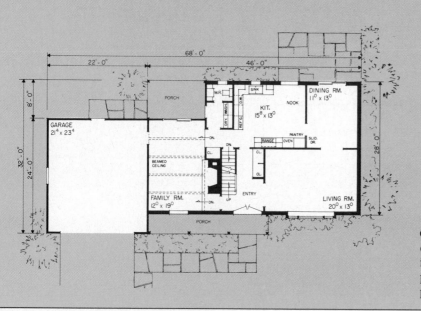

Design 11955
1,192 Sq. Ft. - First Floor
1,192 Sq. Ft. - Second Floor; 32,408 Cu. Ft.

● Here is a design with all of the features a home-owner would want most in a new house. It abounds in exterior appeal and will be a neighborhood show place. Picture yourself relaxing on the front, covered porch after a hard day of work.

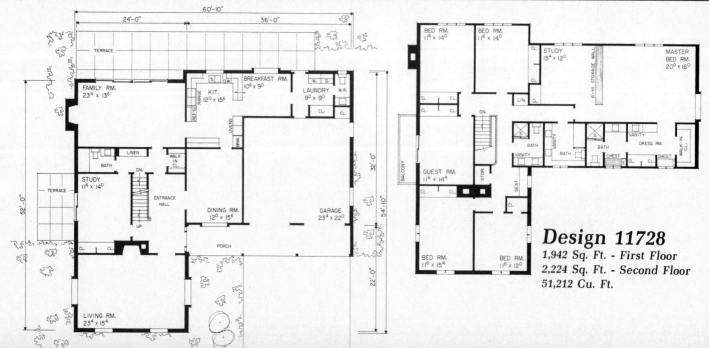

Design 11728
1,942 Sq. Ft. - First Floor
2,224 Sq. Ft. - Second Floor
51,212 Cu. Ft.

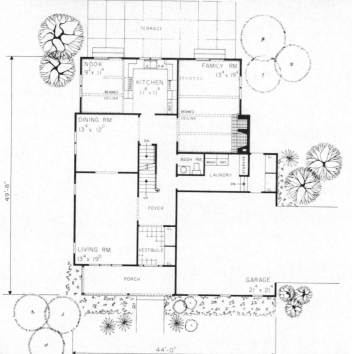

Design 12333

1,411 Sq. Ft. - First Floor
1,152 Sq. Ft. - Second Floor
31,825 Cu. Ft.

Design 12172

1,618 Sq. Ft. - First Floor
1,205 Sq. Ft. - Second Floor
42,667 Cu. Ft.

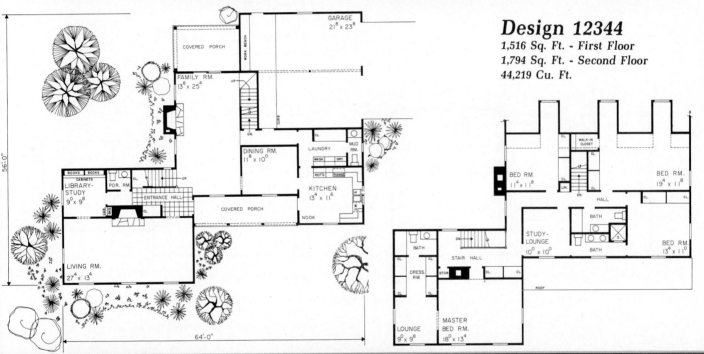

Design 12344

1,516 Sq. Ft. - First Floor
1,794 Sq. Ft. - Second Floor
44,219 Cu. Ft.

Floor plan labels:

GARAGE 21⁸ x 23⁸
COVERED PORCH
WORK BENCH
FAMILY RM. 13⁸ x 25⁴
UP
DN.
CL.
MUD RM.
LAUNDRY
DINING RM. 11⁸ x 10⁰
WASH DRY
REF'G RANGE
KITCHEN 13⁴ x 11⁶
BOOKS BOOKS
CABINETS
LIBRARY-STUDY 9⁰ x 9⁸
PDR. RM.
CL.
ENTRANCE HALL
UP
CAB BKS
CL.
NOOK
COVERED PORCH
LIVING RM. 27⁴ x 13⁴

56'-0"
64'-0"

Second floor labels:

CL.
WALK-IN CLOSET
CL.
BED RM. 11⁴ x 11⁸
LIN.
CL.
CL.
HALL
CL.
BED RM. 19⁴ x 11⁸
DN.
BATH
STUDY-LOUNGE 10⁰ x 10⁰
BATH
BED RM. 13⁴ x 11⁰
BATH
CL.
DRESS. RM.
DN.
STAIR HALL
STOR.
CL.
CL.
ROOF
LOUNGE 9⁰ x 9⁸
MASTER BED RM. 18⁰ x 13⁴

Design 11868

1,190 Sq. Ft. - First Floor
1,300 Sq. Ft. - Second Floor
32,327 Cu. Ft.

● A five bedroom Farmhouse adaptation that is truly a home for family living. The big family room will be everyone's favorite area. Note the master bedroom suite located over the garage.

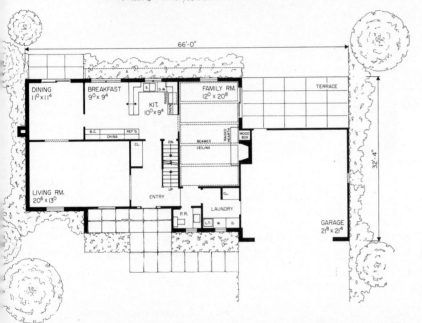

Design 11285

1,202 Sq. Ft. - First Floor
896 Sq. Ft. - Second Floor
27,385 Cu. Ft.

● Laundry, extra powder room, two full baths, four bedrooms, separate dining room, breakfast room and beamed ceiling family room are among the features of this two-story traditional design.

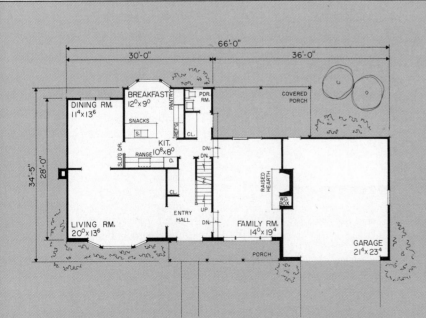

Design 11875

1,200 Sq. Ft. - First Floor
1,186 Sq. Ft. - Second Floor
30,734 Cu. Ft.

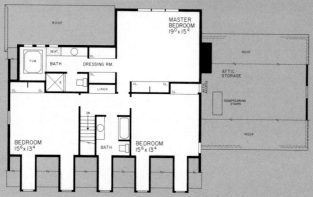

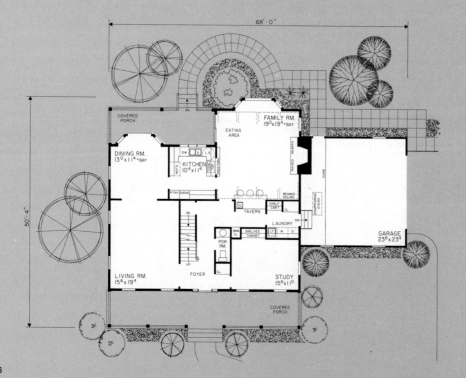

Design 12890

1,612 Sq. Ft. - First Floor
1,356 Sq. Ft. - Second Floor
47,010 Cu. Ft.

● An appealing Farmhouse that is complimented by an inviting front porch. Many memorable summer evenings will be spent here. Entering this house, you will notice a nice-sized study to your right and spacious living room to the left. The adjacent dining room is enriched by an attractive bay window. Just a step away, an efficient kitchen will be found. Many family activities will be enjoyed in the large family room. The tavern/snack bar will make entertaining guests a joy. A powder room and laundry are also on the first floor. Upstairs you'll find a master bedroom suite featuring a bath with an oversized tub and shower and a dressing room. Also on this floor; two bedrooms, full bath and a large attic.

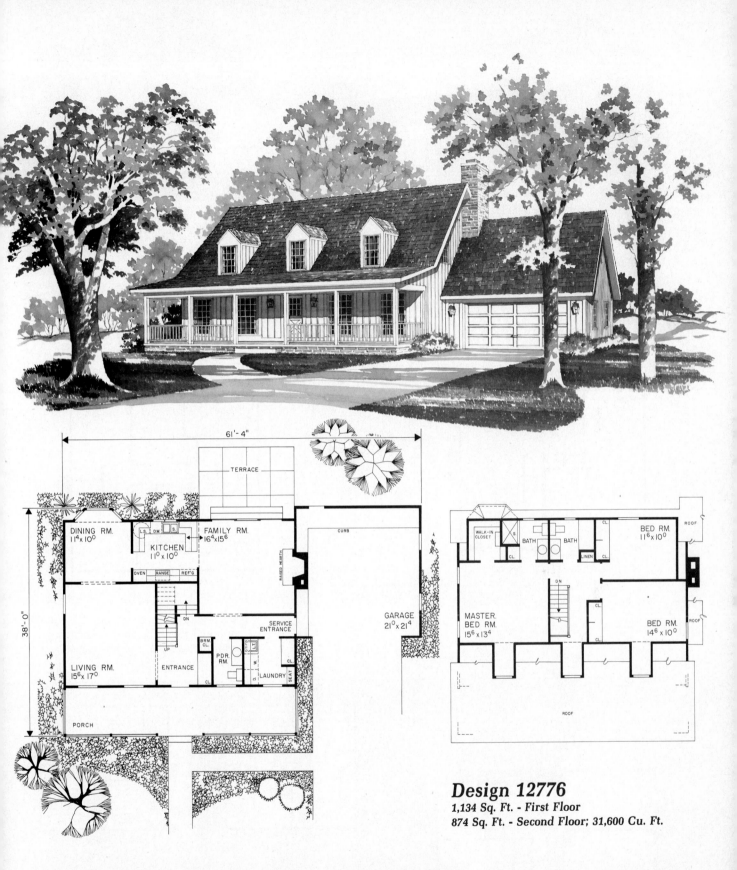

Design 12776

1,134 Sq. Ft. - First Floor
874 Sq. Ft. - Second Floor; 31,600 Cu. Ft.

● This board-and-batten farmhouse design has all of the country charm of New England. The large front covered porch surely will be appreciated during the beautiful warm weather months. Immediately off the front entrance is the delightful corner living room. The dining room with bay window will be easily served by the U-shaped kitchen. Informal family living enjoyment will be obtained in the family room which features a raised hearth fireplace, sliding glass doors to the rear terrace and easy access to the work center of powder room, laundry and service entrance. The second floor houses all of the sleeping facilities. There is a master bedroom with a private bath and walk-in closet. Two other bedrooms share a bath. This is an excellent one-and-a-half story design.

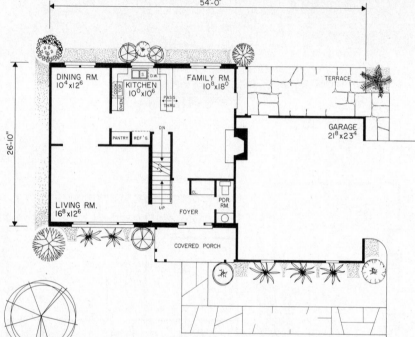

Design 11318

854 Sq. Ft. - First Floor
896 Sq. Ft. - Second Floor
24,420 Cu. Ft.

● Imagine! Five bedrooms, 2½ baths, informal family room, formal living and dining rooms, excellent kitchen, snack bar and a big two-car garage.

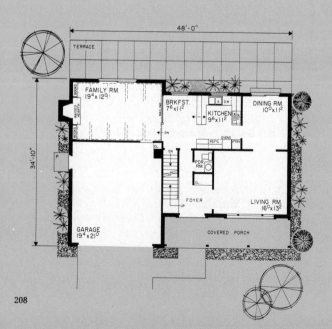

Design 11956 990 Sq. Ft. - First Floor
728 Sq. Ft. - Second Floor; 23,703 Cu. Ft.

● The blueprints for this home include details for both the three bedroom and four bedroom options. The first floor livability does not change.

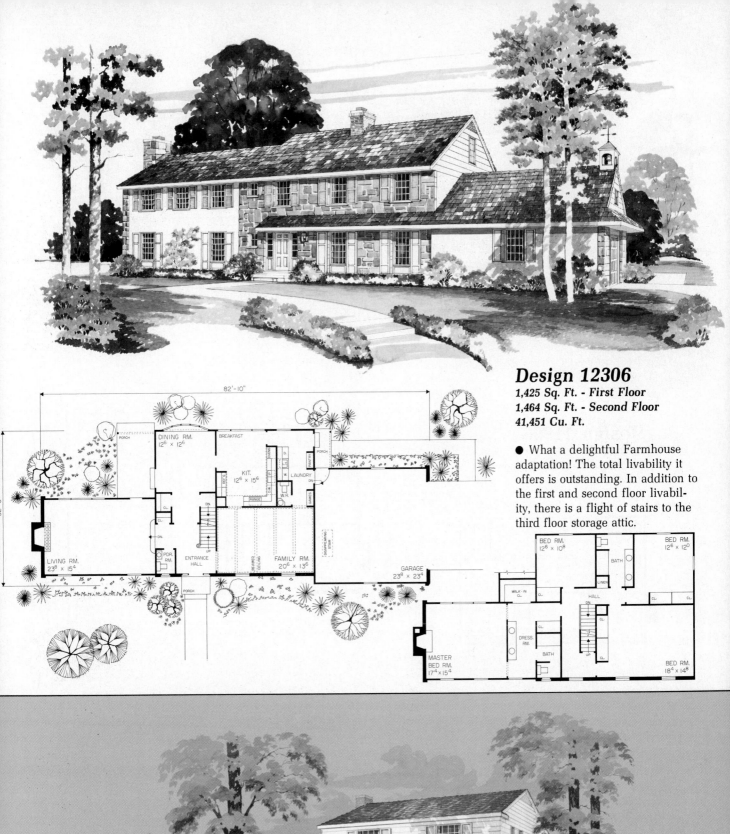

Design 12306

1,425 Sq. Ft. - *First Floor*
1,464 Sq. Ft. - *Second Floor*
41,451 Cu. Ft.

● What a delightful Farmhouse adaptation! The total livability it offers is outstanding. In addition to the first and second floor livability, there is a flight of stairs to the third floor storage attic.

Design 11996

1,056 Sq. Ft. - First Floor
1,040 Sq. Ft. - Second Floor
29,071 Cu. Ft.

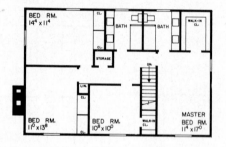

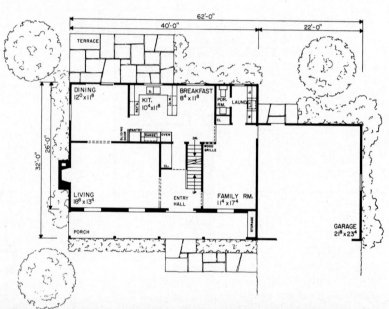

Design 11304

1,120 Sq. Ft. - First Floor
1,120 Sq. Ft. - Second Floor
31,920 Cu. Ft.

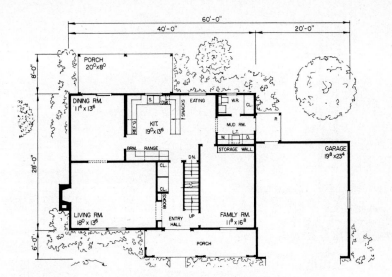

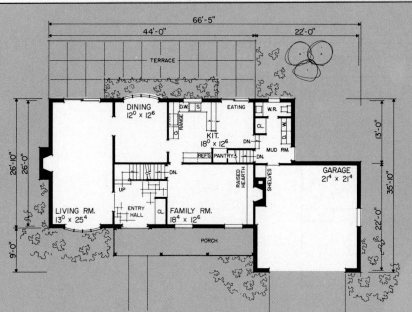

Design 11339

1,292 Sq. Ft. - First Floor
1,232 Sq. Ft. - Second Floor
34,706 Cu. Ft.

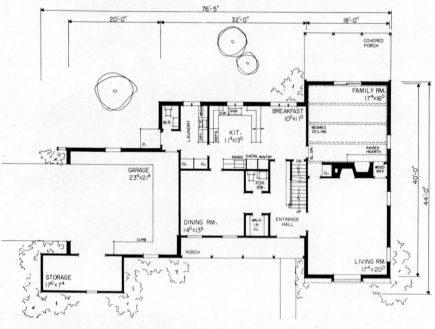

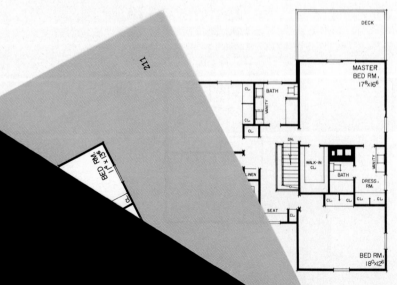

Design 11905
1,596 Sq. Ft. - First Floor
1,574 Sq. Ft. - Second Floor
48,700 Cu. Ft.

● A pleasing Farmhouse adaptation that just looks like it should be catering to the needs of a big, active family. What makes this house so interesting are the various roof lines and projecting wings. The covered front porch and the double front doors add their full measure of charm, too. The traffic patterns of this plan will be a favorite feature for a long time. One whole wing is devoted to living activities. Off the formal entrance hall is the quiet living room. Behind, and functioning with the covered rear porch, is the beamed ceiling family room. It has fine blank wall space and a raised hearth fireplace. The kitchen looks out upon the rear yard and efficiently serves the eating areas. Observe the laundry area with the powder room. Upstairs, four bedrooms!

Design 11857

1,654 Sq. Ft. - First Floor
1,536 Sq. Ft. - Second Floor
44,457 Cu. Ft.

● If ever there was a house of modest size designed for the large and active family, this has to be one of those houses. It would be difficult to decide which floor plan - the first or second - is the most outstanding. The first floor highlights a formal living room and an informal family room. Each has a fireplace. The outstanding kitchen is but a step or two from the formal dining room and the informal breakfast room. Then, there is the separate laundry room with a wash room nearby. But that's not all. In addition, there is the quiet library with an extra powder room next to it. An extremely practical feature are the two flights of stairs to the basement. Note their location. The second floor has six bedrooms! There are two full baths and loads of closets.

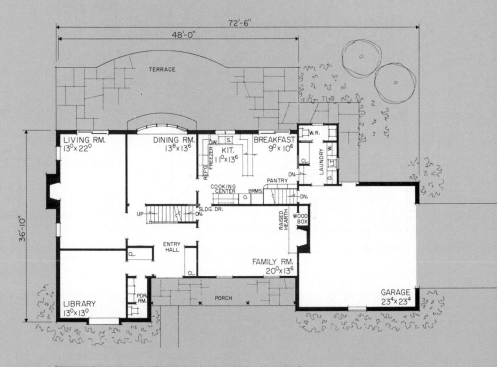

Design 11933

1,184 Sq. Ft. - First Floor
884 Sq. Ft. - Second Floor
27,976 Cu. Ft.

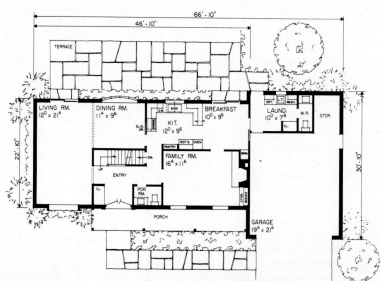

Design 11269

1,232 Sq. Ft. - First Floor
1,232 Sq. Ft. - Second Floor
33,344 Cu. Ft.

Design 11082

1,254 Sq. Ft. - First Floor
1,096 Sq. Ft. - Second Floor
37,239 Cu. Ft.

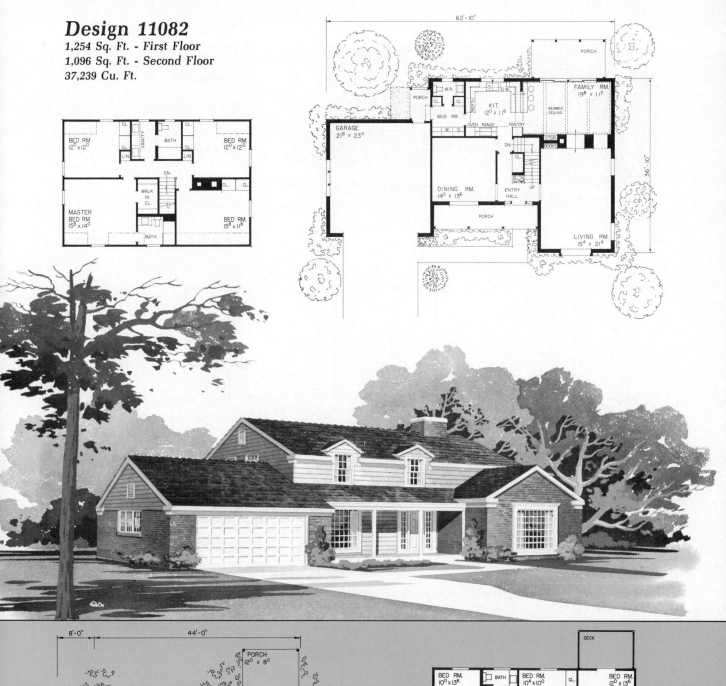

Second Floor (upper left):

BED RM. 12⁰ x 12⁰ — CL. — VANITY — BATH — CL. — BED RM. 12⁰ x 12⁰ — LIN. — LIN.

MASTER BED RM. 15⁸ x 14⁰ — DN. — WALK IN CL. — CL. CL. — BED RM. 15⁸ x 11⁸ — BATH

First Floor (upper right):

62'-10"

PORCH

GARAGE 21⁸ x 23⁴ — PORCH — W.R. — CL. — CL. — REF'G — KIT. 12⁰ x 11⁶ — S. — D.W. — PANTRY — BEAMED CEILING — FAMILY RM. 19⁸ x 11²

MUD RM. — OVEN RANGE — W D — DN. — STOR. — BOOKS

DINING RM. 14⁰ x 13⁶ — ENTRY HALL — UP — LIVING RM. 15⁴ x 21⁴

36'-10"

PORCH

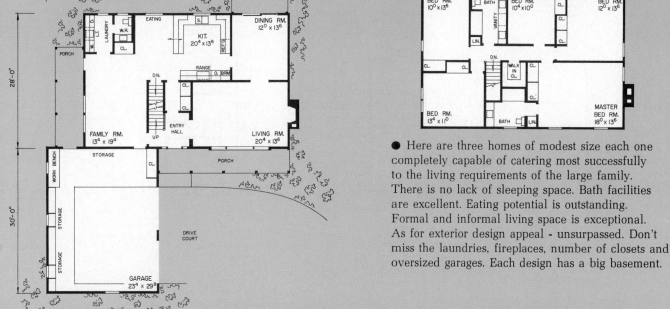

Lower Left Floor Plan:

8'-0" — 44'-0"

PORCH 12⁰ x 8⁰

28'-0"

PORCH — W. — LT. — LAUNDRY — EATING — W.R. — CL. — KIT. 20⁴ x 13⁶ — S. — REF'G — DINING RM. 12⁰ x 13⁶

RANGE — Q. BRM. — DN. — CL.

FAMILY RM. 13⁴ x 19⁴ — ENTRY HALL — UP — CL. — LIVING RM. 20⁴ x 13⁶

STORAGE

WORK BENCH — STORAGE — STORAGE — STORAGE

30'-0"

CL. — PORCH

DRIVE COURT

GARAGE 23⁴ x 29⁸

Lower Right Floor Plan (Second Floor):

DECK

BED RM. 10⁰ x 13⁶ — BATH — BED RM. 10⁴ x 10⁰ — CL. — VANITY — CL. — BED RM. 12⁰ x 13⁶ — LIN.

CL. — CL. — DN. — WALK IN CL. — CL.

BED RM. 13⁴ x 11⁰ — BATH — LIN. — MASTER BED RM. 18⁰ x 13⁶

● Here are three homes of modest size each one completely capable of catering most successfully to the living requirements of the large family. There is no lack of sleeping space. Bath facilities are excellent. Eating potential is outstanding. Formal and informal living space is exceptional. As for exterior design appeal - unsurpassed. Don't miss the laundries, fireplaces, number of closets and oversized garages. Each design has a big basement.

Design 11354
644 Sq. Ft. - First Floor
572 Sq. Ft. - Second Floor
11,490 Cu. Ft.

● Livability galore for the 50 foot building site. The homemaker will enjoy the U-shaped work center with the extra washroom, laundry equipment nearby.

OPTIONAL BASEMENT

BED RM. 13⁰ x 10⁰ · BATH
BED RM. 11⁰ x 12⁸ · BED RM. 10⁰ x 9⁴

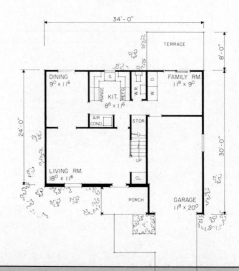

34'-0"
DINING 9⁰ x 11⁶ · KIT. 8⁸ x 11⁶ · FAMILY RM. 11⁸ x 9⁰
TERRACE
LIVING RM. 18⁰ x 11⁶ · STOR. · AIR COND.
PORCH · GARAGE 11⁸ x 20⁰
8'-0" · 24'-0" · 30'-0"

Design 11361
965 Sq. Ft. - First Floor
740 Sq. Ft. - Second Floor
23,346 Cu. Ft.

● An abundance of livability is in this charming, traditional adaptation. It will be most economical to build. Count the numerous features.

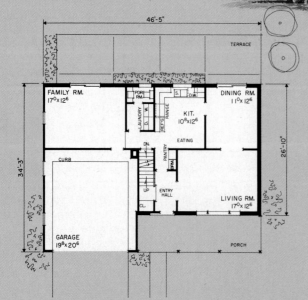

46'-5"
FAMILY RM. 17⁰ x 12⁶ · PDR. RM. · DINING RM. 11⁰ x 12⁶
LAUNDRY · KIT. 10⁸ x 12⁶
EATING · PANTRY
CURB · ENTRY HALL · LIVING RM. 17⁰ x 12⁶
GARAGE 19⁸ x 20⁶ · PORCH
34'-3" · 26'-10"
TERRACE

MASTER BED RM. 15⁰ x 11⁶
BATH · BATH · LIN
BED RM. 11⁰ x 10⁰ · BED RM. 11⁰ x 13⁰

Design 11723

888 Sq. Ft. - First Floor
970 Sq. Ft. - Second Floor
19,089 Cu. Ft.

● You'll not need a large parcel of property to accommodate this home. Neither will you need too large a building budget. Note fourth bedroom.

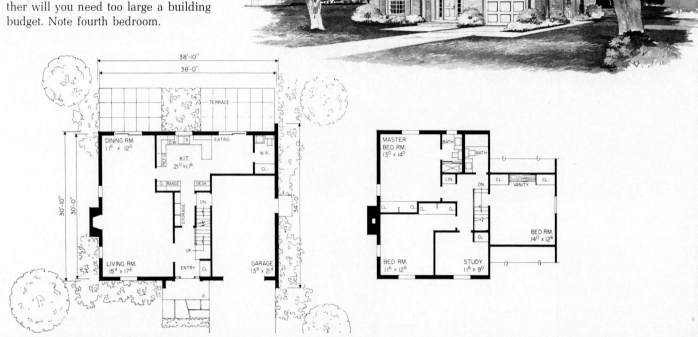

Design 11368

728 Sq. Ft. - First Floor
728 Sq. Ft. - Second Floor
20,020 Cu. Ft.

● Study this outstanding layout. All of the elements are present for fine family living. Four bedrooms, family room, first floor laundry and more are available.

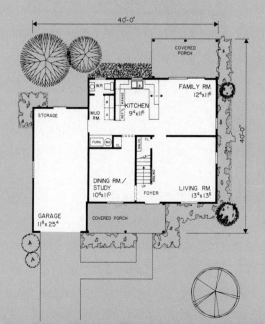

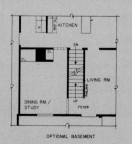

OPTIONAL BASEMENT

BED RM.
11⁰ x 11⁶

CL

SEAT

BATH

BED RM.
9⁸ x 11⁶

CL

DN.

LINEN

CL.

CL.

WALK IN CLOSET

MASTER BED RM.
11⁴ x 17⁶

BATH

S.

BED RM.
12⁰ x 12¹⁰

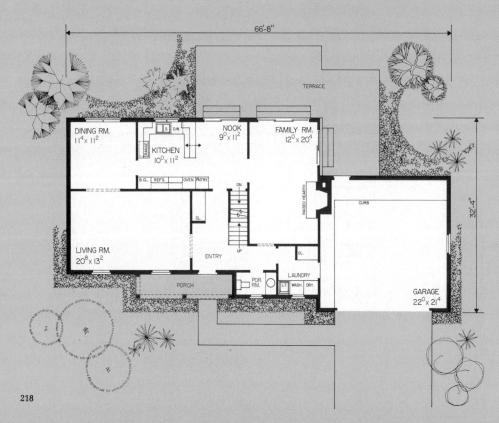

66'-8"

TERRACE

DINING RM.
11⁴ x 11²

KITCHEN
10⁰ x 11²

RANGE

S.

D.W.

NOOK
9⁰ x 11²

FAMILY RM.
12⁰ x 20⁴

B.CL.

REF'G.

OVEN

PNTRY.

DN.

RAISED HEARTH

CURB

LIVING RM.
20⁸ x 13²

CL.

ENTRY

UP

CL.

32'-4"

PORCH

PDR. RM.

LAUNDRY

LT

WASH.

DRY.

GARAGE
22⁰ x 21⁴

Design 12752

1,209 Sq. Ft. - First Floor
960 Sq. Ft. - Second Floor
34,725 Cu. Ft.

● This impressive two-story home is sure to catch the eye of even the most casual of on-lookers. The extended one-story wing adds great appeal to the exterior. The covered porch with pillars also is a charming feature. Now take a walk through the efficient floor plan. The living/dining room is L-shaped with the dining room being convenient to the kitchen. The U-shaped kitchen has a pass-thru to the breakfast nook plus has many built-ins to help ease kitchen duties. The nook, along with the family room, has sliding glass doors to the terrace. Also on the first floor is a powder room and laundry. The second floor houses the three family bedrooms, bath and the master bedroom suite with all the extras. Note the extra curb area in the garage.

Design 12585

990 Sq. Ft. - First Floor
1,011 Sq. Ft. - Second Floor
30,230 Cu. Ft.

● An elegant Colonial! This is a version of a front porch type house. The exterior is highlighted with seven large paned-glass windows and pillars. Note that the second floor overhangs in the front to extend the size of the master bedroom. After entering through the front door one can either go directly to the formal area of the living room and dining room or to the informal area which is the front family room with fireplace. No matter which direction you choose, satisfaction will be found. The U-shaped kitchen will serve the nook area orderly and is just a step away from the wash room. Upstairs one will find all of the sleeping facilities.

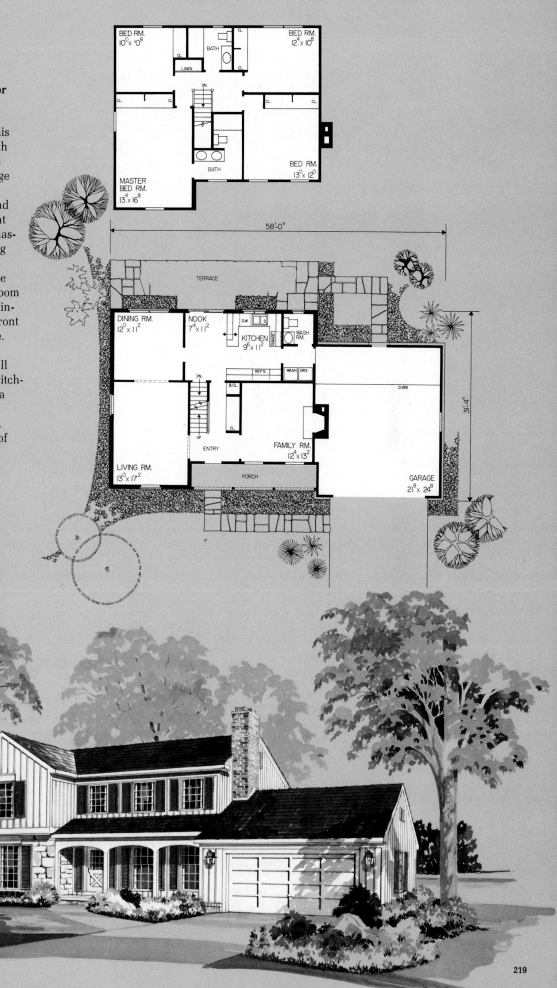

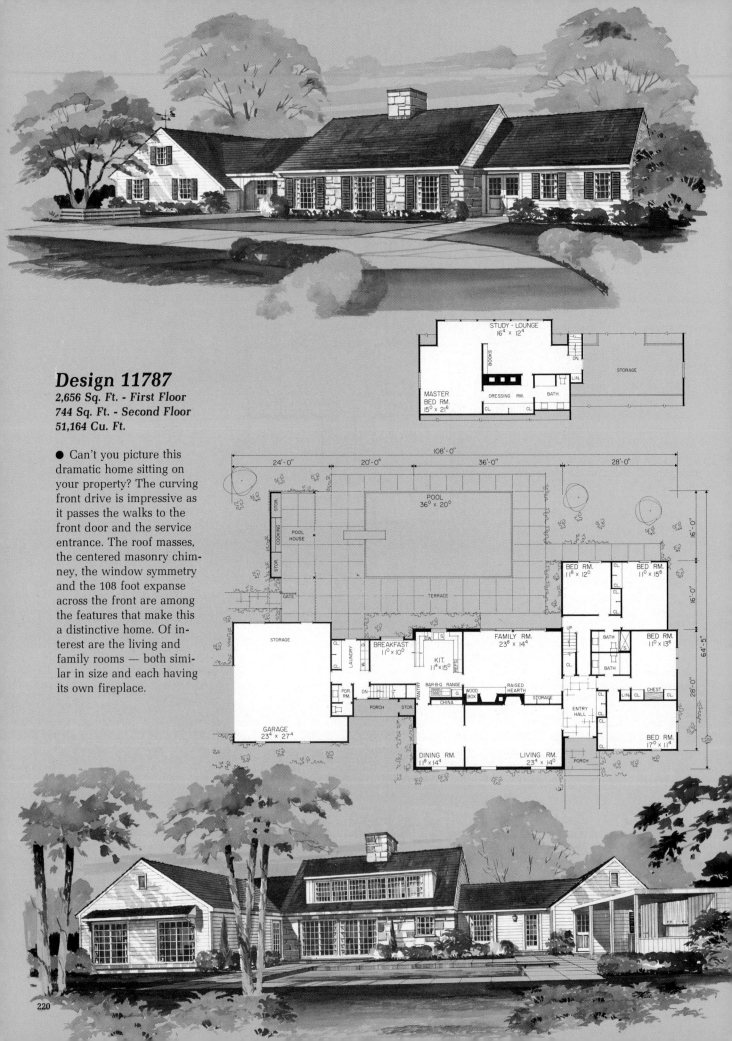

Design 11787

2,656 Sq. Ft. - First Floor
744 Sq. Ft. - Second Floor
51,164 Cu. Ft.

● Can't you picture this dramatic home sitting on your property? The curving front drive is impressive as it passes the walks to the front door and the service entrance. The roof masses, the centered masonry chimney, the window symmetry and the 108 foot expanse across the front are among the features that make this a distinctive home. Of interest are the living and family rooms — both similar in size and each having its own fireplace.

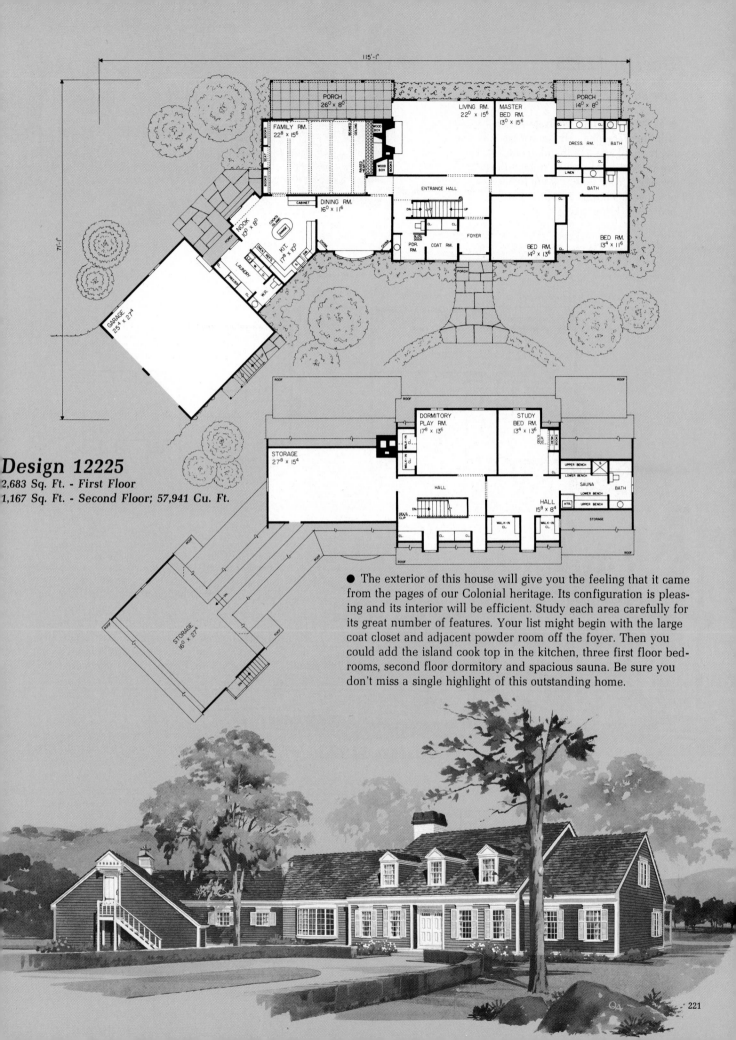

Design 12225
2,683 Sq. Ft. - First Floor
1,167 Sq. Ft. - Second Floor; 57,941 Cu. Ft.

First Floor labels:
- 115'-1"
- 71'-1"
- PORCH 26⁰ x 8⁰
- FAMILY RM. 22⁸ x 15⁶
- WOOD BOX
- WOOD BOX
- LIVING RM. 22⁰ x 15⁶
- MASTER BED RM. 13⁰ x 15⁶
- PORCH 14⁰ x 8⁰
- DRESS. RM.
- BATH
- LINEN
- BATH
- CABINET
- DINING RM. 16⁰ x 11⁶
- NOOK 10⁰ x 8⁰
- RANGE
- KIT. 17⁸ x 10⁰
- LAUNDRY
- W.R.
- ENTRANCE HALL
- SLDG. DOOR
- PDR. RM.
- COAT RM.
- FOYER
- BED RM. 14⁰ x 13⁶
- BED RM. 13⁴ x 11⁶
- GARAGE 25⁴ x 27⁴
- PORCH

Second Floor labels:
- ROOF
- STORAGE 27⁸ x 15⁴
- DORMITORY PLAY RM. 17⁸ x 13⁶
- STUDY BED RM. 13⁴ x 13⁶
- WALK-IN CL.
- HALL
- SAUNA
- UPPER BENCH
- LOWER BENCH
- BATH
- HALL 15⁸ x 8⁴
- HTR.
- UPPER BENCH
- LOWER BENCH
- STORAGE
- WALK-IN CL.
- WALK-IN CL.
- STORAGE 16⁰ x 27⁴
- ROOF

● The exterior of this house will give you the feeling that it came from the pages of our Colonial heritage. Its configuration is pleasing and its interior will be efficient. Study each area carefully for its great number of features. Your list might begin with the large coat closet and adjacent powder room off the foyer. Then you could add the island cook top in the kitchen, three first floor bedrooms, second floor dormitory and spacious sauna. Be sure you don't miss a single highlight of this outstanding home.

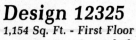

Design 12325

1,154 Sq. Ft. - First Floor
1,188 Sq. Ft. - Second Floor; 29,621 Cu. Ft.

● Here is a modest package which will build economically on a relatively small site. All the elements are present to guarantee tremendous livability. Your family is not likely to outgrow this house. Imagine, four bedrooms, 2½ baths!

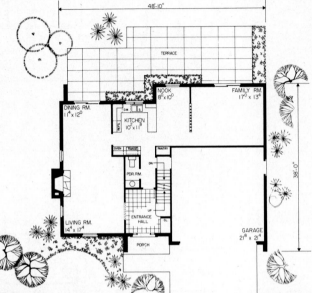

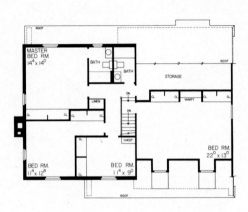

● What an appealingly different type of two-story home! It is one whose grace and charm project an aura of welcome. The large entry hall routes traffic efficiently to all areas. Don't miss the covered porch.

Design 11972 1,286 Sq. Ft. - First Floor; 960 Sq. Ft. - Second Floor
30,739 Cu. Ft.

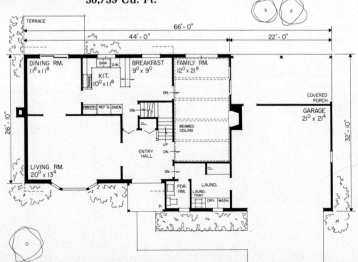

TRADITIONAL DESIGN AS YOU LIKE IT ... and

as seen on the following pages of this section, can be what one chooses to make it. The incorporation of such traditional design features as muntined windows, shutters, panelled doors, glass side lights, gabled roofs, horizontal siding, stone chimneys, bay windows, dovecotes, cupolas, carriage lamps, wood drops or cornice brackets, etc., when tastefully blended with pleasing proportions, can result in an appealing and distinctive facade. Such examples are featured in the following pages along with some Spanish, Western, and Victorian adaptations. Some optional elevation designs illustrate how a Tudor, French, or Georgian exterior can have the same floor plan.

Design 12826
1,112 Sq. Ft. - First Floor
881 Sq. Ft. - Second Floor; 32,770 Cu. Ft.

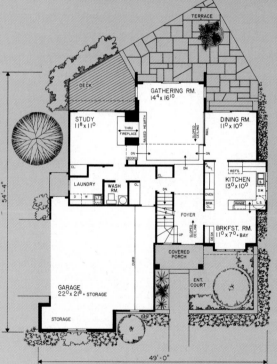

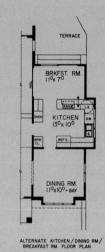

ALTERNATE KITCHEN / DINING RM. / BREAKFAST RM. FLOOR PLAN

● This is an outstanding example of the type of informal, traditional-style architecture that has captured the modern imagination. The interior plan houses all of the features that people want most - a spacious gathering room, formal and informal dining areas, efficient, U-shaped kitchen, master bedroom, two children's bedrooms, second floor lounge, entrance court and rear terrace and deck. Study all areas of this plan carefully.

Design 12535

986 Sq. Ft. - First Floor
1,436 Sq. Ft. - Second Floor; 35,835 Cu. Ft.

● What a great package this is! An enchanting Colonial exterior and an exceptional amount of interior livability. Utilizing the space over the garage results in a fifth bedroom with bath.

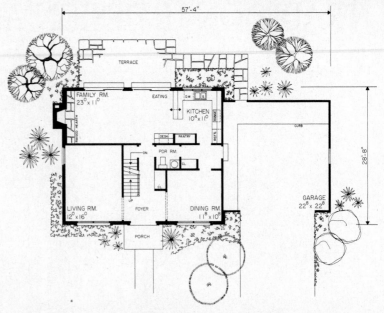

Design 12558

1,030 Sq. Ft. - First Floor
840 Sq. Ft. - Second Floor; 27,120 Cu. Ft.

● This relatively low-budget house is long on exterior appeal and interior livability. It has all the features to assure years of convenient living. Make a list of your favorite features.

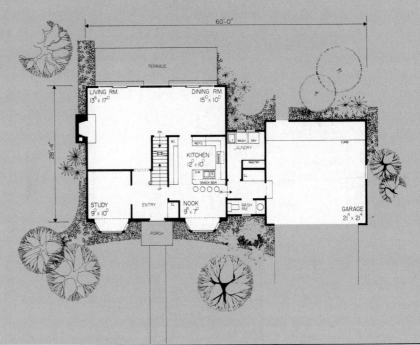

Design 12540

1,306 Sq. Ft. - First Floor
1,360 Sq. Ft. - Second Floor; 40,890 Cu. Ft.

● This efficient Colonial abounds in features. A spacious entry flanked by living areas. A kitchen flanked by eating areas. Upstairs, four bedrooms including a sitting room in the master suite.

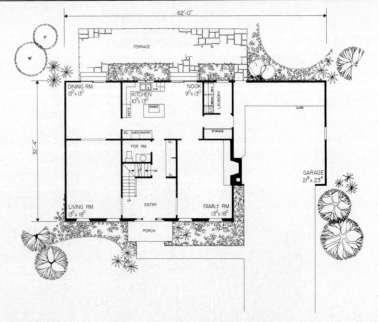

225

Country Style With Contemporary Living

● A country-style home is part of America's fascination with the rural past. This home's emphasis of the traditional country home is in its historic gambrel roof, dormers and fanlight windows. Having a traditional exterior from the street view, this two-story home has large window walls and a greenhouse, which opens the house to the outdoors in a thoroughly contemporary manner. The interior of this design was planned to meet the requirements of today's active family. Like the country houses of the past, this home has a large gathering room for family get-togethers or entertaining. Note its L-shape which accommodates a music alcove. This area is large enough for a grand piano and storage for TV/Stereo equipment.

Design 12883

1,919 Sq. Ft. - First Floor
895 Sq. Ft. - Second Floor; 46,489 Cu. Ft.

The adjacent two-story greenhouse doubles as the dining room. There is a pass-thru snack bar to the country kitchen here. This country kitchen just might be the heart of the house with its two areas - the work zone and the sitting room. A front study is ready for those more quiet retreats.

There are four bedrooms on the two floors - the master bedroom suite on the first floor; and three more on the second floor. A lounge, overlooking the gathering room and front foyer, is also on the second floor. The greenhouse adds 140 sq. ft. and 2,170 cu. ft. to the figures quoted above.

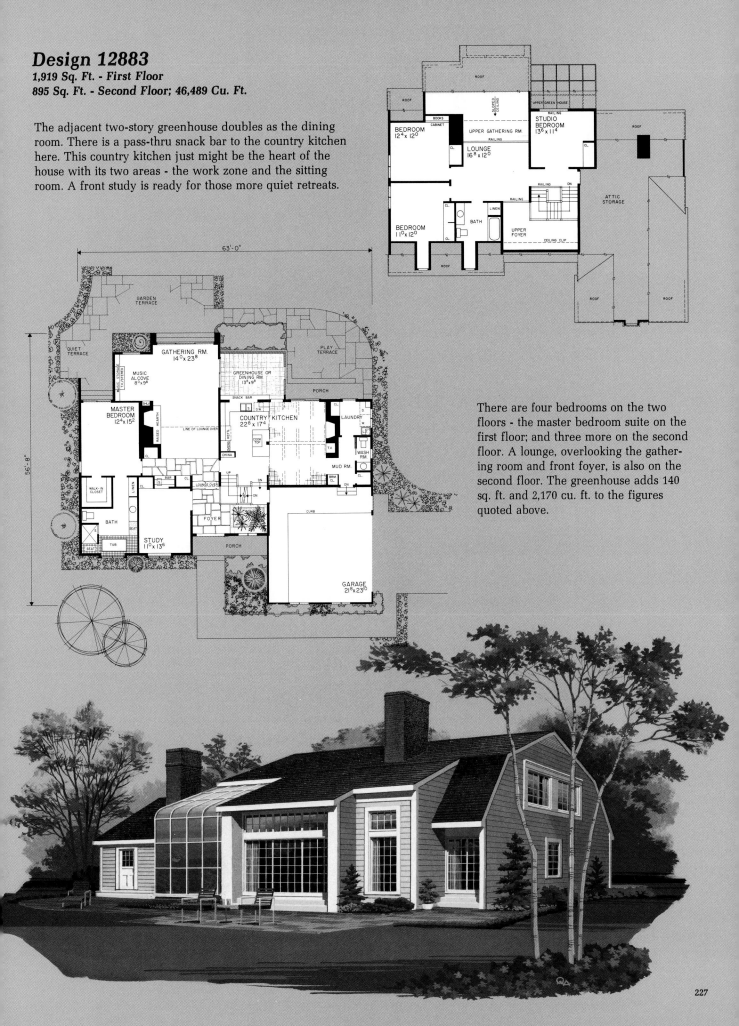

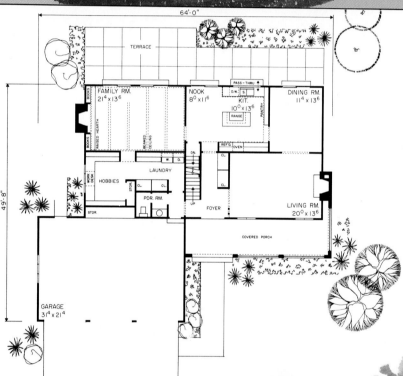

Design 12323 1,430 Sq. Ft. - First Floor
1,172 Sq. Ft. - Second Floor; 36,110 Cu. Ft.

● Five bedrooms on the second floor are serviced by two baths sharing back-to-back plumbing for economical construction. Note that each bath is compartmented to assure privacy. The first floor also has a great deal of living space. The formal living room and the informal family room are both very spacious. Two fireplaces, an island range in the kitchen, two eating areas, a large hobby room with built-ins and an adjacent laundry are some features you won't want to miss. Notice the three-car garage.

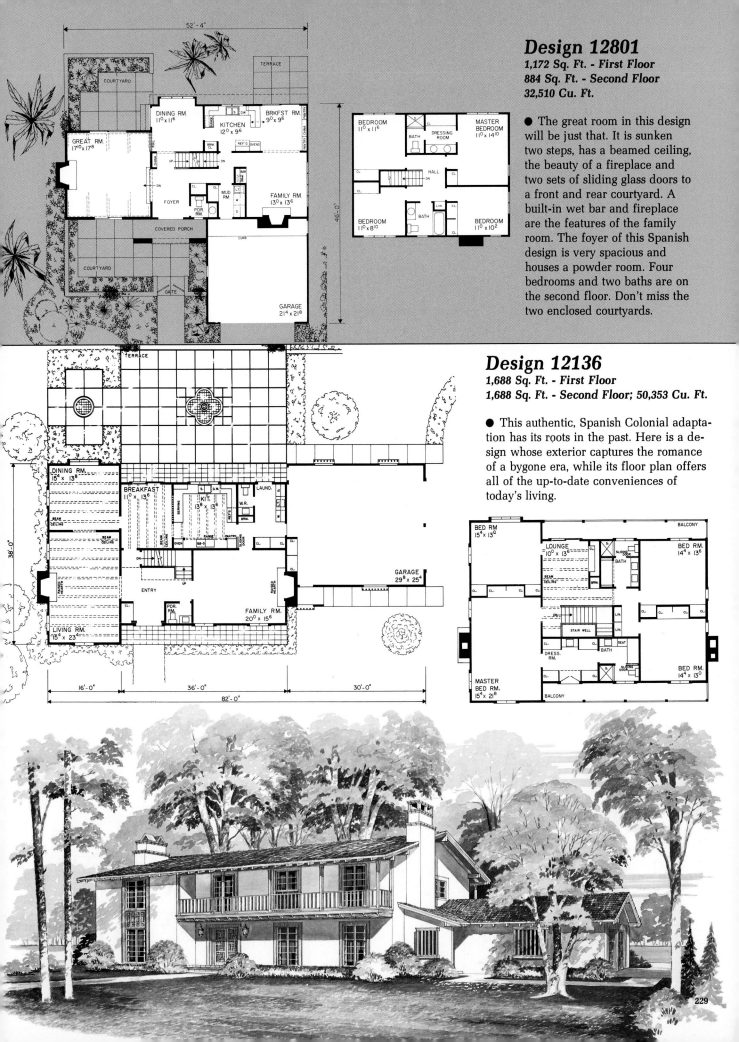

Design 12801
1,172 Sq. Ft. - First Floor
884 Sq. Ft. - Second Floor
32,510 Cu. Ft.

● The great room in this design will be just that. It is sunken two steps, has a beamed ceiling, the beauty of a fireplace and two sets of sliding glass doors to a front and rear courtyard. A built-in wet bar and fireplace are the features of the family room. The foyer of this Spanish design is very spacious and houses a powder room. Four bedrooms and two baths are on the second floor. Don't miss the two enclosed courtyards.

First Floor:
52'-4", 46'-0"
COURTYARD, TERRACE, DINING RM. 11⁰ x 11⁶, KITCHEN 12⁰ x 9⁶, BRKFST. RM. 9⁰ x 9⁶, GREAT RM. 17¹⁰ x 17⁸, FOYER, MUD RM., PDR. RM., FAMILY RM. 13⁰ x 13⁶, COVERED PORCH, CURB, COURTYARD, GATE, GARAGE 21⁴ x 21⁸

Second Floor:
BEDROOM 11⁰ x 11⁶, BATH, DRESSING ROOM, MASTER BEDROOM 11⁰ x 14¹⁰, HALL, BEDROOM 11⁰ x 8¹⁰, BATH, BEDROOM 11⁰ x 10²

Design 12136
1,688 Sq. Ft. - First Floor
1,688 Sq. Ft. - Second Floor; 50,353 Cu. Ft.

● This authentic, Spanish Colonial adaptation has its roots in the past. Here is a design whose exterior captures the romance of a bygone era, while its floor plan offers all of the up-to-date conveniences of today's living.

First Floor:
TERRACE, DINING RM. 15⁴ x 13⁸, BREAKFAST 11⁰ x 13⁶, KIT. 13⁸ x 13⁶, LAUND., W.R., BEAM CEILING, RAISED HEARTH, ENTRY, PDR. RM., FAMILY RM. 20⁰ x 15⁶, GARAGE 29⁸ x 25⁴, LIVING RM. 15⁴ x 23⁴
16'-0", 36'-0", 30'-0", 82'-0", 38'-0"

Second Floor:
BED RM. 15⁴ x 13⁰, BALCONY, LOUNGE 10⁰ x 13⁶, BED RM. 14⁴ x 13⁶, BATH, BEAM CEILING, STAIR WELL, SEAT, BATH, BED RM. 14⁴ x 13⁰, DRESS. RM., MASTER BED RM. 15⁴ x 21⁸, BALCONY

Design 12561

1,655 Sq. Ft. - First Floor
943 Sq. Ft. - Second Floor; 41,738 Cu. Ft.

● A convenient living plan housed in a distinctively appealing exterior. Passing through the double front doors one immediately observes a fine functioning interior. Traffic patterns are efficient, but also flexible. The family room area is sunken a couple of steps below the level of the breakfast nook and entry. The open planning of the kitchen area, and between the living and dining rooms add to the spaciousness. Study the upstairs and how it is open to the family room below. Those are folding doors that provide the bedroom with privacy.

Design 12808

1,540 Sq. Ft. - First Floor; 1,117 Sq. Ft. - Second Floor
605 Sq. Ft. - Apartment; 48,075 Cu. Ft.

● A complete apartment is tucked in the back of this Colonial home. This apartment would be ideal for a live-in relative or supplement your income by becoming a landlord and rent out the apartment. The rest of this house will serve a larger family with great ease. There is a formal living room and an informal family room plus a good-sized study. All of the sleeping facilities are on the efficiently planned second floor.

Design 12609   1,543 Sq. Ft. - First Floor
1,005 Sq. Ft. - Second Floor; 36,800 Cu. Ft.

● Here is an L-shaped two-story with a variety of features that help recall the architectural charm of Colonial America. Observe the massive twin chimneys, contrasting exterior materials, window and door treatment, cupola and picket fence. The interior is designed for real family living. Four bedrooms, two full baths and plenty of closets provide excellent sleeping facilities.

The large, end living room will enjoy its privacy. A study provides that often sought-after haven for the enjoyment of peace and quiet. Beamed ceilings are a highlight of the family room and kitchen. Don't miss the breakfast eating area, the separate dining room, the laundry and the stairs to the basement.

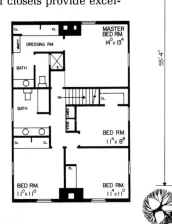

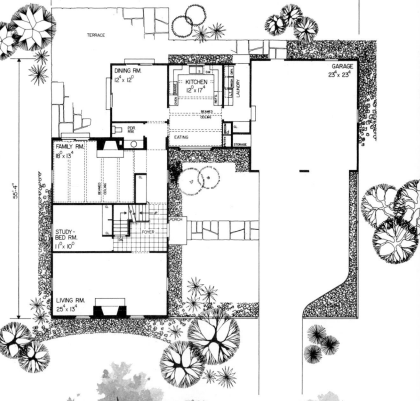

Design 11715 1,276 Sq. Ft. - First Floor; 1,064 Sq. Ft. - Second Floor; 31,295 Cu. Ft.

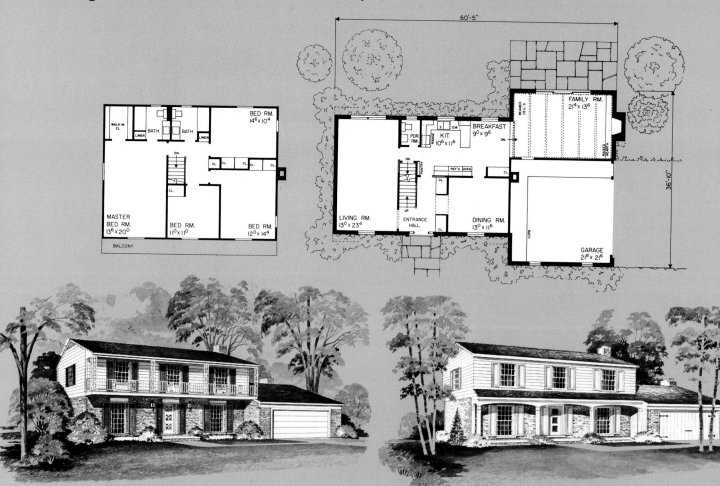

● The blueprints you order for this design show details for building each of these three appealing exteriors. Which do you like best? Whatever your choice, the interior will provide the growing family with all the facilities for fine living.

● Here are three optional elevations that function with the same basic floor plan. No need to decide now which is your favorite since the blueprints for this design include details for each optional exterior.

If yours is a restricted building budget, your construction dollar could hardly return greater dividends in the way of exterior appeal and interior livability. Also, you won't need a big, expensive site on which to build.

In addition to the four bedrooms and 2½ baths, there are two living areas, two places for dining, a fireplace and a basement. Notice the fine accessibility of the rear outdoor terrace.

Design 12366
1,078 Sq. Ft. - First Floor
880 Sq. Ft. - Second Floor
27,242 Cu. Ft.

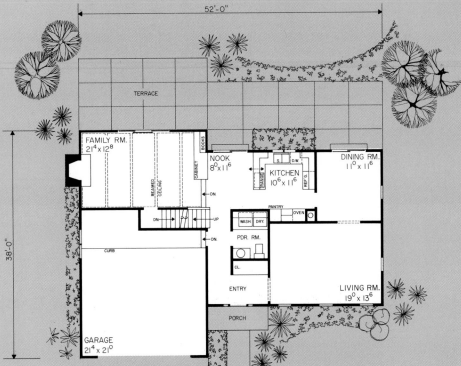

Design 12518

1,630 Sq. Ft. - *First Floor*
1,260 Sq. Ft. - *Second Floor*
43,968 Cu. Ft.

● For those who have a predilection for the Spanish influence in their architecture. Outdoor oriented, each of the major living areas on the first floor have direct access to the terraces. Traffic patterns are excellent.

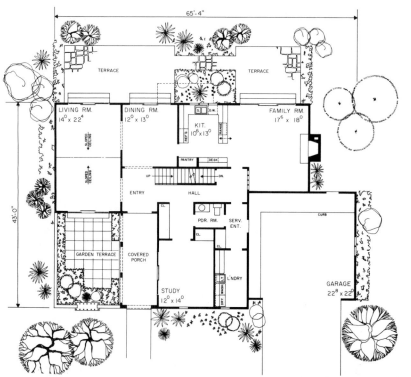

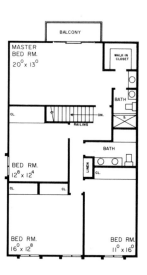

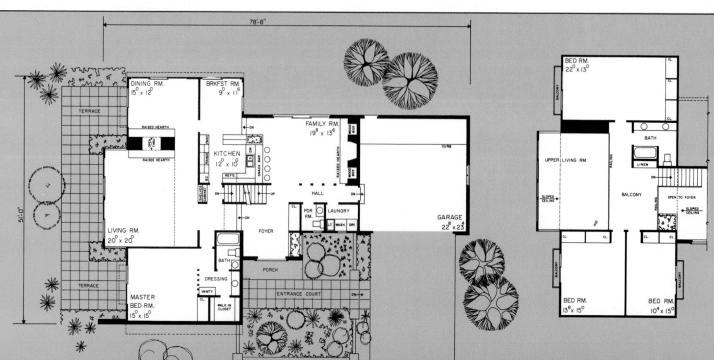

Design 12517

1,767 Sq. Ft. - First Floor
1,094 Sq. Ft. - Second Floor
50,256 Cu. Ft.

● Wherever built - north, east, south, or west - this home will surely command all the attention it deserves. And little wonder with such a well-designed exterior and such an outstanding interior. List your favorite features.

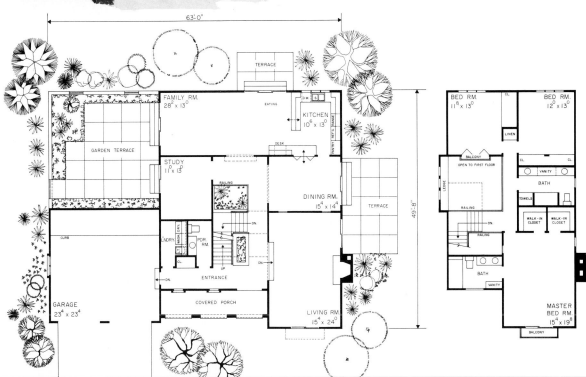

Design 12512

2,074 Sq. Ft. - First Floor
1,116 Sq. Ft. - Second Floor
41,500 Cu. Ft.

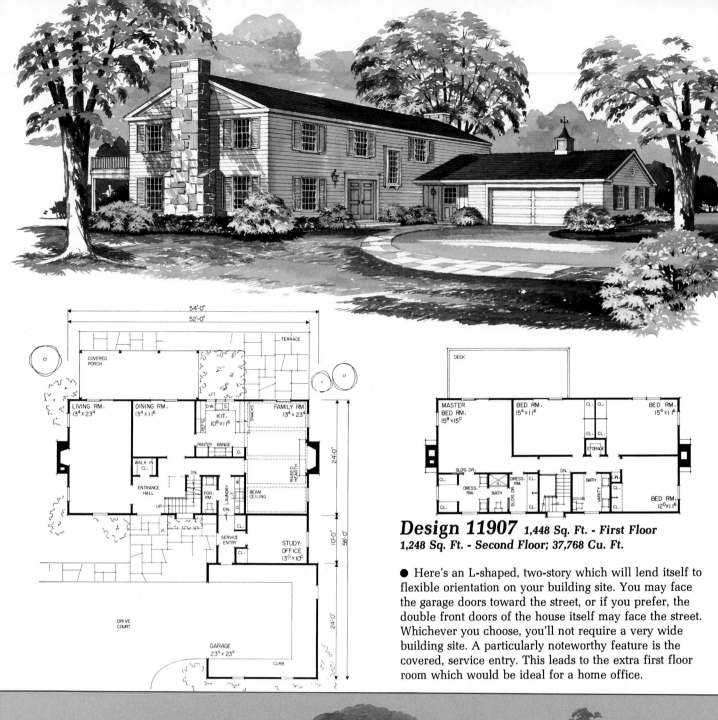

Design 11907 *1,448 Sq. Ft. - First Floor*
1,248 Sq. Ft. - Second Floor; 37,768 Cu. Ft.

● Here's an L-shaped, two-story which will lend itself to flexible orientation on your building site. You may face the garage doors toward the street, or if you prefer, the double front doors of the house itself may face the street. Whichever you choose, you'll not require a very wide building site. A particularly noteworthy feature is the covered, service entry. This leads to the extra first floor room which would be ideal for a home office.

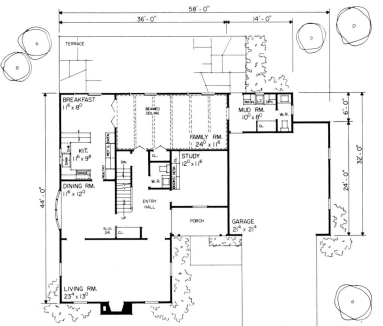

Design 11971

1,460 Sq. Ft. - First Floor
1,056 Sq. Ft. - Second Floor
34,726 Cu. Ft.

First Floor

TERRACE

BREAKFAST
11⁶ x 8⁰

BEAMED CEILING

FAMILY RM.
24⁰ x 11⁶

MUD RM.
10⁰ x 8⁰

WASH. DRY.

W.R.

KIT.
11⁶ x 9⁸

SINK D.W.

REF. G. OVEN

PANTRY

DN.

CL.

STUDY
12⁰ x 11⁶

BOOKS DESK

W.R.

DINING RM.
11⁶ x 12⁰

ENTRY HALL

UP

PORCH

GARAGE
21⁴ x 21⁴

SLID. DR.

CL.

LIVING RM.
23⁴ x 13⁰

58' - 0"

36' - 0"

14' - 0"

44' - 0"

6' - 0"

32' - 0"

24' - 0"

Second Floor

MASTER BED RM.
11⁶ x 17⁰

BED RM.
11⁶ x 11⁶

CL.

WALK-IN CL.

DN.

CL.

VANITY

BATH

DRESS. RM.

LIN.

CL.

PDR. RM.

SHOWER

CL.

BATH

CL.

BED RM.
11⁶ x 14⁴

BED RM.
11⁶ x 11⁰

Design 11966

1,244 Sq. Ft. - First Floor
1,232 Sq. Ft. - Second Floor
34,014 Cu. Ft.

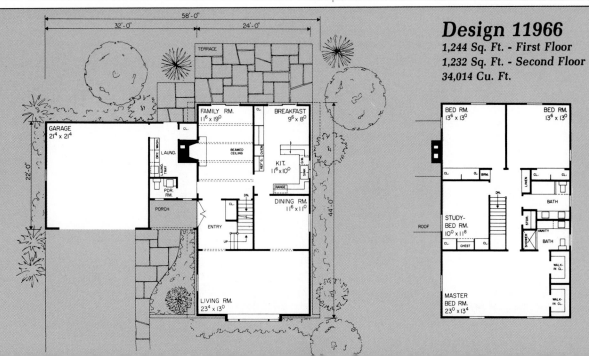

First Floor

58' - 0"

32' - 0"

24' - 0"

TERRACE

GARAGE
21⁴ x 21⁴

FAMILY RM.
11⁶ x 19⁰

CL.

BREAKFAST
9⁶ x 8⁰

DRY. WASH.

LAUND. RM.

LAUNDRY TRAY

PDR. RM.

CL.

BEAMED CEILING

REF. G. OVEN

KIT.
11⁶ x 10⁰

SINK D.W.

RANGE

DINING RM.
11⁶ x 11⁰

22' - 0"

PORCH

DN.

CL.

ENTRY

UP

44' - 0"

LIVING RM.
23⁴ x 13⁰

Second Floor

BED RM.
13⁶ x 13⁰

BED RM.
13⁶ x 13⁰

CL.

BRM.

CL.

LINEN

BATH

ROOF

STUDY-BED RM.
10⁰ x 11⁸

DN.

SHOWER

STOR.

VANITY

BATH

CL.

CHEST

WALK-IN CL.

MASTER BED RM.
23⁰ x 13⁴

WALK-IN CL.

Design 12646
1,274 Sq. Ft. - First Floor
1,322 Sq. Ft. - Second Floor; 42,425 Cu. Ft.

● What a stylish departure from today's usual architecture. This refreshing exterior may be referred to as Neo-Victorian. Its vertical lines, steep roofs and variety of gables remind one of the old Victorian houses of yesteryear. Inside, there is an efficiently working floor plan that is delightfully spacious.

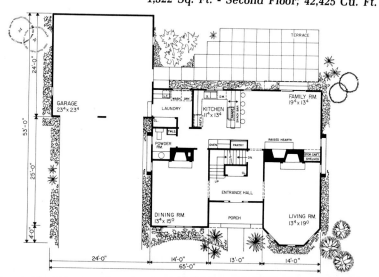

Design 12647 *2,104 Sq. Ft. - First Floor; 1,230 Sq. Ft. - Second Floor; 56,395 Cu. Ft.*

● Another Neo-Victorian, and what an impressive and unique design it is. Observe the roof lines, the window treatment, the use of contrasting exterior materials and the arched, covered front entrance.

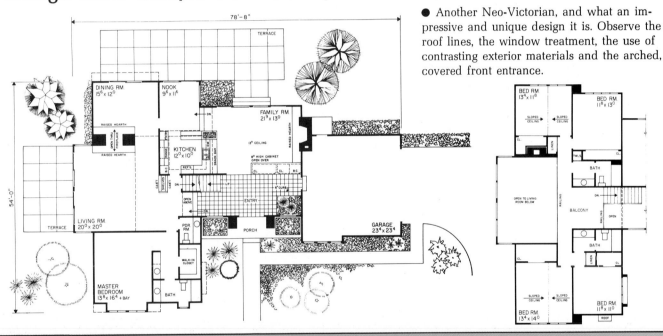

Design 12645 *1,600 Sq. Ft. - First Floor; 1,305 Sq. Ft. - Second Floor 925 Sq. Ft. - Third Floor; 58,355 Cu. Ft.*

● Reminiscent of the Gothic Victorian style of the mid-19th Century, this delightfully detailed, three-story house has a wrap-around veranda for summertime relaxing. The parlor and family room, each with fireplaces, provide excellent formal and informal living facilities. The third floor houses two more great areas plus bath.

239

Design 11831 1,108 Sq. Ft. - First Floor; 992 Sq. Ft. - Second Floor; 31,075 Cu. Ft.

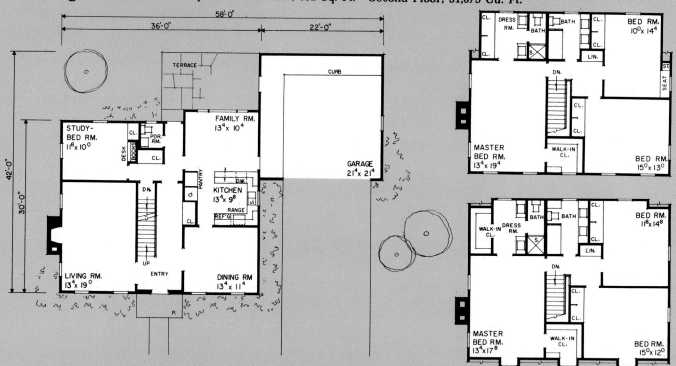

First Floor Plan:

58'-0"
36'-0"
22'-0"
42'-0"
30'-0"

TERRACE

CURB

STUDY-BED RM. 11⁸ x 10⁰

CL.
PDR. RM.
DESK
BOOKS
CL.

FAMILY RM. 13⁴ x 10⁴

GARAGE 21⁴ x 21⁴

DN.
UP
ENTRY

PANTRY
CL.
KITCHEN 13⁴ x 9⁸
D.W.
RANGE
REF'G.

LIVING RM. 13⁴ x 19⁰

DINING RM. 13⁴ x 11⁴

P.

Second Floor Plan (upper):

CL.
DRESS RM.
BATH
BATH
CL.
BED RM. 10⁰ x 14⁴
CL.
S.
LIN.
DN.
MASTER BED RM. 13⁴ x 19⁴
CL.
CL.
WALK-IN CL.
SEAT
BED RM. 15⁰ x 13⁰

Second Floor Plan (lower):

WALK-IN CL.
DRESS RM.
BATH
BATH
CL.
BED RM. 11⁸ x 14⁸
S.
CL.
LIN.
DN.
MASTER BED RM. 13⁴ x 17⁸
CL.
CL.
WALK-IN CL.
BED RM. 15⁰ x 12⁰

Design 11832 1,108 Sq. Ft. - First Floor; 1,018 Sq. Ft. - Second Floor; 31,342 Cu. Ft.

Design 11833 1,152 Sq. Ft. - First Floor; 958 Sq. Ft. - Second Floor; 31,386 Cu. Ft.

Four Authentic Exteriors Go With
This Practical Family Living Plan . . .

● . . . which one do you prefer? Each of these delightful exteriors - the New England Salt Box, Design 11831; the Connecticut Gambrel, Design 11832; the French Mansard, Design 11833; the Georgian, Design 11834 - will provide you with a proud link with the past. Pride of ownership will be yours forever! The efficient first floor plan is common to each of these four designs. The second floor, however, varies with each exterior style. While each house features three sizeable bedrooms, excellent bath facilities and fine storage potential, a study of the various bedroom dimensions reveals difference in sizes. This is due to the varying characteristics of the roof structures. Observe the center entrance and how the main hall effectively routes traffic to all areas. The efficient work center is strategically located between the separate dining room and the informal family room. The formal living room will be entirely free of unnecessary traffic. Note the fireplace and all that blank space for flexible furniture placement. Don't miss the extra room which may be used as a study or fourth bedroom.

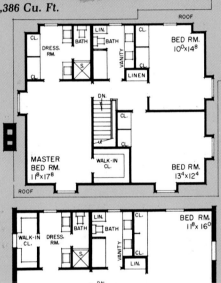

Design 11834 1,150 Sq. Ft. - First Floor; 1,120 Sq. Ft. - Second Floor; 34,460 Cu. Ft.

Design 12367
1,356 Sq. Ft. - First Floor
780 Sq. Ft. - Second Floor
31,230 Cu. Ft.

70'-0"

32'-0"

TERRACE

NOOK
8⁰ x 11⁶

KITCHEN
10⁶ x 11⁶

WASH. DRY.
LT.

PANTRY

STORAGE

REF'G. RANGE
S. D.W.

MUD RM.
6⁶ x 11⁴

CL. CL.

FAMILY RM.
21⁸ x 13⁶

BEAMED CEILING

DN.

PDR. RM.

CL.

UP

DINING RM.
12⁰ x 13⁶

ENTRANCE HALL

LIVING RM.
21⁸ x 13⁶

PORCH

GARAGE
21⁸ x 23⁴

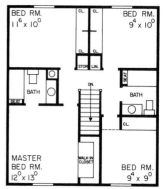

BED RM.
11⁶ x 10⁰

CL. CL.

BED RM.
9⁴ x 10⁰

CL. CL.

STOR. LIN.

SEAT

BATH

SEAT

DN.

BATH

CL.

MASTER BED RM.
12⁰ x 13⁰

WALK IN CLOSET

BED RM.
9⁴ x 9⁰

● This attractively proportioned two-story is a good study in effective zoning. Observe how the various areas function independently as well as together.

Design 12634 1,308 Sq. Ft. - First Floor
1,047 Sq. Ft. - Second Floor; 32,600 Cu. Ft.

● The second floor of this fine home overhangs the first floor. Four bedrooms and two baths are located here. This home will be an outstanding investment.

MASTER BED RM.
16⁰ x 12⁴

DRESSING RM.

CL. CL.

BED RM.
13⁴ x 12⁴

BATH

DN.

HALL

LINEN

BED RM.
11⁰ x 12⁰

CL.

VANITY

BATH

BED RM.
10⁰ x 12⁰

CL.

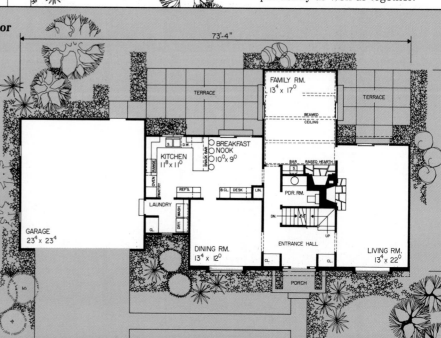

73'-4"

36'-9"

TERRACE

FAMILY RM.
13⁴ x 17⁰

TERRACE

BEAMED CEILING

KITCHEN
11⁸ x 11⁰

OVEN RANGE

BREAKFAST NOOK
10⁰ x 9⁰

SNACK BAR

S. D.W.

BAR

RAISED HEARTH

PANTRY

REF'G.

B.CL. DESK LIN.

PDR. RM.

LAUNDRY

WASH. DRY.

DN.

BAR

UP

GARAGE
23⁴ x 23⁴

DINING RM.
13⁴ x 12⁰

ENTRANCE HALL

LIVING RM.
13⁴ x 22⁰

PORCH

Design 12108 1,188 Sq. Ft. - First Floor
720 Sq. Ft. - Second Floor; 27,394 Cu. Ft.

● This design features a full two-story section flanked by one-story wings. The livability offered in this home is interesting and practical. It has separated the functions to assure convenient living.

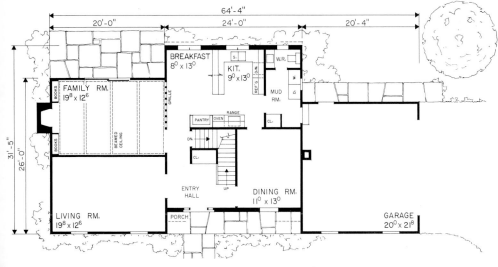

BED RM. 14⁰ x 13⁶	BATH	BATH	DRESSING RM.
BED RM. 14⁰ x 15²	SITTING RM.- BED RM. 14⁴ x 10⁰	MASTER BED RM. 12⁴ x 20⁰

Design 12599

2,075 Sq. Ft. - First Floor
1,398 Sq. Ft. - Second Floor
55,000 Cu. Ft.

● This traditional two-story with its projecting one-story wings is delightfully proportioned. The symmetrical window treatment is most appealing. The massive field-stone arch projects from the front line of the house providing a sheltered front entrance. Inside, there is the large foyer with the curving, open staircase to the second floor. Flexibility will be the byword to describe the living patterns. Not only are there the formal living and informal family rooms, but there is the quiet study and the upstairs sitting room. As for eating, there is a sizeable breakfast nook and a separate dining room. The second floor offers the option to function as either a three, or four, bedroom sleeping zone. That's a fine master bedroom suite when the sitting room is included.

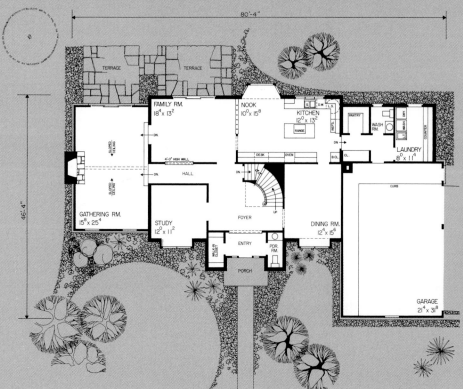

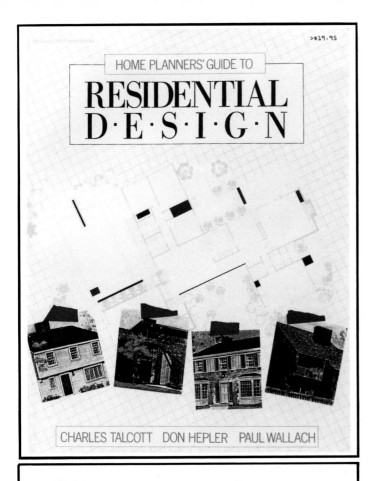
Announcing-

A "MUST" Book for Anyone Involved in the Planning of a New Home

This book features a wealth of information vital to the successful planning of a new home. Discussed in a highly illustrated manner, is a great variety of subjects concerning residential design and planning. Written and edited specifically for use during the early planning and pre-construction stages of the building program, this book may save you many times its cost. In addition to giving a layman's overview of the architectural side of residential design, it helps the reader give due consideration to the innumerable budgetary and livability aspects of the planning process. A CHECKLIST FOR PLAN SELECTION lists over 650 items that will guide and help assure proper decision-making which involve the myriad of subjects influencing proper residential design and planning.

224 pages, soft cover.

A Most Rewarding and Money-Saving Book.

$19.95
Postpaid

Contents

Design 12619

1,269 Sq. Ft. - First Floor
1,064 Sq. Ft. - Second Floor
29,195 Cu. Ft.

● The Southwest is captured ideally in this two-story, hip-roofed house. It has many fine features which will aide a family to easy living. The formal and informal areas are outstanding. Note the large 13 x 23 foot living room and separate dining room. Upstairs, there are three bedrooms, bath and master bedroom.

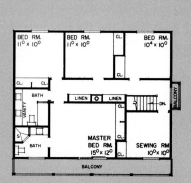

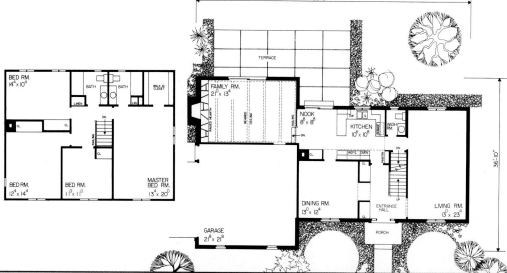

Design 11753

1,580 Sq. Ft. - First Floor
1,008 Sq. Ft. - Second Floor
26,484 Cu. Ft.

● The charm of the old Spanish Southwest is captured by the rugged individualism characterized by this design. The family, dining and living rooms will cater to the family's informal and formal group activities most adequately. Four bedrooms and a sewing room are on the second floor. Make the sewing room into a fifth bedroom if it is needed.

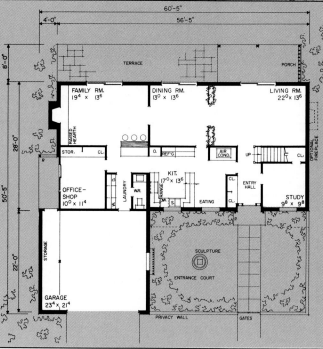

Design 12214

3,011 Sq. Ft. - First Floor
2,297 Sq. Ft. - Second Floor; 78,585 Cu. Ft.

● A Spanish hacienda with all the appeal and all the comforts one would want in a new home. This is a house that looks big and really is big. Measuring 100 feet across the front with various appendages and roof planes.

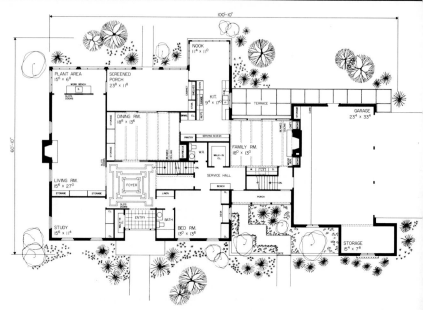

Design 11957 1,042 Sq. Ft. - First Floor; 780 Sq. Ft. - Second Floor; 24,982 Cu. Ft.

● When you order your blueprints for this design you will receive details for the construction of each of the three charming exteriors pictured above. Whichever the exterior you finally decide to build, the floor plan will be essentially the same except the location of the windows. This will be a fine home for the growing family. It will serve well for many years. There are four bedrooms and two full baths (one with a stall shower) upstairs.

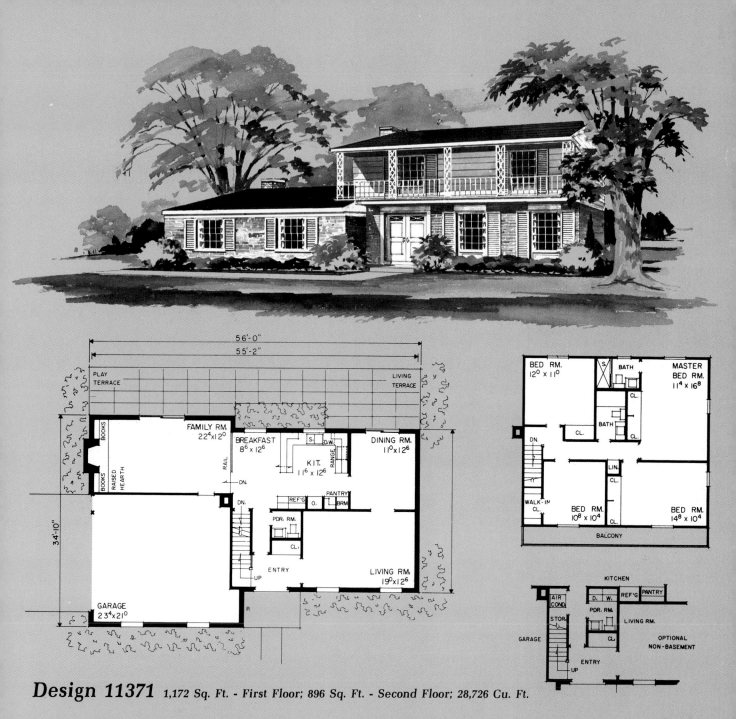

Design 11371 1,172 Sq. Ft. - First Floor; 896 Sq. Ft. - Second Floor; 28,726 Cu. Ft.

Floor plan labels:

First floor:
- 56'-0"
- 55'-2"
- 34'-10"
- PLAY TERRACE
- LIVING TERRACE
- FAMILY RM. 22⁴ x 12⁰
- BOOKS
- RAISED HEARTH
- RAIL
- DN.
- DN.
- BREAKFAST 8⁶ x 12⁶
- KIT. 11⁶ x 12⁶
- RANGE
- DINING RM. 11⁰ x 12⁶
- REF'G
- O.
- PANTRY
- BRM
- PDR. RM.
- CL.
- ENTRY
- UP
- LIVING RM. 19⁰ x 12⁶
- GARAGE 23⁴ x 21⁰
- P.

Second floor:
- BED RM. 12⁰ x 11⁰
- S.
- BATH
- MASTER BED RM. 11⁴ x 16⁸
- CL.
- BATH
- CL.
- DN.
- LIN.
- CL.
- WALK-IN CL.
- BED RM. 10⁸ x 10⁴
- BED RM. 14⁸ x 10⁴
- BALCONY

Optional non-basement:
- KITCHEN
- AIR COND.
- STOR.
- D.
- W.
- REF'G
- PANTRY
- PDR. RM.
- LIVING RM.
- GARAGE
- CL.
- ENTRY
- UP
- OPTIONAL NON-BASEMENT

● If you like traditional charm and the tried and true living patterns of the conventional two-story idea, you'll not go wrong in selecting this design as your next home. In fact, when you order blueprints for Design 11371 you'll receive details for building all three optional elevations. So, you needn't decide which front exterior is your favorite right now. Any one of these will surely add a touch of class to your new neighborhood.

Design 12149
988 Sq. Ft. - First Floor
952 Sq. Ft. - Second Floor; 30,438 Cu. Ft.

● Any one of these exteriors can be built with the floor plan below. If you like the traditional version to the left, order blueprints for 12149; if you prefer the Farmhouse adaptation below, order 12150; should your choice be for the Tudor variation at the bottom, order 12151. Whatever your selection, you'll appreciate your new home.

Design 12150
991 Sq. Ft. - First Floor
952 Sq. Ft. - Second Floor; 27,850 Cu. Ft.

● In each of these designs the attached two-car garage adds to the appeal as its roof continues to provide a covered porch for the front doors. A professional builder could hardly do better than to find a place for these charming houses in his subdivision. The basically rectangular shape of the main house will mean economical construction.

Design 12151
991 Sq. Ft. - First Floor
952 Sq. Ft. - Second Floor; 28,964 Cu. Ft.

● The blueprints you order will show details for building either the four or the five bedroom version. Which will serve your family best? In addition to the two baths of the second floor, there is an extra powder room. Further, there is a laundry, separate dining room, family room, U-shaped kitchen and basement. A great plan for the modest budget.

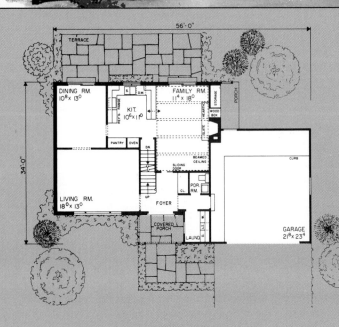

OPTIONAL 4 BEDROOM PLAN

Design 12488 *1,113 Sq. Ft. - First Floor*
543 Sq. Ft. - Second Floor; 36,055 Cu. Ft.

● A cozy cottage for the young at heart! Whether called upon to serve the young, active family as a leisure-time retreat at the lake, or the retired couple as a quiet haven in later years, this charming design will perform well. As a year round second home, the upstairs with its two sizable bedrooms, full bath and lounge area, looking down into the gathering room below, will ideally accommodate the younger generation.

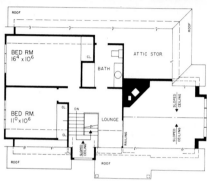

● Natural stone, board-and-batten, multi-paned windows, overhanging eaves and the covered front porch highlight the exterior of this two-story home. Not only is the exterior well designed, but so is the interior. The sunken gathering room's ceiling is open to the second floor and is sloped for an even more dramatic appeal. Note the efficiency of the kitchen and dining area. A skylight will illuminate this area.

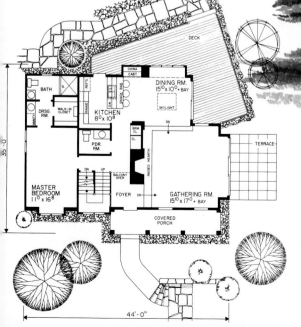

Design 12853
1,161 Sq. Ft. - First Floor
475 Sq. Ft. - Second Floor
28,715 Cu. Ft.

251

Design 12829

2,044 Sq. Ft. - First Floor
1,962 Sq. Ft. - Second Floor; 74,360 Cu. Ft.

● The architecture of this design is Post-Modern with a taste of Victorian styling. Detailed with gingerbread woodwork and a handsome double-width chimney, this two-story design is breathtaking. Enter this home to the large, tiled receiving hall and begin to explore this very livable floor plan. Formal areas consist of the front living room and the dining room. Each has features to make it memorable. The living room is spacious, has a fireplace and access to the covered porch; the dining room has a delightful bay window and is convenient to the kitchen for ease in meal serving. The library is tucked between these two formal areas. Now let's go to the informal area. The family room will welcome many an explorer. It will be a great place for many family activities. Note the L-shaped snack bar with cabinets below. Onward to the second floor, where the private area will be found. Start with the two bedrooms that have two full bathrooms joining them together. The older children will marvel at this area's efficiency and privacy. A third family bedroom is nearby. Then, there is the master bedroom suite. Its list of features is long, indeed. Begin with the "his" and "her" baths and see how many features you can list. A guest bedroom and bath are on the first floor.

All The "TOOLS" You And Your Builder Need

. . . to, first select an exterior and a floor plan for your new house that satisfy your tastes and your family's living patterns . . .

. . . then, to review the blueprints in great detail and obtain a construction cost figure . . . also, to price out the structural materials required to build . . . and, finally, to review and decide upon the specifications to which your home is to be built. Truly, an invaluable set of "tools" to launch your home planning and building programs.

1. THE PLAN BOOKS

Home Planners' unique Design Category Series makes it easy to look at and study only the types of designs for which you and your family have an interest. Each of six plan books features a specific type of home, namely: Two-Story, 1½ Story, One-Story Over 2000 Sq. Ft., One-Story Under 2000 Sq. Ft., Multi-Levels and Vacation Homes. In addition to the convenient Design Category Series, there is an impressive selection of other current titles. While the home plans featured in these books are also to be found in the Design Category Series, they, too, are edited for those with special tastes and requirements. Your family will spend many enjoyable hours reviewing the delightfully designed exteriors and the practical floor plans. Surely your home or office library should include a selection of these popular plan books. Your complete satisfaction is guaranteed.

2. THE CONSTRUCTION BLUEPRINTS

There are blueprints available for each of the designs published in Home Planners' current plan books. Depending upon the size, the style and the type of home, each set of blueprints consists of from five to ten large sheets. Only by studying the blueprints is it possible to give complete and final consideration to the proper selection of a design for your next home. The blueprints provide the opportunity for all family members to familiarize themselves with the features of all exterior elevations, interior elevations and details, all dimensions, special built-in features and effects. They also provide a full understanding of the materials to be used and/or selected. The low-cost of our blueprints makes it possible and indeed, practical, to study in detail a number of different sets of blueprints before deciding upon which design to build.

3. THE MATERIALS LIST

A list of materials is an integral part of the plan package. It comprises the last sheet of each set of blueprints and serves as a handy reference during the period of construction. Of course, at the pricing and the material ordering stages, it is indispensable.

4. THE SPECIFICATION OUTLINE

Each order for blueprints is accompanied by one Specification Outline. You and your builder will find this a time-saving tool when deciding upon your own individual specifications. An important reference document should you wish to write your own specifications.

The Design Category Series

360 TWO STORY HOMES

English Tudors, Early American Salt Boxes, Gambrels, Farmhouses, Southern Colonials, Georgians, French Mansards, Contemporaries. Interesting floor plans for both small and large families. Efficient kitchens, 2 to 6 bedrooms, family rooms, libraries, extra baths, mud rooms. Homes for all budgets.

1.

288 Pages, $6.95

150 1½ STORY HOMES

Cape Cod, Williamsburg, Georgian, Tudor and Contemporary versions. Low budget and country-estate feature sections. Expandable family plans. Formal and informal living and dining areas along with gathering rooms. Spacious, country kitchens. Indoor-outdoor livability with covered porches and functional terraces.

2.

128 Pages, $3.95

210 ONE STORY HOM OVER 2,000 Sq. Ft.

All popular styles. Includ Spanish, Western, Tud French, and other traditio versions. Contemporari Gracious, family living p terns. Sunken living roo master bedroom suites, a ums, courtyards, pools. Fi indoor-outdoor living re tionships. For modest country-estate budgets.

3.

192 Pages, $4.95

315 ONE STORY HOMES UNDER 2,000 Sq. Ft.

A great selection of traditional and contemporary exteriors for medium and restricted budgets. Efficient, practical floor plans. Gathering rooms, formal and informal living and dining rooms, mud rooms, indoor-outdoor livability. Economically built homes. Designs with bonus space livability for growing families.

4.

192 Pages, $4.95

215 MULTI-LEVEL HOMES

For new dimensions in family living. A captivating variety of exterior styles, exciting floor plans for flat and sloping sites. Exposed lower levels. Balconies, decks. Plans for the active family. Upper level lounges, excellent bath facilities. Sloping ceilings. Functional outdoor terraces. For all building budgets.

5.

192 Pages, $4.95

223 VACATION HOM

Features A-Frames, Chal Hexagons, economical rect gles. One and two stories p multi-levels. Lodges for y 'round livability. From 480 3238 sq. ft. Cottages sleepin to 22. For flat or sloping si Spacious, open planning. O 600 illustrations. 120 Pages full color. Cluster hom selection. For lakeshore woodland leisure living.

6.

176 Pages, $4.95

The Exterior Style Series

120 EARLY AMERICAN PLANS

and Other Colonial Adaptations is an outstanding and unique plan book for the home and professional library. Devoted exclusively to Early American architectural interpretations adapted for today's living patterns. Exquisitely detailed exteriors retain all the charm of a proud heritage. One-story, 1½ and two-story and multi-level designs for varying budgets.

7.

112 Pages, $2.95

125 CONTEMPORARY HOME PLANS

Here is an exciting book featuring a wide variety of home designs for the 1980's and far beyond. The exteriors of these delightfully illustrated houses are refreshing with their practical and progressive "new look". The floor plans offer new dimensions in living highlighting such features as gathering rooms, cathedral ceilings and interior balconies. House designs of all sizes.

8.

112 Pages, $2.95

135 ENGLISH TUDOR HOMES

and other Popular Fami Plans is a favorite of man The current popularity of t English Tudor home design phenomenal. Here is a bo which is loaded with Tud for all budgets. There a one-story, 1½ and two-sto designs, plus multi-levels a hillsides from 1,176 to 3,849 s ft. There is a special 20 pa section of Early America Adaptations.

9.

104 Pages, $2.95

The Budget Series

175 LOW BUDGET HOMES

A special selection of home designs for the modest or restricted building budget. An excellent variety of Traditional and Contemporary designs. One-story, 1½ and two-story and split-level homes. Three, four and five bedrooms. Family rooms, extra baths, formal and informal dining rooms. Basement and non-basement designs. Attached garages and covered porches.

11.

96 Pages, $2.95

165 AFFORDABLE HOME PLANS

This outstanding book was specially edited with a wide selection of houses and plans for those with a medium building budget. While none of these designs are considered low-cost; neither do they require an unlimited budget to build. Square footages range from 1,428. Exteriors of Tudor, French, Early American, Spanish and Contemporary are included.

12.

112 Pages, $2.95

142 HOME DESIGNS FOR EXPANDED BUILDING BUDGETS

A family's ability to finan and need for a larger hor grows as its size and incor increases. This selection hig lights designs which house average square footage 2,551. One-story plans avera 2,069; two-stories, 2,73 multi-levels, 2,825. Spacio homes featuring raised hear fireplaces, open planning a efficient kitchens.

13.

112 Pages, $2.95

The Full Color Series

116 TRADITIONAL and CONTEMPORARY PLANS

A beautifully illustrated home plan book in complete, full color. One, 1½, two-story and split-level designs featured in all of the most popular exterior styles. Varied building budgets will be satisfied by the numerous plans for all budget sizes. Designs for flat and hillside sites, including exposed lower levels. It will make an ideal gift item.

14.

96 Pages in Full Color, $5.95

122 HOME DESIGNS

This book has full color throughout. More than 120 eye-pleasing, colored illustrations. Tudor, French, Spanish, Early American and Contemporary exteriors featuring all design types. The interiors house efficient, step-saving floor plans. Formal and informal living areas along with convenient work centers. Two to six bedroom sleeping areas. A delightful book for one's permanent library.

15.

96 Pages in Full Color, $5.95

114 TREND HOMES

Heritage Houses, Energy Designs, Family Plans - these, along with Vacation Homes, are in this new plan book in full color. The Trend Homes feature unique living patterns. The revered Heritage Houses highlight the charm and nostalgia of Early America. Solariums, greenhouses, earth-sheltered and super-insulated houses are the Energy Designs. Vacation homes feature A-frames and chalets.

16.

104 Pages in Full Color, $5.95

450 HOUSE PLANS

For those who wish to review and study perhaps the largest selection of designs available in a single volume. This edition will provide countless hours of enjoyable family home planning. Varying exterior styles, plus interesting and practical floor plans for all building budgets. Formal, informal living patterns; indoor-outdoor livability; small, growing and large family facilities.

17.

320 Pages, $8.95

136 SPANISH & WESTERN HOME DESIGNS

Stucco exteriors, arches, tile roofs, wide-overhangs, courtyards and rambling ranches are characteristics which make this design selection distinctive. These sun-country designs highlight indoor-outdoor relationships. Solar oriented livability is featured. Their appeal is not limited to the Southwest region of our country.

10.

120 Pages, $2.95

The Plan Books

. . . are a most valuable tool for anyone planning to build a new home. A study of the hundreds of delightfully designed exteriors and the practical, efficient floor plans will be a great learning and fun-oriented family experience. You will be able to select your preferred styling from among Early American, Tudor, French, Spanish and Contemporary adaptations. Your ideas about floor planning and interior livability will expand. And, of course, after you have selected an appealing home design that satisfies your long list of living requirements, you can order the blueprints for further study of your favorite design in greater detail. Surely the hours spent studying the portfolio of Home Planners' designs will be both enjoyable and rewarding ones.

1 Frontal Sheet

2 Foundation Plan

3 Detailed Floor Plan

FIRST FLOOR PLAN

SECOND FLOOR PLAN

4 House Cross-Sections

CROSS SECTION C-C

CROSS SECTION DD

ATTIC

5 Interior Elevations

6 Exterior Elevations

LEFT SIDE

7 Material List

The Blueprints

1. FRONTAL SHEET.
Artist's landscaped sketch of the exterior and ink-line floor plans are on the frontal sheet of each set of blueprints.

2. FOUNDATION PLAN.
¼" Scale basement and foundation plan. All necessary notations and dimensions. Plot plan diagram for locating house on building site.

3. DETAILED FLOOR PLAN.
¼" Scale first and second floor plans with complete dimensions. Cross-section detail keys. Diagrammatic layout of electrical outlets and switches.

4. HOUSE CROSS-SECTIONS.
Large scale sections of foundation, interior and exterior walls, floors and roof details for design and construction control.

5. INTERIOR ELEVATIONS.
Large scale interior details of the complete kitchen cabinet design, bathrooms, powder room, laundry, fireplaces, paneling, beam ceilings, built-in cabinets, etc.

6. EXTERIOR ELEVATIONS.
¼" Scale exterior elevation drawings of front, rear, and both sides of the house. All exterior materials and details are shown to indicate the complete design and proportions of the house.

7. MATERIAL LIST.
Complete lists of all materials required for the construction of the house as designed are included in each set of blueprints.

THIS BLUEPRINT PACKAGE
will help you and your family take a major step forward in the final appraisal and planning of your new home. Only by spending many enjoyable and informative hours studying the numerous details included in the complete package, will you feel sure of, and comfortable with, your commitment to build your new home. To assure successful and productive consultation with your builder and/or architect, reference to the various elements of the blueprint package is a must. The blueprints, material list and specification outline will save much consultation time and expense. Don't be without them.

The Material List

With each set of blueprints you order you will receive a material list. Each list shows you the quantity, type and size of the non-mechanical materials required to build your home. It also tells you where these materials are used. This makes the blueprints easy to understand.

Influencing the mechanical requirements are geographical differences in availability of materials, local codes, methods of installation and individual preferences. Because of these factors, your local heating, plumbing and electrical contractors can supply you with necessary material take-offs for their particular trades.

Material lists simplify your material ordering and enable you to get quicker price quotations from your builder and material dealer. Because the material list is an integral part of each set of blueprints, it is not available separately.

Among the materials listed:

• Masonry, Veneer & Fireplace • Framing Lumber • Roofing & Sheet Metal • Windows & Door Frames • Exterior Trim & Insulation • Tile Work, Finish Floors • Interior Trim, Kitchen Cabinets • Rough & Finish Hardware

The Specification Outline

This fill-in type specification lists over 150 phases of home construction from excavating to painting and includes wiring, plumbing, heating and air-conditioning. It consists of 16 pages and will prove invaluable for specifying to your builder the exact materials, equipment and methods of construction you want in your new home. One Specification Outline is included free with each order for blueprints. Additional Specification Outlines are available at $3.00 each.

CONTENTS
• General Instructions, Suggestions and Information • Excavating and Grading • Masonry and Concrete Work • Sheet Metal Work • Carpentry, Millwork, Roofing, and Miscellaneous Items • Lath and Plaster or Drywall Wallboard • Schedule for Room Finishes • Painting and Finishing • Tile Work • Electrical Work • Plumbing • Heating and Air-Conditioning

Before You Order

1. STUDY THE DESIGNS . . . found in Home Planners current publications. As you review these delightful custom homes, you should keep in mind the total living requirements of your family — both indoors and outdoors. Although we do not make changes in plans, many minor changes can be made prior to the period of construction. If major changes are involved to satisfy your personal requirements, you should consider ordering one set of blueprints and having them redrawn locally. Consultation with your architect is strongly advised when contemplating major changes.

2. HOW TO ORDER BLUEPRINTS . . . After you have chosen the design that satisfies your requirements, or if you have selected one that you wish to study in more detail, simply clip the accompanying order blank and mail with your remittance. However, if it is not convenient for you to send a check or money order, you can use your credit card, or merely indicate C.O.D. shipment. Postman will collect all charges, including postage and C.O.D. fee. C.O.D. shipments are not permitted to Canada or foreign countries. Should time be of essence, as it sometimes is with many of our customers, your telephone order usually can be processed and shipped in the next day's mail. Simply call toll free 1-800-521-6797, (Michigan residents call collect 0-313-477-1854).

3. OUR SERVICE . . . Home Planners makes every effort to process and ship each order for blueprints and books within 48 hours. Because of this, we have deemed it unnecessary to acknowledge receipt of our customers orders. See order coupon for the postage and handling charges for surface mail, air mail or foreign mail.

4. A NOTE REGARDING REVERSE BLUEPRINTS . . . As a special service to those wishing to build in reverse of the plan as shown, we do include an extra set of reversed blueprints for only $25.00 additional with each order. Even though the lettering and dimensions appear backward on reversed blueprints, they make a handy reference because they show the house just as it's being built in reverse from the standard blueprints — thereby helping you visualize the home better.

5. OUR EXCHANGE POLICY . . . Since blueprints are printed up in specific response to your individual order, we cannot honor requests for refunds. However, the first set of blueprints in any order (or the one set in a single set order) for a given design may be exchanged for a set of another design at a fee of $10.00 plus $3.00 for postage and handling via surface mail; $4.00 via air mail.

TO: HOME PLANNERS, INC., 23761 RESEARCH DRIVE FARMINGTON HILLS, MICHIGAN 48024

Please rush me the following:

_____ SET(S) BLUEPRINTS FOR DESIGN NO(S). _____ $_____
Single Set, $95.00; Additional Identical Sets in Same Order $25.00 ea.
4 Set Package of Same Design, $145.00 (Save $25.00)
7 Set Package of Same Design, $180.00 (Save $65.00)
(Material Lists and 1 Specification Outline included)
_____ SPECIFICATION OUTLINES @ $3.00 EACH . . . . $_____

Michigan Residents add 4% sales tax $_____

| FOR POSTAGE AND HANDLING PLEASE CHECK ✔ & REMIT | ☐ $3.00 Added to Order for Surface Mail (UPS) - Any Mdse. ☐ $4.00 Added for Priority Mail of One-Three Sets of Blueprints. ☐ $6.00 Added for Priority Mail of Four or more Sets of Blueprints. ☐ For Canadian orders add $2.00 to above applicable rates | } $_____ |

☐ C.O.D. PAY POSTMAN
(C.O.D. Within U.S.A. Only)   TOTAL in U.S.A. funds $_____

PLEASE PRINT
Name _____
Street _____
City _____ State _____ Zip _____

CREDIT CARD ORDERS ONLY: Fill in the boxes below   Prices subject to change without notice

Credit Card No. [ ][ ][ ][ ][ ][ ][ ][ ][ ][ ][ ][ ][ ][ ][ ][ ]   Expiration Date Month/Year [ ][ ][ ][ ]

CHECK ONE: ☐ **VISA**   ☐ **MasterCard**

Order Form Key NCV1   Your Signature _____

BLUEPRINT ORDERS SHIPPED WITHIN 48 HOURS OF RECEIPT!

TO: HOME PLANNERS, INC., 23761 RESEARCH DRIVE FARMINGTON HILLS, MICHIGAN 48024

Please rush me the following:

_____ SET(S) BLUEPRINTS FOR DESIGN NO(S). _____ $_____
Single Set, $95.00; Additional Identical Sets in Same Order $25.00 ea.
4 Set Package of Same Design, $145.00 (Save $25.00)
7 Set Package of Same Design, $180.00 (Save $65.00)
(Material Lists and 1 Specification Outline included)
_____ SPECIFICATION OUTLINES @ $3.00 EACH . . . . $_____

Michigan Residents add 4% sales tax $_____

| FOR POSTAGE AND HANDLING PLEASE CHECK ✔ & REMIT | ☐ $3.00 Added to Order for Surface Mail (UPS) - Any Mdse. ☐ $4.00 Added for Priority Mail of One-Three Sets of Blueprints. ☐ $6.00 Added for Priority Mail of Four or more Sets of Blueprints. ☐ For Canadian orders add $2.00 to above applicable rates | } $_____ |

☐ C.O.D. PAY POSTMAN
(C.O.D. Within U.S.A. Only)   TOTAL in U.S.A. funds $_____

PLEASE PRINT
Name _____
Street _____
City _____ State _____ Zip _____

CREDIT CARD ORDERS ONLY: Fill in the boxes below   Prices subject to change without notice

Credit Card No. [ ][ ][ ][ ][ ][ ][ ][ ][ ][ ][ ][ ][ ][ ][ ][ ]   Expiration Date Month/Year [ ][ ][ ][ ]

CHECK ONE: ☐ **VISA**   ☐ **MasterCard**

Order Form Key NCV1   Your Signature _____

How many sets of blueprints should be ordered?

This question is often asked. The answer can range anywhere from 1 to 7 sets, depending upon circumstances. For instance, a single set of blueprints of your favorite design is sufficient to study the house in greater detail. On the other hand, if you are planning to get cost estimates, or if you are planning to build, you may need as many as seven sets of blueprints. Because the first set of blueprints in each order is $95.00, and because additional sets of the same design in each order are only $25.00 each (and with package sets even more economical), you save considerably by ordering your total requirements now. To help you determine the exact number of sets, please refer to the handy check list.

How Many Blueprints Do You Need?

_____ OWNER'S SET

_____ BUILDER (Usually requires at least 3 sets: 1 as legal document; 1 for inspection; and at least 1 for tradesmen — usually more.)

_____ BUILDING PERMIT (Sometimes 2 sets are required.)

_____ MORTGAGE SOURCE (Usually 1 set for a conventional mortgage; 3 sets for F.H.A. or V.A. type mortgages.)

_____ SUBDIVISION COMMITTEE (If any.)

_____ TOTAL NO. SETS REQUIRED

Blueprint Ordering Hotline –

Phone toll free: 1-800-521-6797. Orders received by 11 a.m. (Detroit time) will be processed the same day and shipped to you the following day. Use of this line restricted to blueprint ordering only. Michigan residents simply call collect 0-313-477-1854.

Kindly Note: When ordering by phone, please state Order Form Key No. located in box at lower left corner of blueprint order form.

In Canada Mail To:
Home Planners, Inc., 20 Cedar St. North Kitchener, Ontario N2H 2W8
Phone: (519) 743-4169

CONTEMPORARY HOMES . . . are known for, and

often identified by, their lack of exterior adornment. Simple, uncluttered lines generally highlight their exteriors. Often, irregular shapes and soaring roof lines achieve a visual impact that is, indeed, dramatic. And as appealing as many of these contemporary forms are, so too are their accompanying, refreshing living patterns. Open planning, dual and multi-use space, sunken living areas, indoor balconies and lounges, cathedral ceilings, effective uses of glass, and functional indoor-outdoor living relationships can all complement one another to assure outstanding family living patterns. The contemporary home can offer an exciting break from the conventions of the past.

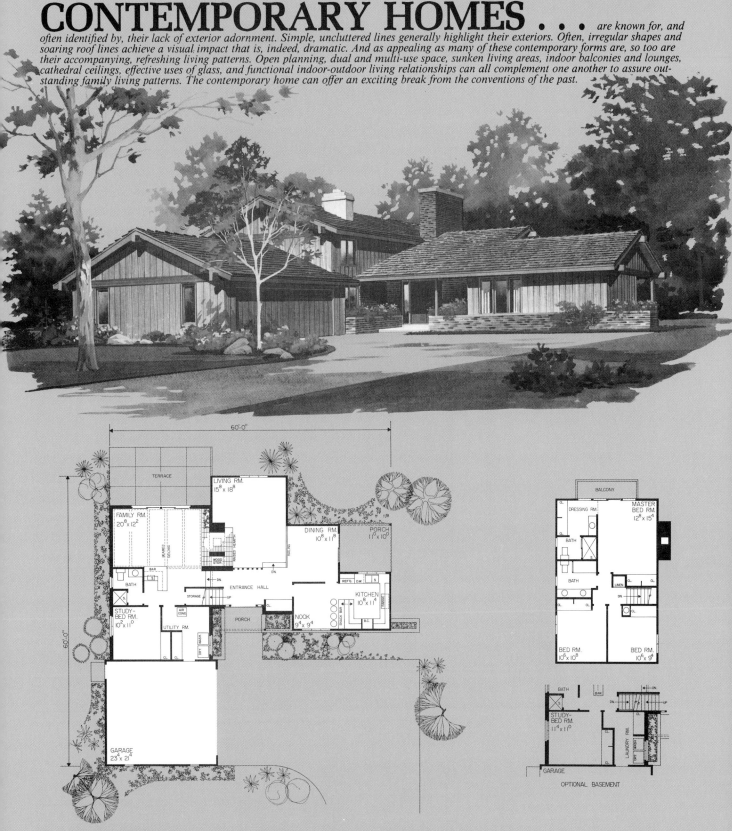

Design 12379 1,525 Sq. Ft. - First Floor; 748 Sq. Ft. - Second Floor; 26,000 Cu. Ft.

● A house that has "everything" may very well look just like this design. Its exterior is well-proportioned and impressive. Inside the inviting double front doors there are features galore. The living room and family room level are sunken. Separating these two rooms is a dramatic thru fireplace. A built-in bar, planter and beamed ceiling highlight the family room. Nearby is a full bath and a study which could be utilized as a fourth bedroom. The fine functioning kitchen has a pass-thru to the snack bar in the breakfast nook. The adjacent dining room overlooks the living room and has sliding doors to the covered porch. Upstairs three bedrooms, two baths and an outdoor balcony. Blueprints for this design include optional basement details.

Design 12711 975 Sq. Ft. - First Floor
1,024 Sq. Ft. - Second Floor; 31,380 Cu. Ft.

● Special features! A complete master suite with a private balcony plus two more bedrooms and a bath upstairs. The first floor has a study with a storage closet. A convenient snack bar between kitchen and dining room. The kitchen offers many built-in appliances. Plus a gathering room and dining room that measures 31 feet wide. Note the curb area in the garage and fireplace in gathering room.

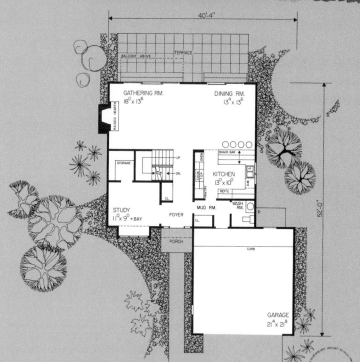

Design 12748
1,232 Sq. Ft. - First Floor
720 Sq. Ft. - Second Floor
27,550 Cu. Ft.

● This four bedroom contemporary will definitely have appeal for the entire family. The U-shaped kitchen-nook area with its built-in desk, adjacent laundry/wash room and service entrance will be very efficient for the busy kitchen activities. The living and family rooms are both sunken one step.

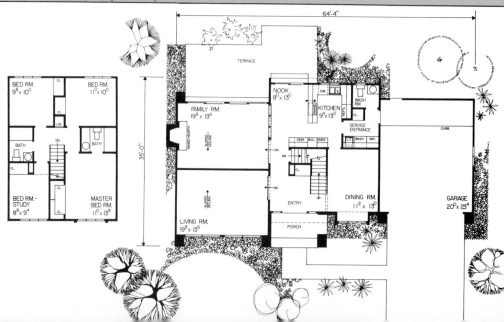

Design 12701 1,909 Sq. Ft. - First Floor
891 Sq. Ft. - Second Floor; 50,830 Cu. Ft.

● A snack bar in the kitchen! Plus a breakfast nook and formal dining room. Whether it's an elegant dinner party or a quick lunch, this home provides the right spot. There's a wet bar in the gathering room. Built-in bookcases in the study. And between these two rooms, a gracious fireplace. Three large bedrooms. Including a luxury master suite. Plus a balcony lounge overlooking gathering room below.

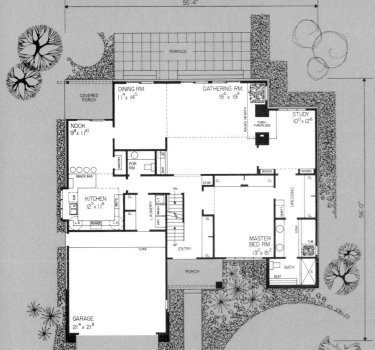

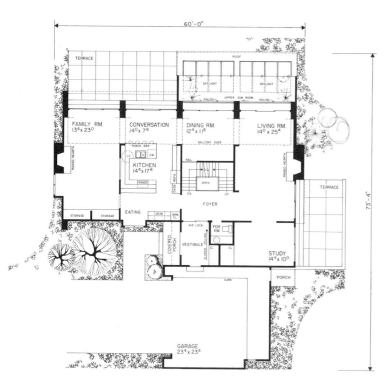

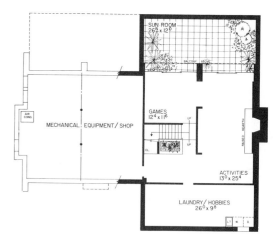

Design 12834

1,775 Sq. Ft. - First Floor; 1,041 Sq. Ft. - Second Floor
1,128 Sq. Ft. - Lower Level; 55,690 Cu. Ft.

● This passive solar design offers 4,200 square feet of livability situated on three levels. The primary passive element will be the lower level sun room which admits sunlight for direct-gain heating. The solar warmth collected in the sun room will radiate into the rest of the house after it passes the sliding glass doors. During the warm summer months, shades are put over the skylight to protect it from direct sunlight. This design has the option of incorporating active solar heating panels to the roof. The collectors would be installed on the south-facing portion of the roof. They would absorb the sun's warmth for both domestic water and supplementary space heating. An attic fan exhausts any hot air out of the house in the summer and circulates air in the winter. With or without the active solar panels, this is a marvelous two-story contemporary.

Design 12831
1,758 Sq. Ft. - First Floor
1,247 Sq. Ft. - Second Floor
44,265 Cu. Ft.

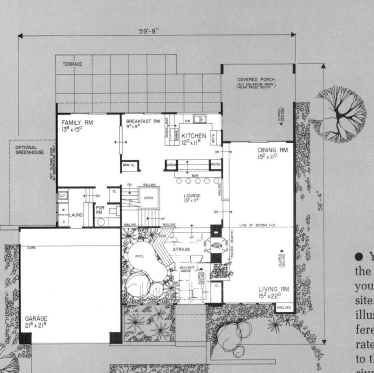

● You can incorporate energy-saving features into the elevation of this passive solar design to enable you to receive the most sunlight on your particular site. Multiple plot plans (included with the blueprints) illustrate which elevations should be solarized for different sites and which extra features can be incorporated. The features can include a greenhouse added to the family room, the back porch turned into a solarium or skylights installed over the entry.

Design 12123

1,624 Sq. Ft. - First Floor
1,335 Sq. Ft. - Second Floor
42,728 Cu. Ft.

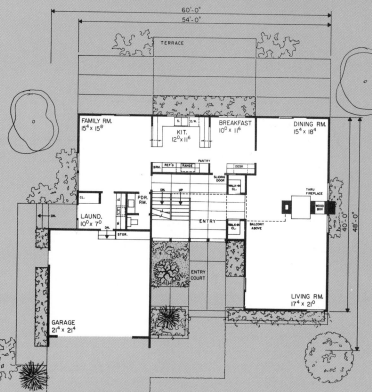

● Inside there is close to 3,000 square feet of uniquely planned floor area. The spacious, well-lighted entry has, of course, a high sloping ceiling. The second floor ceiling also slopes and, consequently, adds to the feeling of spaciousness.

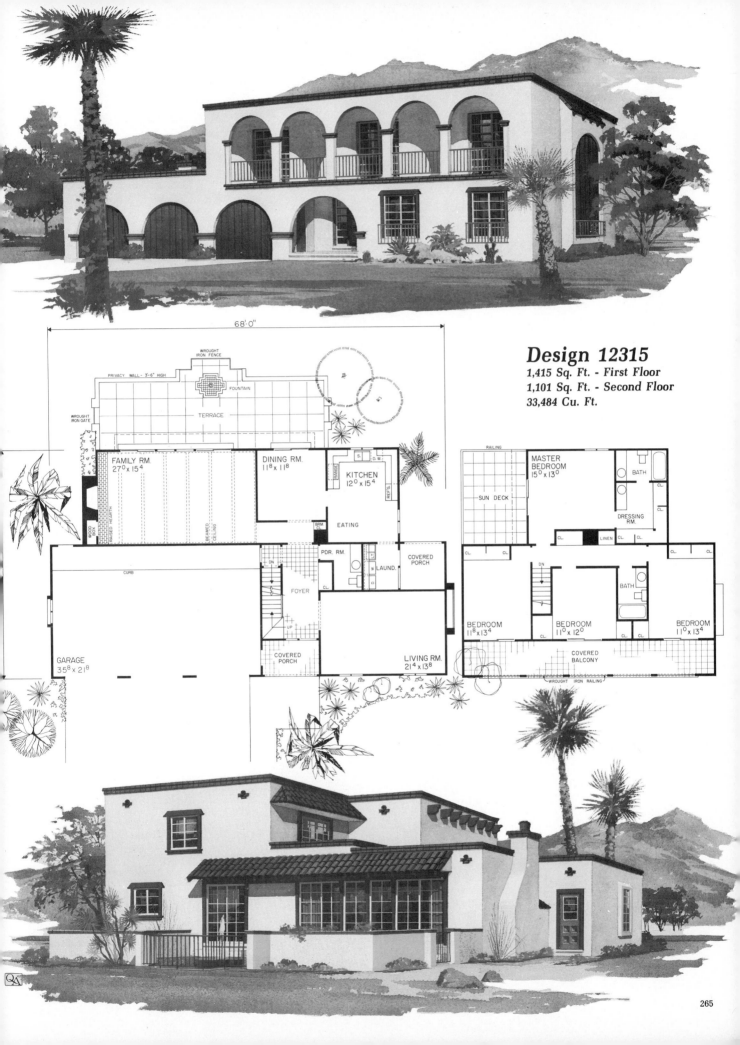

Design 12315

1,415 Sq. Ft. - First Floor
1,101 Sq. Ft. - Second Floor
33,484 Cu. Ft.

68'-0"

WROUGHT IRON FENCE

PRIVACY WALL - 3'-6" HIGH

FOUNTAIN

WROUGHT IRON GATE

TERRACE

FAMILY RM.
27⁰ x 15⁴

DINING RM.
11⁸ x 11⁸

KITCHEN
12⁰ x 15⁴

RANGE

REFG.

WOOD BOX

RAISED HEARTH

BEAMED CEILING

BRM CL

EATING

CURB

DN

PDR. RM.

LAUND.

COVERED PORCH

GARAGE
35⁸ x 21⁸

FOYER

CL

UP

COVERED PORCH

LIVING RM.
21⁴ x 13⁸

RAILING

MASTER BEDROOM
15⁰ x 13⁰

BATH

CL

SUN DECK

DRESSING RM.

CL

CL

LINEN

CL

CL

DN

BATH

BEDROOM
11⁸ x 13⁴

BEDROOM
11⁰ x 12⁰

CL

BEDROOM
11⁰ x 13⁴

COVERED BALCONY

WROUGHT IRON RAILING

265

Design 12339 2,068 Sq. Ft. - First Floor; 589 Sq. Ft. - Second Floor; 27,950 Cu. Ft.

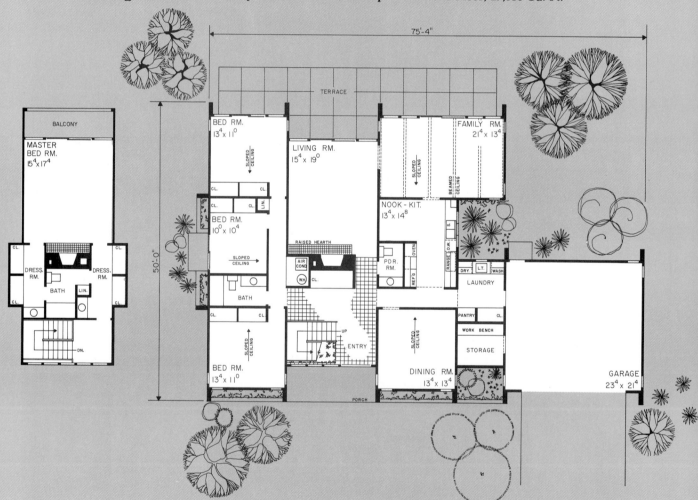

● Here, the influence of the Spanish Southwest comes into clear view. The smooth texture of the stucco exterior contrasts pleasingly with the roughness of the tile roofs. Contributing to the appeal of this contemporary design are the varying roof planes, the interesting angles and the blank wall masses punctuated by the glass areas. Whether called upon to function as a two-story home, or a one-story ranch with an attic studio, this design will deliver interesting and enjoyable living patterns. Sloping ceilings and generous glass areas foster a feeling of spaciousness. Traffic patterns are excellent and the numerous storage facilities are outstanding. Fireplaces are the focal point of the living room and the second floor master bedroom. Three more bedrooms are on the first floor.

Design 12130 *1,608 Sq. Ft. - First Floor; 924 Sq. Ft. - Second Floor; 34,949 Cu. Ft.*

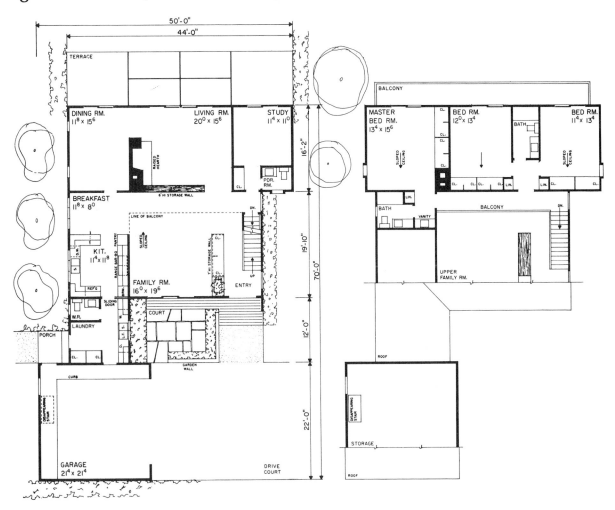

● Ring in the new. Here is a fresh forward-looking design which exemplifies some of the up-to-date imagery of today's architecture. This contemporary is a good study in the interest developed by the introduction of angles. These angles, plus the varying roof planes, blank wall masses, simple glass areas and the overall shape resulting from the orientation of the living components, make this an outstanding design. Inside, the floor planning will offer a lifetime of enjoyable living patterns. Study the various room relationships. Notice the practical zoning which results in a separation of functions to guarantee convenient living. Observe the homemaker's kitchen/laundry area. Also, formal dining, living rooms.

● This refreshing two-story has just enough individuality - both inside and out - to assure its own full measure of distinction. Sliding glass doors provide the living, dining and family rooms with direct access to their own terrace areas. You can look down into the foyer and the dining room from the second floor.

Design 12252

1,810 Sq. Ft. - First Floor
1,033 Sq. Ft. - Second Floor; 38,346 Cu. Ft.

Design 11978 1,280 Sq. Ft. - First Floor

960 Sq. Ft. - Second Floor; 24,031 Cu. Ft.

● Why not make your next two-story home one with a contemporary facade? Surely, it can be agreed that such an exterior can be as attractive, well-proportioned and distinctive as its traditional counterpart. Study each floor carefully. This design has much to offer in the way of total comfort for the family. Particularly noteworthy are the sleeping and bath accommodations on the second floor. Study the entire plan.

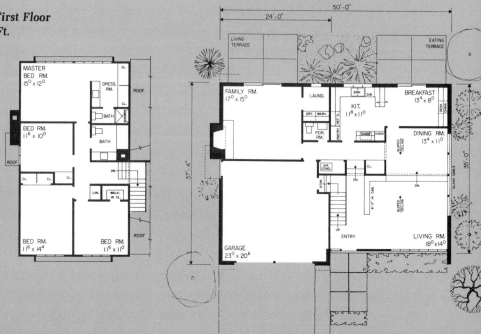

Design 12552 1,437 Sq. Ft. - First Floor
1,158 Sq. Ft. - Second Floor; 43,000 Cu. Ft.

● This is a flexible, two-story design. By having the exposed basement to the rear, this home has an additional level of livability. After the development of this area, your family will enjoy an additional 1,056 square feet of informal living space. The second floor hall and master bedroom look down into the living room.

TWO COUPLES/SINGLES RESIDENCE

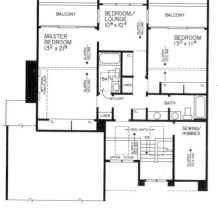

CONVERTIBLE ONE-FAMILY RESIDENCE

Design 12828
First Floor: 817 Sq. Ft. - Living Area; 261 Sq. Ft. - Foyer & Laundry
Second Floor: 852 Sq. Ft. - Living Area; 214 Sq. Ft. - Foyer & Storage; 34,690 Cu. Ft.

● This contemporary home has been designed as a two-couples/singles residence. A home of this type could be bought jointly by two couples or one couple could buy the entire home and rent out one of the units. Complete livability is offered on each floor of this two-story. Each floor has a living room, dining room, interior kitchen, bedroom and bath. At a later date this home could be converted into a one-family residence. The second floor unit would now be a bedroom area.

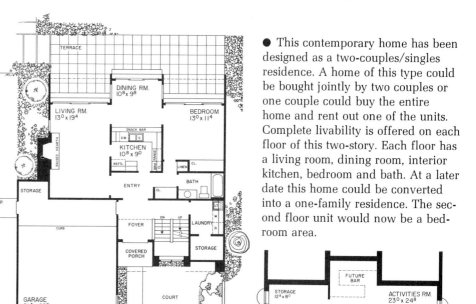

Design 12884 1,855 Sq. Ft. - First Floor
837 Sq. Ft. - Second Floor; 50,137 Cu. Ft.

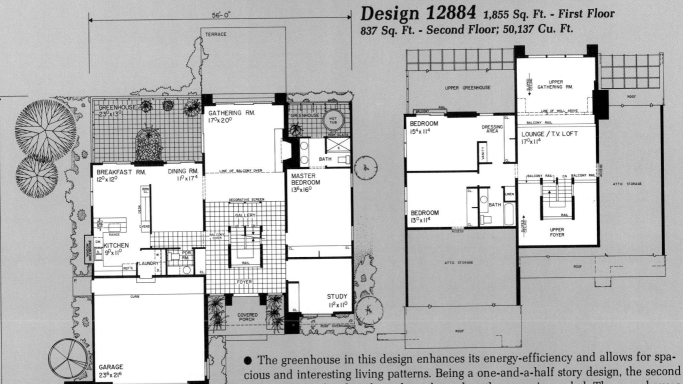

● The greenhouse in this design enhances its energy-efficiency and allows for spacious and interesting living patterns. Being a one-and-a-half story design, the second floor could be developed at a later date when the space is needed. The greenhouses add an additional 418 sq. ft. and 8,793 cu. ft. to the above quoted figures.

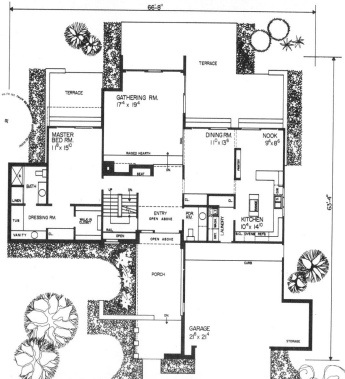

Design 12729 1,590 Sq. Ft. - First Floor
756 Sq. Ft. - Second Floor; 39,310 Cu. Ft.

● Entering this home will be a pleasure through the sheltered walk-way to the double front doors. And the pleasure and beauty does not stop there. The entry hall and sunken gathering room are open to the upstairs for added dimension. There is fine indoor-outdoor living relationships in this design. Note the private terrace, a living terrace plus the balcony.

Design 11783
2,412 Sq. Ft. - First Floor
640 Sq. Ft. - Second Floor
36,026 Cu. Ft.

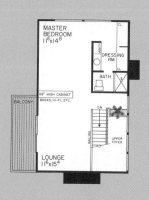

Design 12178 _1,441 Sq. Ft. - First Floor; 1,415 Sq. Ft. - Second Floor; 40,206 Cu. Ft._

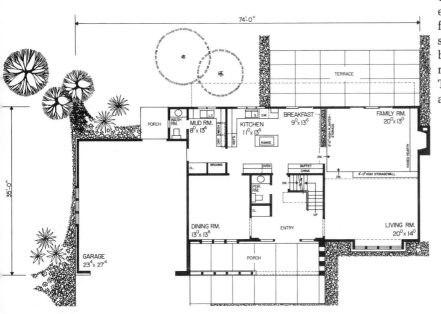

● The spacious, front entry routes traffic most effectively to all of the areas of this wonderfully livable home. The front living room is separated from the sunken, rear family room by the four foot high built-in storage wall. The result is a tremendously spacious living zone. The kitchen is big and efficient. Upstairs there are four large bedrooms and three full baths.

273

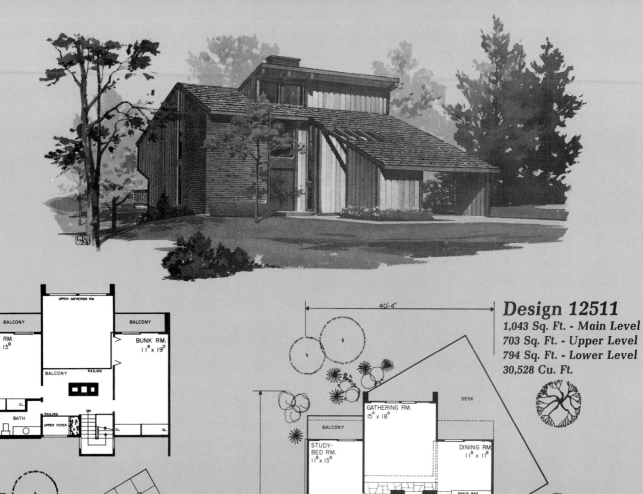

Design 12511

1,043 Sq. Ft. - Main Level
703 Sq. Ft. - Upper Level
794 Sq. Ft. - Lower Level
30,528 Cu. Ft.

Upper Level floor plan labels:
BALCONY
BED RM. 11⁸ x 13⁸
BUNK RM. 11⁸ x 19⁰
BALCONY
UPPER GATHERING RM.
BALCONY
RAILING
CL. CL.
BATH
RAILING
UPPER FOYER
DN.
CL. CL.

Main Level floor plan labels:
40'-4"
52'-0"
DECK
GATHERING RM. 15⁴ x 18⁴
BALCONY
STUDY-BED RM. 11⁸ x 13⁸
DINING RM. 11⁸ x 11⁸
LINEN
CL.
BATH
FOYER
SNACK BAR
KITCHEN 11⁸ x 9⁸
DN. UP
CL.
PANTRY REF'G RANGE
PORCH
ENTRANCE COURT
OPEN TRELLIS
STORAGE
CARPORT 11⁸ x 20⁰

Lower Level floor plan labels:
TERRACE
ACTIVITIES RM. 15⁴ x 18⁴
BUNK RM. OPTIONAL 11⁴ x 15⁸
BASEMENT
RAISED HEARTH
AIR COND.
BATH
STORAGE CABINETS
UP
CL. L.T. WASH. DRY.

● Study this outstanding multi-level with its dramatic outdoor deck and balconies. This home is ideal if you are looking for a home that is new and exciting. The livability that it offers will efficiently serve your family.

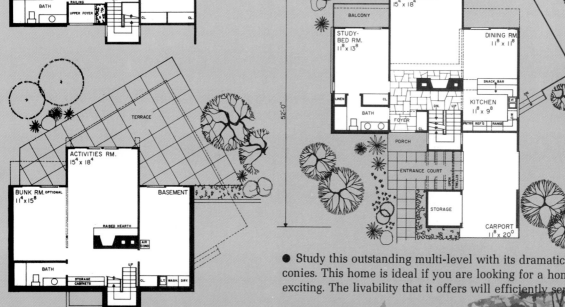

Design 12823

1,370 Sq. Ft. - First Floor
927 Sq. Ft. - Second Floor
34,860 Cu. Ft.

● The street view of this contemporary design features a small courtyard entrance as well as a private terrace off the study. Inside the livability will be outstanding. This design features spacious first floor activity areas that flow smoothly into each other. In the gathering room a raised hearth fireplace creates a dramatic focal point. An adjacent covered terrace, featuring a skylight, is ideal for outdoor dining and could be screened in later for an additional room.

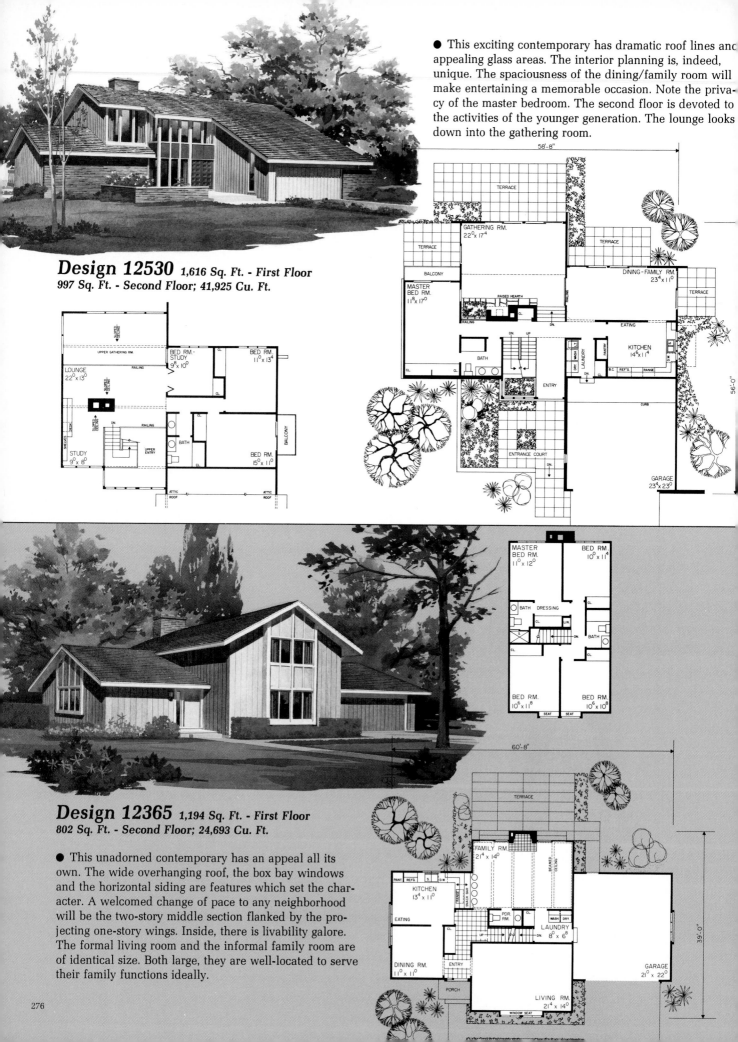

● This exciting contemporary has dramatic roof lines and appealing glass areas. The interior planning is, indeed, unique. The spaciousness of the dining/family room will make entertaining a memorable occasion. Note the privacy of the master bedroom. The second floor is devoted to the activities of the younger generation. The lounge looks down into the gathering room.

Design 12530 *1,616 Sq. Ft. - First Floor*
997 Sq. Ft. - Second Floor; 41,925 Cu. Ft.

Design 12365 *1,194 Sq. Ft. - First Floor*
802 Sq. Ft. - Second Floor; 24,693 Cu. Ft.

● This unadorned contemporary has an appeal all its own. The wide overhanging roof, the box bay windows and the horizontal siding are features which set the character. A welcomed change of pace to any neighborhood will be the two-story middle section flanked by the projecting one-story wings. Inside, there is livability galore. The formal living room and the informal family room are of identical size. Both large, they are well-located to serve their family functions ideally.

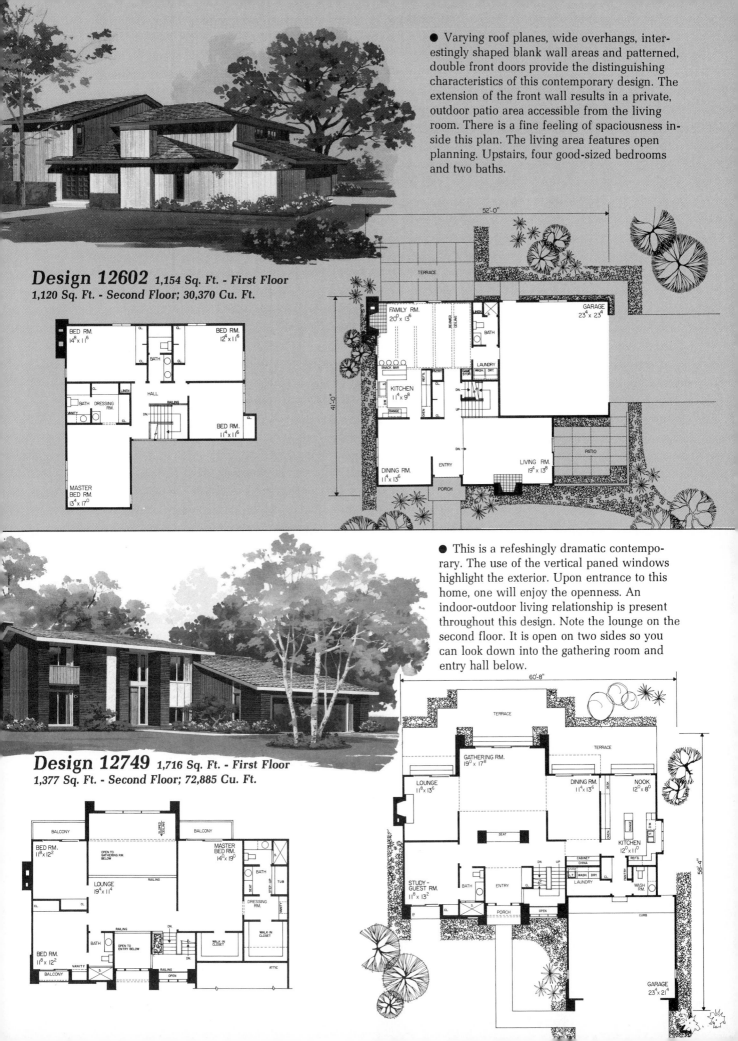

● Varying roof planes, wide overhangs, inter-
estingly shaped blank wall areas and patterned,
double front doors provide the distinguishing
characteristics of this contemporary design. The
extension of the front wall results in a private,
outdoor patio area accessible from the living
room. There is a fine feeling of spaciousness inside this plan. The living area features open
planning. Upstairs, four good-sized bedrooms
and two baths.

Design 12602 1,154 Sq. Ft. - First Floor
1,120 Sq. Ft. - Second Floor; 30,370 Cu. Ft.

● This is a refreshingly dramatic contemporary. The use of the vertical paned windows
highlight the exterior. Upon entrance to this
home, one will enjoy the openness. An
indoor-outdoor living relationship is present
throughout this design. Note the lounge on the
second floor. It is open on two sides so you
can look down into the gathering room and
entry hall below.

Design 12749 1,716 Sq. Ft. - First Floor
1,377 Sq. Ft. - Second Floor; 72,885 Cu. Ft.

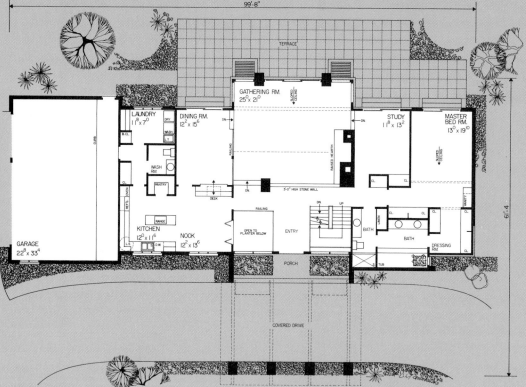

Design 12562

2,884 Sq. Ft. - First Floor
864 Sq. Ft. - Second Floor
73,625 Cu. Ft.

● Here is an exciting contemporary design for the large, active family. It can be called upon to function as either a four or five bedroom home. As a four bedroom home the parents will enjoy a wonderful suite with study and exceptional bath facilities. Note stall shower, plus sunken tub. The upstairs features the children's bedrooms and a spacious balcony lounge which looks down to the floor below. The sunken gathering room will be just that with its sloped beamed ceiling, dramatic raised hearth fireplace and direct access to the rear terrace.

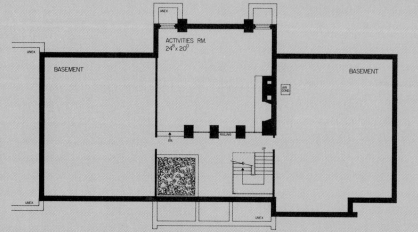

Design 12709

2,471 Sq. Ft. - First Floor
2,038 Sq. Ft. - Second Floor
73,125 Cu. Ft.

● A lower-level conversation pit! Above, a skylight. And on the first and second floors, open balconies. . .offering a view of both the conversation pit and skylight. That's just the beginning. Develop the basement area around the conversation pit and add 1,435 square feet to your informal living area. The gathering room features a balcony overlooking an indoor garden . . . part of the scenery in the family room. Fireplace in both those rooms. An enormous kitchen with a walk-in pantry, island range, built-in desk. Four large bedrooms, including a luxury master suite. Observe the storage potential.

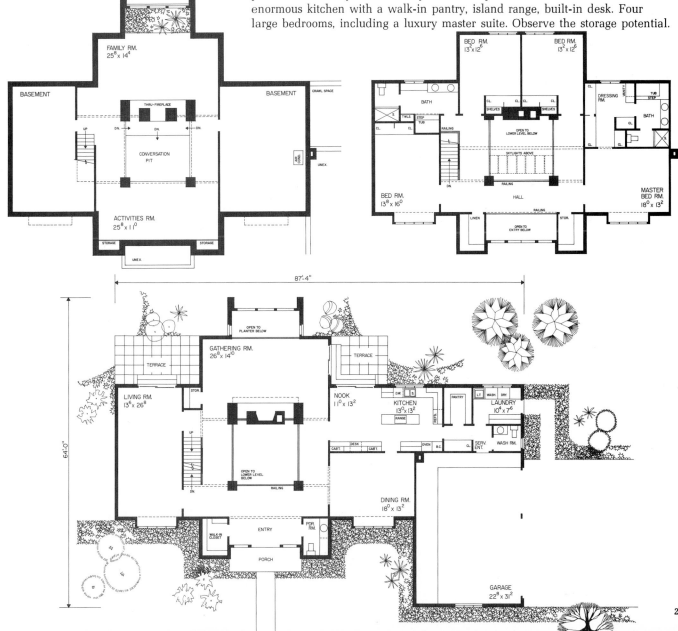

Design 11879

1,008 Sq. Ft. - First Floor
1,008 Sq. Ft. - Second Floor
27,518 Cu. Ft.

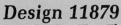

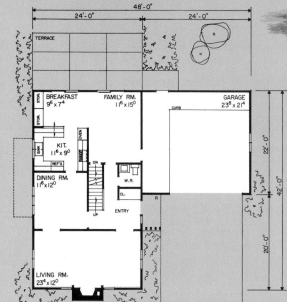

● This contemporary two-story will be most economical to build. Thus, the return on your construction dollar will be weighted in your favor. Consider: four bedrooms - three for the kids and one for the parents; one main bath and one private bath with dressing room for Mr. and Mrs.; two distinct eating areas - the informal breakfast room and the formal dining room; a family room only a step removed from the rear terrace and a quiet living room off by itself.

● Here is another contemporary, two-story design which offers fine contemporary living patterns. There are four bedrooms, 2½ baths and formal and informal living and dining areas. The fireplace with its raised hearth in the family room is flanked with bookshelves. Blueprints for this design include details for an optional non-basement.

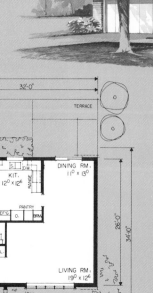

Design 11908

1,122 Sq. Ft. - First Floor
896 Sq. Ft. - Second Floor; 27,064 Cu. Ft.

● This two-story contemporary offers a variety of living patterns for your family. To the right of the spacious entrance hall, you will find a large living room with a fireplace. A few steps away is a nice-sized dining room with adjacent kitchen and breakfast area. Note, the bar and pantry. A spacious family room with beamed ceiling and fireplace is ideal for entertaining guests. Also featured on this floor is a laundry room and adjacent washroom. Three bedrooms are upstairs, along with a full bath and the master bedroom with full bath and dressing room. Notice the luxury of the private balcony.

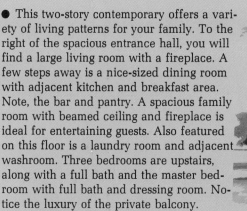

Design 11878 1,384 Sq. Ft. - First Floor
1,320 Sq. Ft. - Second Floor; 37,384 Cu. Ft.

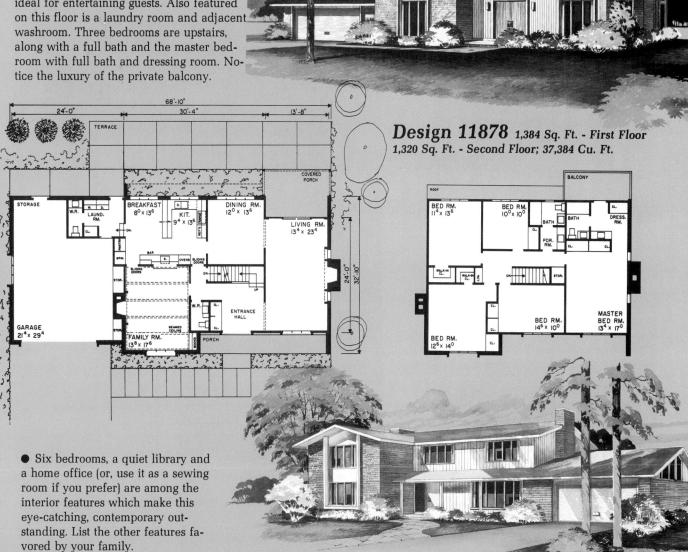

● Six bedrooms, a quiet library and a home office (or, use it as a sewing room if you prefer) are among the interior features which make this eye-catching, contemporary outstanding. List the other features favored by your family.

Design 11899 1,790 Sq. Ft. - First Floor
1,514 Sq. Ft. - Second Floor; 47,058 Cu. Ft.

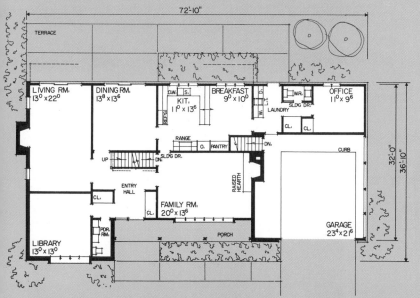

Design 12377 1,170 Sq. Ft. - First Floor
815 Sq. Ft. - Second Floor; 22,477 Cu. Ft.

● What an impressive, up-to-date home. Its refreshing configuration will command a full measure of attention. Note that all of the back rooms on the first floor are a couple steps lower than the entry and living room area. Separating the living room and the slightly lower level is a thru-fireplace, which has a raised hearth in the family room. Four bedrooms, serviced by two full baths, comprise the second floor which looks down into the living room.

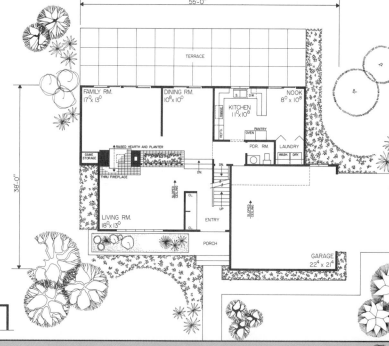

Design 12390 1,368 Sq. Ft. - First Floor
1,428 Sq. Ft. - Second Floor; 37,734 Cu. Ft.

● If yours is a large family and you like the architecture of the Far West, don't look further. Particularly if you envision building on a modest sized lot. Projecting the garage to the front contributes to the drama of this two-story. Its stucco exterior is beautifully enhanced by the clay tiles of the varying roof surfaces. The focal point, of course, is the five bedroom, three bath second floor. Four bedrooms have access to the outdoor balcony.

Design 12309
1,719 Sq. Ft. - First Floor
456 Sq. Ft. - Second Floor; 22,200 Cu. Ft.

● Study this floor plan carefully. The efficiency of the kitchen could hardly be improved upon. It is strategically located to serve the formal dining room, the family room and even the rear terrace. The sleeping facilities are arranged in a most interesting manner. The master bedroom with its attached bath and dressing room will enjoy a full measure of privacy on the first floor. A second bedroom is also on this floor and has a full bath nearby. Upstairs, there are two more bedrooms and a bath.

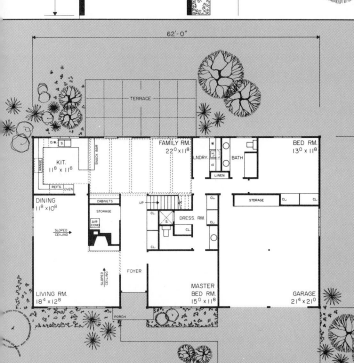

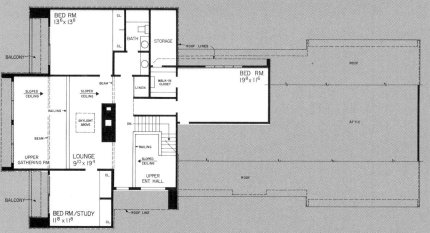

Floor plan labels (second floor):
BED RM. 13⁶ x 13⁸ — written as BED RM. 13^6 x 13^8
CL.
BATH
STORAGE
BALCONY
ROOF LINES
ROOF
SLOPED CEILING
RAILING
BEAM
SKYLIGHT ABOVE
BEAM
UPPER GATHERING RM.
LOUNGE 9^{10} x 19^4
DN.
RAILING
SLOPED CEILING
BALCONY
BED RM./STUDY 11^8 x 11^8
CL.
LINEN
WALK-IN CLOSET
BED RM. 19^8 x 11^6
ATTIC
SLOPED CEILING
UPPER ENT. HALL
ROOF LINE
ROOF

Design 12781

2,132 Sq. Ft. - First Floor
1,156 Sq. Ft. - Second Floor
47,365 Cu. Ft.

● This beautifully designed two-story could be considered a dream house of a lifetime. The exterior is sure to catch the eye of anyone who takes sight of its unique construction. The front kitchen features an island range, adjacent breakfast nook and pass-thru to formal dining room. The master bedroom suite with its privacy and convenience on the first floor has a spacious walk-in closet and dressing room. The side terrace is accessible through sliding glass doors from the master bedroom, gathering room and study. The second floor has three bedrooms and storage space galore. Also notice the lounge which has a sloped ceiling and a sky-light above. This delightful area looks down into the gathering room. The out-door balconies overlook the wrap-around terrace. Surely an outstanding trend house for decades to come.

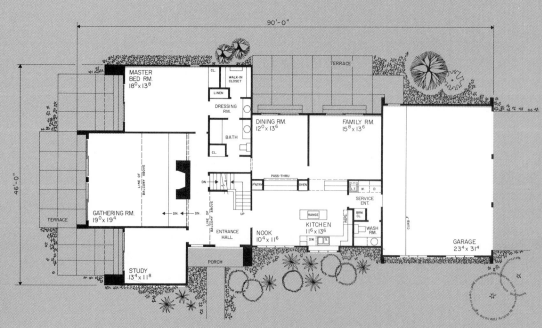

Floor plan labels (first floor):
90'-0"
46'-0"
MASTER BED RM. 18^0 x 13^8
CL.
WALK-IN CLOSET
LINEN
TERRACE
DRESSING RM.
BATH
CL.
DINING RM. 12^0 x 13^6
FAMILY RM. 15^8 x 13^6
PASS-THRU
OVEN
LINE OF BALCONY ABOVE
DN.
DN.
PNTRY
SERVICE ENT.
W. D.
GATHERING RM. 19^0 x 19^4
TERRACE
LINE OF BALCONY ABOVE
UP
RANGE
REFG.
BRM. CL.
KITCHEN 11^6 x 13^6
WASH RM.
ENTRANCE HALL
NOOK 10^4 x 11^6
DW.
GARAGE 23^4 x 31^4
CURB
STUDY 13^4 x 11^8
PORCH

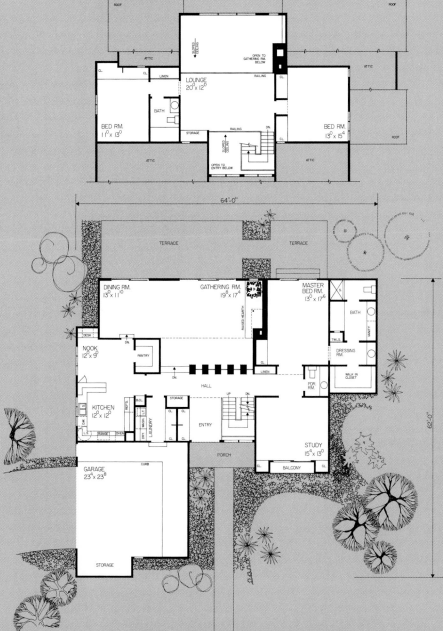

Design 12708
2,108 Sq. Ft. - First Floor
824 Sq. Ft. - Second Floor
52,170 Cu. Ft.

● Here is a one-and-a-half story home whose exterior is distinctive. It has a contemporary feeling, yet it retains some of the fine design features and proportions of traditional exteriors. Inside the appealing double front doors there is livability galore. The sunken rear living-dining area is delightfully spacious and is looked down into from the second floor lounge. The open end fireplace, with its raised hearth and planter, is another focal point. The master bedroom features a fine compartmented bath with both shower and tub. The study is just a couple steps away. The U-shaped kitchen is outstanding. Notice the pantry and laundry. Upstairs provides children with their own sleeping, studying and TV quarters. Absolutely a great design! Study all the fine details closely with your family.

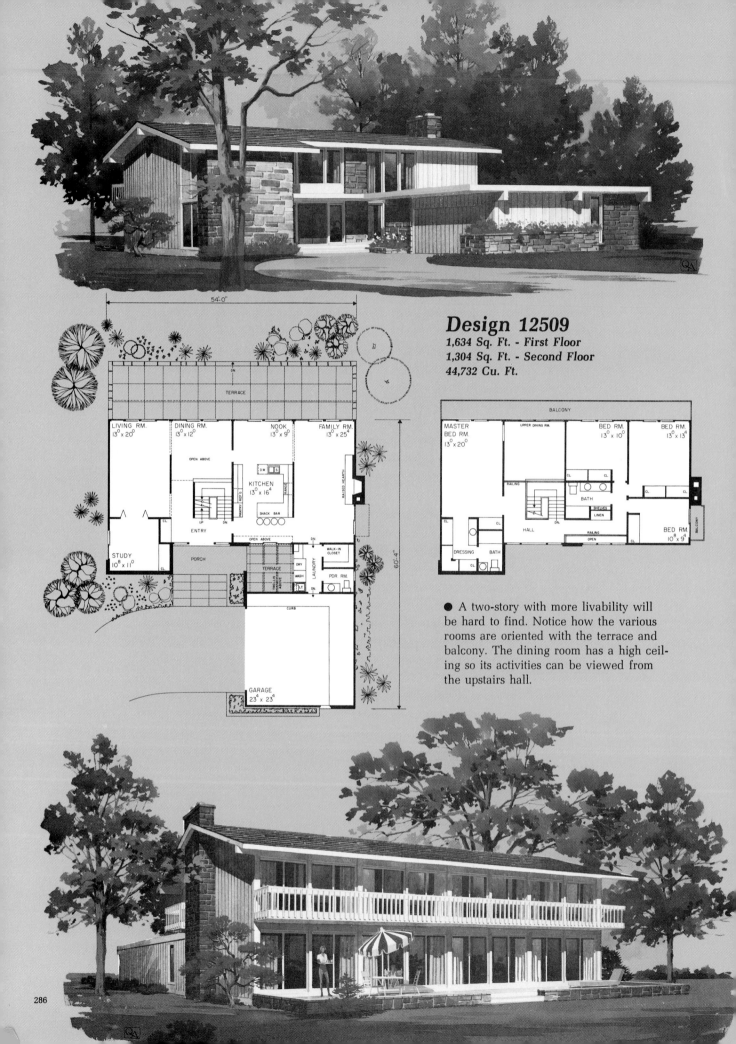

Design 12509

1,634 Sq. Ft. - First Floor
1,304 Sq. Ft. - Second Floor
44,732 Cu. Ft.

● A two-story with more livability will be hard to find. Notice how the various rooms are oriented with the terrace and balcony. The dining room has a high ceiling so its activities can be viewed from the upstairs hall.

Design 12822
1,363 Sq. Ft. - First Floor
351 Sq. Ft. - Second Floor
36,704 Cu. Ft.

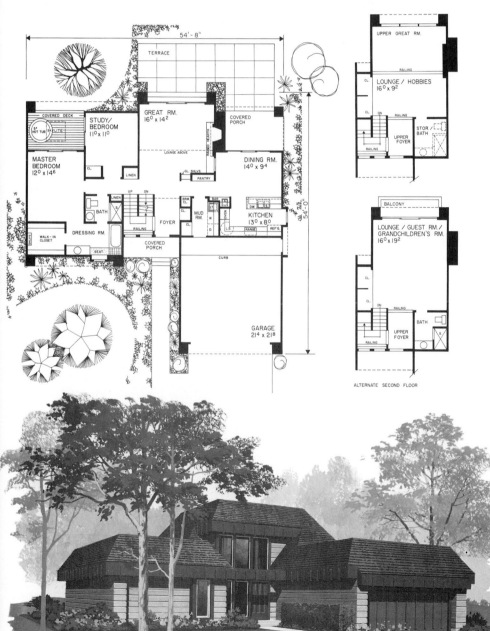

● Here is a truly unique house whose interior was designed with the current decade's economies, lifestyles and demographics in mind. While functioning as a one-story home, the second floor provides an extra measure of livability when required. Note the two optional layouts. The second floor may serve as a lounge, studio or hobby area overlooking the great room. Or, it may be built to function as a complete private guest room. It would be a great place for the visiting grandchildren. Don't miss the outdoor balcony. In addition, this two-story section adds to the dramatic appeal of both the exterior and the interior. Within only 1,363 square feet, this contemporary delivers refreshing and outstanding living patterns for those who are buying their first home, those who have raised their family and are looking for a smaller home and those in search of a retirement home. The center entrance routes traffic effectively to the great room. The adjacent covered porch will provide an ideal spot for warm weather, outdoor dining. The sleeping area may consist of one bedroom and a study, or two bedrooms. Each room functions with the sheltered wood deck - a perfect location for a hot tub.

Design 12821
1,363 Sq. Ft. - First Floor
351 Sq. Ft. - Second Floor
37,145 Cu. Ft.

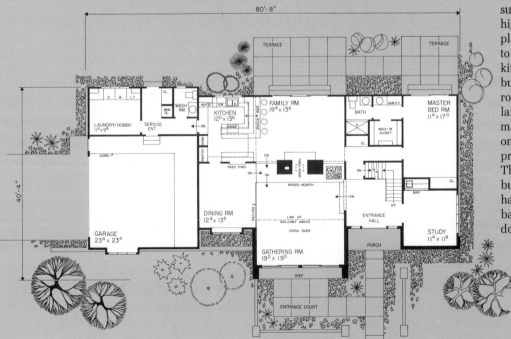

Design 12782

2,060 Sq. Ft. - First Floor
897 Sq. Ft. - Second Floor
47,750 Cu. Ft.

● What makes this such a distinctive four bedroom design? Let's list some of the features. This plan includes great formal and informal living for the family at home or when entertaining guests. The formal gathering room and informal family room share a dramatic raised hearth fireplace. Other features of the sunken gathering room include: high, sloped ceilings, built-in planter and sliding glass doors to the front entrance court. The kitchen has a snack bar, many built-ins, a pass-thru to dining room and easy access to the large laundry/washroom. The master bedroom suite is located on the main level for added privacy and convenience. There's even a study with a built-in bar. The upper level has three more bedrooms, a bath and a lounge looking down into the gathering room.